Ralph Guldahl

RALPH GULDAHL

*The Rise and Fall
of the World's Greatest Golfer*

KEVIN KENNY

McFarland & Company, Inc., Publishers
Jefferson, North Carolina

ISBN (print) 978-1-4766-6262-6
ISBN (ebook) 978-1-4766-2456-3

LIBRARY OF CONGRESS CATALOGUING DATA ARE AVAILABLE

BRITISH LIBRARY CATALOGUING DATA ARE AVAILABLE

Front cover: Guldahl completes his hat-trick of Western Open
wins in 1938 (courtesy the Western Golf Association)

Printed in the United States of America

*McFarland & Company, Inc., Publishers
Box 611, Jefferson, North Carolina 28640
www.mcfarlandpub.com*

For Celia, Jo, Stephen,
Heather and Matthew

Acknowledgments

There are many people to whom I am deeply indebted in regard to the completion of this book. In terms of research, the staff at the USGA Museum of Golf in Far Hills, New Jersey, were very helpful, especially Nancy Stulack, Victoria Student, Hilary Coe and Mike Trostel. I am also grateful to Nick Pepe and his team of willing volunteers at the PGA Museum of Golf in Port St. Lucie, Florida. And a special thanks also to Audrey Moriarty and Kay Lund at the Tufts Archives, Pinehurst. I also received great support from the LA84 library in California as well as the archivists at the University of Florida and the University of Texas.

In no particular order, I also wish to place on record my thanks to the following—Betsy Drazner; Scott Sayers; Ben Crenshaw; Jim Healey; Kent Ahlf; Mike Moretti; Vincent Daversa; Melanie Hauser; Samantha Dodd; Beverly Carver; Cathy Spitzenberger; Kevin Hood; Cindy Cutler; Marty Kavanaugh; Clayton Derr; Marque and Walter Guldahl; Penny Harris Healy; and Paul Gwynne.

In the course of researching a subject such as this, I am consistently struck by the generosity and enthusiasm of so many clubs throughout the world of golf. In this regard, I can thank the Inverness Club, Toledo; the Wildwood Country Club; Cherry Hills Country Club; North Shore Country Club; and Southport and Ainsdale Golf Club, England.

Finally, my sincere thanks to my family—Celia, Jo, Stephen, Heather and Matthew—for their support and encouragement during the writing and completion of this book.

Table of Contents

Preface

Last year, I completed a book on American golf during the Great Depression. My motivation for doing this was primarily to try to bring to life the stories of some of the wonderful players who were active during this era. I am thinking particularly of golfers such as Henry Picard, Horton Smith, Denny Shute, and many, many more. I believed that these players had not always been sufficiently recognized by the chroniclers of golf's history. However, in this group, for me at least, one name stood out above all the others: Ralph Guldahl, who for a brief period could justifiably claim the title of "the world's best golfer." His record, which is well documented here, backs up this claim.

The words "comet" or "shooting star" are often used as headlines by sportswriters to describe a top-class athlete who emerges for a short period and then disappears. And after their disappearance, we are faced with the question of "whatever happened to" so-and-so. Ralph Guldahl certainly qualified for these headlines on all counts, as for a period of roughly four years at the end of the 1930s he was *the* best player in golf. Certainly Byron Nelson and especially Sam Snead had arrived on the scene, and Gene Sarazen was still a regular winner. But it was Guldahl who was the game's most feared competitor, especially in the month of June, when the U.S. Open was played. He is one of a handful of players to win this coveted title in successive years. In this period, he earned the respect of his peers such as Hagen, Armour, Jones, Snead, and many more. And then, he faded from view... gradually at first, until, in the 1950s, he became an insurance salesman and occasional golfer.

These facts provide just a brief outline as to why I felt this was a story worth telling, as in the history of the game not many reach such heights and then fall so spectacularly in such a short time. In order to try to provide some answers, I trace the life of Ralph Guldahl from the caddy yards in Dallas; to early success in golf; to a slump which saw him almost broke; to the pinnacle of the game; to his gradual withdrawal from golf; and eventually to a contented return to golf in the later years of his life. I hope that lovers of golf history will relish his story as much as I enjoyed researching and writing this book.

Introduction

The year 1912 was one of the more celebrated in golf's history as Ben Hogan, Byron Nelson and Sam Snead were all born then. And in his wonderful *American Triumvirate*, James Dodson describes it as a "Year of Wonders."[1] It is hard to disagree. The previous year, 1911, has understandably never been accorded the same significance, although there were some important happenings that year. For example, John McDermott became the first American-born winner of the U.S. Open when he defeated Mike Brady and George Simpson in a play-off at the Chicago Club with a score of 80 against the 82 from Brady and the 85 of Simpson. His prize was the (then) sizeable sum of $300. McDermott was not just the first "national" to win the U.S. Open, he was also the first home pro to openly (and vocally) challenge the notion that British professionals were best. Arguably his win was a prelude to the start of American golfing dominance, confirmed by Francis Ouimet's victory over Vardon and Ray at Brookline two years later. McDermott was 19 years old and remains the youngest player to win the title.

In contrast, the U.S. Amateur title was won by Harold Hilton, who became the first and only British-born player to win the British and American trophies in the same year. Across the water, Harry Vardon won his fifth Open Championship at Sandwich by defeating Arnaud Massey in a 36-hole play-off. The White House incumbent that year was William Howard Taft, who is generally regarded as the nation's first golfing president. During his stay in 1600 Pennsylvania Avenue, rather than disguise his playing the game, in case voters felt he was neglecting his duties, Taft was more than open about his love of golf, and there were regular newspaper reports on the state of his game. Later, his military aide, Archie Butt, confirmed the president's passion in a series of letters to his sister, written during the summer of 1910. On July 29, 1910, he wrote, "The President

3

played golf with Frick this morning, but when he finished the game his ankle was so sore he could scarcely walk." On July 30, 1910: "The President went to Myopia to play golf with Judge Grant this morning, but his ankle was so painful that he could not make a start." And on August 1, 1910: "Dear Clara: I went by for the President at nine and found Frank Kellogg there, waiting on the porch with his golf bag. We drove to Myopia, where he and the President played together and I played alone just behind them."[2] Archie Butt later died a hero when the *Titanic* sank in 1912.

As well as being an enthusiastic golfer, Taft also called for more municipal courses to be built, and in a speech in Newhaven he laid out his vision. "I hope," he said, "to see that time not far distant when public courses will be offered, as in Scotland, for those who cannot pay for costly club privileges. I would have the funds raised by taxation. Golf is pre-eminently a game for the people and they should be allowed to play it.... Properly played it brings a self-restraint that not even the churches can exert."[3] His views on taxation could be seen as quite daring for a Republican, but he was committed to the cause, and long after he left office, he wrote articles to advance the case for more municipal courses. His call to make the game more affordable is seen as having done much to popularize the game in America.

A further and often-forgotten footnote in the history of American golf is the fact that Ralph Guldahl was born in 1911, and it is clear that he, along with Hogan, Snead and Nelson, was born into a country where golf was expanding at all levels of society.

If the American Triumvirate were all born in 1912, their respective rates of progress varied. Sam Snead and Byron Nelson made their mark quicker than Ben Hogan as each became prolific winners in the 1930s. Nelson, for example, won the regional New Jersey Open in 1935 and followed up by winning the Metropolitan Open the next year, his first win in a recognized tour event. He also won the 1937 Masters and the 1939 National Open as well as a number of other tournaments. Snead had to wait until the next decade for his first major, but from the time he won the Oakland Open in 1937 and followed this with four more victories, he was the favorite for just about every event during the Depression years. The favorite's tag was justified as he won eight times in 1938 and had three victories in 1939. In contrast, Hogan had just one win in this decade, and that was the Hershey Four-ball with Vic Ghezzi in 1938. His first individual win came in 1940 and sparked one of the greatest careers in golf.

When writing of the emergence of Nelson and Snead during the Depression era, the eminent U.S. Open historian Robert Somers wrote,

"Though Sam and soon Byron were getting all the attention, Guldahl was the best player in the game."[4] In 1939, Tommy Armour claimed that "Ralph Guldahl is the most underrated golfer I ever knew.... Guldahl, for some reason, has never received one half the publicity he deserves. Yet he is not only one of the best golfers in the world today, but one of the best of all time."[5] And his great rival, and exhibition and four-ball partner, Sam Snead, later claimed, "The greatest I ever saw for a grooved swing was Ralph Guldahl."[6] Such praise from his peers was not unwarranted.

Just a few years later, in the early 1940s, the sportswriters were exhausting all possible sporting analogies to describe what went wrong. Ralph Guldahl was described as "golf's forgotten man" and was likened to "the heavyweight fighter who realizes that nothing happens when he hits the other bloke." Or "the miler who, for no reason he can explain, gets precisely nowhere in a jiffy when he tries desperately to turn it on in the last lap. The kick is gone."[7] Baseball was perhaps the sport which provided most material, as he was referred to as "the pitcher whose swift one disappears overnight."[8] And following on with the baseball analogies: "The glittering golf evaporated almost as abruptly as it had come on and his game became so commonplace that historians pinched themselves to see whether they had dreamed it. So did Guldahl. It was like leading the major leagues in home runs three years in a row and suddenly not being able to get a foul tip in the three-eye league."[9] And Fred Corcoran put it succinctly when he said, "He was the greatest golfer in the world and he lost it overnight. He woke up one morning and it was gone. In one year he went from Who's Who to Who's He."[10]

The tribute "greatest golfer in the world" was not handed out lightly by as experienced a figure as Fred Corcoran. Originally from Boston, here was a man with a wonderful golfing pedigree, from caddying for Alexa Stirling when she won the U.S. Women's Amateur title in 1916; to introducing and operating scoreboards for the USGA at its Amateur and Professional Championships; to becoming friends with greats such as Hagen and Sarazen; to PGA tournament director. Fred was also Sam Snead's manager and would go on to co-found what is now the LPGA tour. There were many other multiple major winners during the 1930s, and yet at no time were their names put forward for this accolade. We are talking here of Denny Shute, who won the Open Championship at St. Andrews and two PGA titles: Henry Picard, who won the Masters and the PGA; and Horton Smith, who won the first Masters in 1934 and then another two years later. And Byron Nelson won both the Masters and the National Open during this period.

The reason for Corcoran's tribute (and he was not alone) was that Ralph Guldahl was *different* in that he dominated the game for a period, and the story of how he went from being the best player in the world in the late 1930s to golfing oblivion in the matter of a few years is without doubt seen as one of golf's greatest mysteries. During the space of five years, he won back to back U.S. Opens in 1937 and 1938 and he also had two runner-up finishes at Augusta before he finally won the Masters in 1939. In addition he won three successive Western Opens at a time when this event was considered golf's fifth major. He was also a Ryder Cup player in 1937 with a 100 percent record, and he won numerous other titles. And all of this before he reached the age of 30. Theories on what happened have abounded and range from his writing an instructional book which affected his natural way of playing the game, to a loss of interest and a desire to spend more time with his family. It is hoped that this book will find some answers to the question of what happened.

1

The Texas Rangers

When Jordan Spieth won the 2015 Masters at Augusta and followed this with a victory in the U.S. Open, he was not only winning his first two major titles. He was also maintaining a long and honorable tradition, as one of the notable features of American golf in the first half of the twentieth century was the number of top players who came from the Lone Star State of Texas. Indeed, Herbert Warren Wind described Texas as the "New Scotland," such was the regularity with which outstanding golfers emerged from the state. Why this was the case is a matter of conjecture, but what is not in doubt is that the origins of the game in Texas were to be found in Great Britain. From the year 1888, when John Reid from Dunfermline established the first golf club in America at Yonkers, New York, it was Scotland, as the game's "home," which was responsible for sending over men who would advance the game in America. This list included professionals such as Jock Hutchison and Willie Anderson, and course designers such as Donald Ross. However, in the case of Texas, it was two transplanted Englishmen who were responsible.

The first course in Texas was a six-hole project laid out in Dallas in 1896 by Richard Potter and Harry Edwards. Potter and Edwards saw how golf was developing in their native England and decided to try out the game in Dallas.[1] It was reported that having laid out the course, the two men sent to Boston for some clubs and balls to get them started.[2] This rudimentary course would slowly evolve into the Oak Lawn Club, with a clubhouse being built in 1903. The delay before opening a clubhouse was because Potter and Edwards were not certain as to how the locals would take to this new "imported" game. Before that, golfers rented a room in a nearby cottage where they could store their clubs. The cost of this was $5 per month. However, it quickly became clear that it was not just "furrinners" who were attracted to the game, but many Dallasites too. The club grew rapidly and eventually became the Dallas Golf and Country Club. Harry Edwards would go on to become a founder member of the Texas Golf Association and was regarded as the "father of golf in Texas."

The initiative shown by Potter and Edwards coincided with what was happening socially and economically in the Lone Star State. Towards the end of the nineteenth century, and like most of America, Texas benefited from the growth of railways, which saw the state's economy quickly change from a rural to an industrial model. Dallas profited accordingly and grew from a population of just 3,000 people in 1872 to 158,976 in 1920. This economic and demographic growth saw the city thrive and become a center for banking, insurance, large department stores, garment manufacturing and aviation in the early decades of the twentieth century. And underpinning much of this economic expansion was oil.

Sport in general thrived and became "not only acceptable but a necessary part of the American way of life."[3] In the previous century, sport was usually the preserve of the private sector, but in the early decades of the twentieth century, "Cities across the nation began to provide athletic fields, equipment, training, leadership and encouragement for a broad spectrum of the population."[4] Dallas was not left behind in this regard, and the city saw many parks either built or transformed to provide sporting facilities which would enhance "the American way of life." The sports that were especially popular included boxing, baseball and athletics.

Golf also gained from this rapid increase in wealth and progressive thinking. After the modest beginnings of the Oak Lawn Club, the game exploded, especially in the second decade of the twentieth century. A.W. Tillinghast, the future creator of Bethpage Black, Baltusrol, and Winged Foot, designed the state's first public course, which opened in 1916. This was at Brackenridge in San Antonio, and the course would host the Texas Open on many occasions. Many more public courses would follow and so make the game more affordable, and it was the municipal courses where many of the state's future stars (including Ralph Guldahl) would cut their golfing teeth.

This era also saw the arrival of Texas's first resident professional course architect, John Bredemus. Bredemus was an "Easterner" with an academic background in Princeton, from which he graduated with a degree in civil engineering. He was also a noted athlete at Princeton. In this regard, he captured the national AAU for best all-round athlete, and in the 1912 AAU championship, he competed against Jim Thorpe, who won two gold medals in that year's Olympics in Stockholm. In the race for the decathlon title, Thorpe won but was later disqualified for playing semi-pro football. Bredemus got Thorpe's AAU medals. Not long after this, in 1914, Bredemus discovered golf at America's first public course, Van Cortlandt, New York. He moved quickly in his adopted sport, and apart from becoming a good player, he was present, along with Rodman Wanamaker, Francis Ouimet, and others, when the PGA was founded in 1916 at the Taplow Club, New York. However, he migrated to Texas at the start of the 1920s and made a huge impact as a course designer, professional, celebrated teacher, co-founder and secretary of the Texas PGA, and tournament organizer. One of his projects was at Ben Hogan's Colonial, which he co-designed with Parry Maxwell. The course would host the U.S. Open of 1941. A good friend of Harvey Penick, Bredemus died penniless in 1946. While Harry Edwards had the official title of "father of golf" in Texas, Bredemus ran him close.

Tom Bendelow was also influential. Tom came from Aberdeen and was one of the many Scots who brought their golfing expertise to America in the late nineteenth century. He designed hundreds of courses in his adopted land, a number of which were in Texas. These included Lakewood, where Ralph Guldahl started caddying and where he would play a lot of golf in his early days. The growth in the number of courses was also used to promote Texas as a tourist destination: because of its benign climate, the state could offer visitors "all year 'round" golf. By 1926, for example, Dallas could boast sixteen courses "all open and in use 52 weeks a year." Included in these figures were five public courses where 125,000 were recorded as having played the previous year.[5] There were also "child friendly" courses where youngsters could learn to play the game.

The professional game also benefited from this popularity and money in the form of the Texas Open, which was first held in 1922, and was co-founded by newspaperman Jack O'Brien and John Bredemus. For years, O'Brien was sports editor with the *San Antonio News*, and so he was used to generating publicity. And, Bredemus was especially active in terms of drumming up support from the leading players. His job, of course, was made easier with the $5,000 purse on offer. Noted golf historian Al Barkow drew comparisons between the more conservative attitudes to prize money in the eastern states to those in Texas. "This was Texas," Barkow wrote, "and the sense of largesse always associated with Texans expanded golf's personality, giving it a broader, deeper aspect more fully reflective of the American character."[6] Seeing this munificence as being reflective of a broader American identity may seem a little exaggerated, but there was no doubting the founders' desire to put both the state and the Texas Open on the golfing map, and money would be a sure way of doing this.

Jack O'Brien spelled his approach out by announcing that the "prizes won't be cups, they're useless nowadays, but will be those silver discs produced at Mister Uncle Sam's factory. The king will be crowned with 1,500 cool iron men."[7] O'Brien saw the money available to prize fighters, and reasoned, why not golf? Bredemus, who was now assistant professional at Brackenridge, used his contacts back east and helped attract the big names, with Hagen, Sarazen, Kirkwood and Barnes among those taking part. In regard to making the long journey south, Sarazen said, "For that money we'd play in a pasture."[8] In the event, it was Bob MacDonald who took home the 1,500 "cool iron men" as first-place money when he beat future National Open winner Cyril Walker by one shot. MacDonald was another immigrant Scotsman who hailed from Dornoch, the same birthplace as Donald Ross, and was an influential figure in the early days of professional golf. He was one of the PGA's founding members and he also wrote a seminal instruction book for this era titled *Golf*. Golfers who availed of his teaching skills included Horton Smith, Gene Sarazen and Babe Zaharias. In the 1920s, $1,500 was serious cash, and far exceeded the figures on offer for winning the National Open, the PGA Championship or the Western Open. Second prize was $750 and third was $500, with the first twenty guaranteed some cash. The players were also treated to some lavish hospitality in the hotels downtown. After the tournament, double major winner Jock Hutchison offered this very complimentary assessment: "San Antonio is now on the map of winter golf tournaments. More towns in the country should follow the example of this enterprising Texas town."[9]

The following year, 1923, Walter Hagen took time off from his exhibition travels to play in and win the Texas Open. The first prize again was $1,500. In the final round, Hagen came from six back (65–71) to catch Mehlhorn and beat him next day. The East Coast papers, attracted by the name of Hagen and his performance, picked up the story and helped cement the Texas Open. Golf historian and Hagen biographer Stephen Lowe claimed, "The Texas Open has been widely regarded as the birthplace of modern tour golf. The event was the first permanent 'big money' tournament and became the anchor for a winter circuit."[10] All these years later, the Texas Open is still going strong, and it is now sponsored by the Valero Energy Corporation.

Then, in 1927, the state received further affirmation of its growing reputation in golf when it hosted its first-ever major championship. Since its first staging in 1916, the PGA Championship immediately assumed its place as golf's third major after the British and U.S. Opens. In 1927, the title was contested at the Tillinghast-designed Cedar Crest Club in Dallas, a place which would feature prominently in the development of Ralph Guldahl. This was the first time a major had been held that far west and that far south, and it took all of John Bredemus's powers of persuasion to convince the PGA to host its tournament so far from its usual surroundings. However, Bredemus needed help, and this came from Sol Dreyfuss, a Dallas entrepreneur and banker, who had established the Cedar Crest Club, and whose guarantee of $12,000 ultimately convinced the PGA that Texas was ready to host its first major. At the end of the week, Hagen, who clearly relished Texas, claimed his fourth successive title with a one-up win over Joe Turnesa in the 36-hole final. A strong case can be made, therefore, to suggest that money, facilities, and climate all contributed to the rapid development of the game in Texas.

More insightful and technical views regarding the Texan production line came from many of the game's leading players. For example, three-time major winner Denny Shute claimed that learning to play off Texas "hard pan" produced excellent strikers of the ball, as golfers learned how to "hold" their shots. On the other hand, Byron Nelson's view was that Texans grew up playing relatively open courses and so learned to develop their swings in an uninhibited manner. Byron also believed that the golfing environment had something to do with it. "When you start out playing for nickels and dimes that mean something," he said, "you're going to learn to play winning golf or have to quit the game entirely."[11] The evidence to support this view is quite persuasive when you consider the caddy yard games at Glen Garden between himself and Ben Hogan or those of Guldahl, Ray Mangrum and "Spec" Goldman at Randall Park. Nelson elaborated on this theme and recalled: "When I grew up, I played in an amateur tournament every single week. We could play in a tournament every week, all summer long. We played on different golf courses, different putting surfaces: sand greens, Bermuda greens, bent greens, and rye greens. We played in wind conditions, heat conditions, hard ground and soft ground, everything golf has to offer.... There is something about the competition and the background of golf in Texas that has produced the good players from 1928 until now. It's almost like one generation is built upon the next."[12] This argument is persuasive, when you consider Nelson's own generation which, apart from Hogan and Demaret, also included Lloyd Mangrum; followed by Jackie Burke Jr.; then Tom Kite and Ben Crenshaw; and now Jordan Spieth.

Jimmy Demaret voiced a similar opinion to Nelson's. Demaret believed that in junior and amateur events in Texas, the competition was so intense that only the best would survive. And the ever-quotable Gene Sarazen had his say on courses in the southwest and their impact: "Down there the courses, particularly the greens, are hard and fast. The Nelsons and the Guldahls learned golf the hard way—playing shots that had to stick to fast greens."[13] Regardless of *why*, the group included Ben Hogan, Byron Nelson, and Jimmy Demaret, and America's most eminent golf writer of that era, Grantland Rice, called them the "Texas Rangers." Ralph Guldahl was another "Texas Ranger," and combined, this group won twenty of the game's majors. However, there is a significant difference between the images of these men and between their legacies.

Hogan won nine majors, with three of these being in his stellar year of 1953. That year he did not enter the PGA as it overlapped with the Open Championship. This achievement was the nearest to a professional grand slam until Tiger Woods held all four majors at the same time (2000–01), although not in the same calendar year. Hogan was and remains generally recognized as the greatest ball striker in the history of the game, and even today his *Five Lessons* book remains the seminal work on golf technique. There was also the occasional appearance at Augusta in the 1960s during which the public was once again reminded of his greatness. And there was his 1965 *Shell's Wonderful World of Golf* match versus Sam Snead, which is generally regarded as being a golfing master class. (Ben won.) The DVD of this classic encounter is considered a "must" for both teachers and students of the game. In addition, he is the only American professional to be honored by Hollywood, with *Follow the Sun* charting his career and his remarkable recovery from a near-fatal car crash. And for many years, the Hogan irons, made under *his* supervision at *his* firm, were brand leaders in the equipment industry. Right up to his death in 1997, the Hogan *mystique* endured, with his absence from public life, if anything, adding to the Hogan legend.

Nelson, with five majors and owner of "the streak" of 1945,[14] is regarded as the father of the modern golf swing, and remained visible long after his playing career through his Ryder Cup captaincy in 1965; his television commentary work; and his mentoring of players such as Tom Watson and Ken Venturi. And the Byron Nelson Classic, which has raised millions for worthy causes, has been a favored tour stop since the inaugural event in 1969. Byron acted as a very visible host for the event, and competitors were always quick to shake the hand of the great man at the back of the 18th green. And for many years he was an observable presence at the Masters, where he acted as honorary starter, often in the company of Sam Snead and Gene Sarazen.

Demaret won the Masters three times in a total of thirty-one tour victories, and he was good enough, at age 52, to tie Tommy Jacobs for the 1964 Palm Springs Classic. (He lost the play-off.) History has judged him to be a most colorful player in the game's past because of his attire and his personality, and because of his fine singing voice, which was not out of place in the company of Bing Crosby, with whom he had a lasting friendship. This image was reinforced by his appearances as commentator on *All Star Golf* and *Shell's Wonderful World of Golf*, which did so much to popularize the game in the 1960s. Jimmy also co-founded the Champions Club in Houston with Jackie Burke Jr., which had the honor of hosting the Ryder Cup in 1967 and the National Open of 1969.

And so, through a variety of ways, these three Texans remained in golfing consciousness through the ages. Yet Ralph Guldahl, despite an outstanding record, is rarely mentioned, and when he is, it is often in reference to his seemingly dour personality; his demise; or his disappearance from golf for a number of years. However, his story is worthy of serious consideration in the glittering history of American golf.

Ralph Guldahl was born on November 22, 1911, in Dallas, one year before Hogan, Snead and Nelson. His home was on South Glasgow Drive about a mile from the Tenison Park and Lakewood golf courses. The location of the Guldahl house would become an important detail in the years ahead. In the early to mid-twentieth century, the American "melting pot" concept was well underway in the world of golf. Olin Dutra and his brother Mortie were of Spanish ancestry, and Billy Burke (formerly Burkowski) was of Lithuanian origin. Most prominent, however, were the Italian-Americans, many of whom would go on to make their mark in golf. This group included the Espinosa and Turnesa brothers as well as major winners Gene Sarazen, Johnny Revolta and Tony Manero. Guldahl, however, was the first to come from immigrant Norwegian stock, with his father being Olaf Guldahl and his mother Anna Nordy.

Norwegians began coming to America in numbers in the nineteenth century. Immigration figures were at their highest in the late nineteenth and early twentieth centuries. If jobs were relatively scarce in Norway, the demand for labor in the United States was growing. "The Norwegians and Swedes gravitated usually in family groups to Wisconsin and Minnesota, where the climate and woodlands reminded them of home."[15] In addition, these states were suited to their native skills of farming. These talents, as well as the fact that the immigrants were mostly Lutherans or Quakers, made it relatively easy for Norwegians to integrate into American society. Certainly expressions of anti–Norwegian sentiments were rare.

In terms of Norwegians in Dallas, the census of 1900 shows that 1,356 lived in the city. Olaf Guldahl came to America in 1899, when he was 22, and apart from a few years "up north" he lived in Dallas and worked with the Continental Gin Company, where he was a timekeeper and a stockman. The Guldahls were comfortably off, but no more than that, and golf was certainly not on the family radar. Then in 1922 came a life-changing and life-threatening moment when Ralph Guldahl contracted double pneumonia. Later, and in the golfing vernacular of the era, he claimed, "The Grim Reaper had me dormie and the doctors thought he would win the match. But I beat him on the extra hole."[16]

Part of the recommended recovery process was to spend as much time as possible in the fresh air to strengthen his lungs, and it was this which took Guldahl and his older brother Howard and the "baby" Herbert to the nearby Lakewood club to start caddying. In time, both Herbert and Howard became accomplished players and featured prominently in local golf tournaments. Howard, for example, was ahead of Ralph in making his mark when, in 1925, he won the prestigious Dallas Municipal Championship. In this three-round event, he beat Ray Mangrum by one shot with a score of 226 to 227. And like Ralph, he also represented the Woodrow Wilson School. Howard would later become a teaching professional in the city.

So it was health and not nickels and dimes, as was the case with Sarazen, Hogan and Nelson, that started Guldahl in caddying and then into the world of golf. And, as was common with players from the caddy yard, he never had formal lessons but learned the game mostly by observation and quickly found the swing which would serve him so well in the coming years. Very soon he became a formidable player and well able to play par golf. Guldahl played golf for the Woodrow Wilson High School, whom he captained to victory in the state championship of 1929. Here he easily won the individual title with a score of 144 at Tenison Park.

Tenison Park was the first municipal course in Dallas, and its existence owed much to the generosity of banker E.O. Tenison and his wife Annie. In 1923, Tenison bought land and donated it to the city fathers where they might construct a place "for recreation and the healthful amusements that an outdoor playground affords."[17] These "amusements" included golf, and in 1925, the course, designed by Syd Cooper and Jack Burke, was opened. Cooper would later figure prominently in Guldahl's life, and Burke was one of the most significant figures in the history of golf in Texas. Among his accomplishments was finishing joint second, one shot behind Ted Ray, in the 1920 U.S. Open at Inverness.

Over the years, Tenison Park became a significant part of Texas's golfing lore as the center of high-stakes money matches in Dallas. The legend is in no small way due to the exploits of renowned gambler Titanic Thompson back in the 1920s and 1930s, and more recently, the role such games played in the development of a young Dallasite: Lee Trevino. Despite a significant age difference, the two men got to know each other and Thompson (a fine golfer) was one of the first to recognize just how good Trevino's unorthodox swing was. He also staked him in money matches in which Lee would play some unsuspecting "pigeon" with a Dr Pepper bottle—and beat him. "Trevino's split," it was recorded, "would be a hundred dollars, sometimes two hundred if Ti was feeling generous."[18] Trevino was so good that Thompson wanted him to go with him on the "hustler's tour."[19] Instead Lee opted for the more orthodox way of making a living from golf.

Tenison was also the place where Ralph Guldahl's real golfing education began. Guldahl could not easily afford the playing dues at Tenison, but because he won the club championship regularly, he could forego the prizes and instead come to an arrangement with the club which enabled him to play all year round. It was also where Guldahl first came into contact with Syd Cooper, a transplanted English professional who had an impeccable golfing pedigree, having served part of his apprenticeship with Old Tom Morris at St. Andrews. He was also professional at the beautiful Aberdovey course in Wales, where he often played with Ted Ray and J.H. Taylor, in addition to Britain's foremost golf writer, Bernard Darwin. His son Harry would later recall how, in Aberdovey, the sheep kept the fairways trimmed. In time, Syd followed the well-worn route to North America, where he worked in Canada before he became a much sought-after teacher as well as a course designer in Texas. Syd was friendly with A.W. Tillinghast and learned a great deal from him. During his formative years, Guldahl received a great deal of advice and encouragement from Syd, who also ran the junior program at Tenison and put on lots of competitions for aspiring youngsters.

Syd's son, Harry, was also a player of some promise, and to say that he was steeped in golf would be an understatement. As well as being taught the basics by his father, his mother Alice was also known to give lessons, apart from helping Syd with his other professional duties. Harry started playing when he was three, and at age 5, he could drive the ball 100 yards. At age 11, Harry equaled the record for the nine-hole course at Cedar Crest. The record was held by Syd, and Harry's score was 38. Harry was a few years older than Guldahl, and, as Ralph would later say, became an

A teenage Ralph Guldahl in Dallas circa 1928—the days of hickory shafts and plus-fours or knickers (courtesy *Fort Worth Star-Telegram* Collection, Special Collections, University of Texas at Arlington Library).

idol for him and the others at Tenison. Harry turned pro in the early 1920s and was good enough to win the regional Texas PGA in 1923 at age 19 before winning his first tour event, the Los Angeles Open in 1926. He went on to become a winner of thirty-one tour events and the first holder of the Vardon Trophy; he had several near misses in the majors, including two runner-up finishes in the National Open. He was also regarded as one of the great stylists of his era. Unfortunately for Cooper, his achievements did not gain him a Ryder Cup place; having been born in England, he was ineligible. Cooper would later feature prominently in Guldahl's professional career.

As we saw above, Texas had a reputation for producing home-grown talent, and later in life, Guldahl would claim that the level of competition he faced up to in his formative golfing years was vital in his development. For example, when the local council built a nine-hole course at Randall Park, Ralph came up against Ray Mangrum. Later, in the 1930s, Guldahl and Mangrum locked horns on tour on a number of occasions, notably at the Western Open of 1936, when Ralph beat his fellow Dallasite into second place. Later that year, however, Mangrum beat Guldahl into fourth place at the Oregon Open. In total, Ray won five times on tour as well as achieving some high finishes in the majors. His younger brother, Lloyd, would go on to become National Open champion and a Ryder Cup player and captain.

Guldahl also met up with Gus Moreland, who, early in his career, was tipped for amateur stardom. In 1928, Guldahl defeated Moreland 4–3 in the final of the much coveted Bob-O-Link tournament in Dallas. He shot a 67 in the morning round, and later that year at the same Bob-O-Link course, he shot another 67 which contained only 19 putts. "Don't make the mistake," one report read, "of trying to tell Texans that Moreland, 20-year-old links star and 1931 Texas golf king, isn't the greatest fairway product turned out in the south since Bobby's younger days. Texas is convinced that Gus is the lad who will take over Jones' crown in amateur golf."[20] Moreland didn't go on to match the achievements of Jones (nobody did), but he did enjoy an outstanding career which saw him finish joint seventh in the 1933 National Open. In addition, in the 1932 Texas Open, he tied second with Gene Sarazen, just one shot behind winner Clarence Clark. Moreland also played on two Walker Cup teams and finished with an unbeaten record, and he had the distinction of defeating Ben Hogan in the final of the 1929 Southwestern Amateur, one of many titles he won.

Another contemporary at Randall Park was "Spec" Goldman, who recognized Guldahl's abilities early on when recalling that "we used to make some bets. It had been 50 cents per nine until Guldahl came along. But he won so regularly that everyone was getting cleaned out of pocket money. Pretty soon we reduced the bets to 25 cents and finally 10 cents."[21] "Spec" was a good enough player to reach the U.S. Amateur final of 1934. There he lost to the best amateur in the world at that time, Lawson Little.

Guldahl's last amateur victory was a 8–7 thrashing of "Spec" in the Dallas City Championship of 1929. Guldahl, however, was on the receiving end from Goldman and Moreland in a tournament which taught him a valuable lesson. He was just 16 when he came up against his fellow Dallasites in a three-man play-off for the Municipal Course Championship of Dallas. The tournament required one round to be played on each of the finalist's home courses. Guldahl's was Tenison Park; Moreland's was Oak Grove; and Goldman's was Stevens Park. Guldahl shot 75 and 70 on his opponents' courses, which left him one behind Goldman and three ahead of Moreland. With the final round at Tenison Park, where he had shot 64 on a number of occasions, Guldahl figured that he was good as home and dry. Back in the late 1920s, dieticians, any more than swing gurus, had not entered the golfer's lexicon. Players mostly had to work things out by trial and error. And so a very confident Guldahl decided to have a sizeable Scandinavian meal at Sunday lunchtime of beef, potatoes and ice cream. He shot 87 that afternoon and lost out, but he gained some invaluable experience. After that he stuck to a light diet before rounds. As he later recalled, "One of the old boys in the game told me once that tournaments were won on toast and tea, and lost on fruit and milk."[22]

In addition to Moreland and Goldman, when Guldahl played outside Dallas, he again came up against Ben Hogan, as well as Byron Nelson at nearby Fort Worth. When you add Harry Cooper to this group, we can see what a formidable golfing education Guldahl had. What is also apparent is that from the age of 16, Guldahl was a fierce competitor. In a series of local amateur events or in one-day tournaments when he first turned professional in 1930, he was the man to beat and demonstrated an ability to shoot low scores, as in 1928 when he recorded an amateur record of 64 at the Tenison course. He was just 17 years old. It was also in 1928 that he landed a particularly prized title: that of the Dallas Junior Golf Championship.

In February 1930, he moved up to the big league when he and Gus Moreland entered for the Texas Open, an event which would shape his career. At that time it was not unusual for amateurs to play in professional tournaments, especially if they were local. In addition, there was very little regulation regarding an amateur turning pro. Byron Nelson, for example, became a professional by simply paying a $5 entrance fee for the 1932 Texarkana Open. Some years later, after his first U.S. Open win in 1937, Guldahl admitted, "I had no idea of turning professional when I went to San Antonio the following February to play in the Texas Open. I was still attending Woodrow Wilson High School at home and I didn't think I was quite ready to play against professionals."[23] As it turned out, he shot 289 to finish 11th, 12 shots behind winner Denny Shute, and when hearing that the prize money for this finish was worth $100, he decided there and then to take the money (instead of the amateur trophy) and relinquish his amateur status. This gesture, as he later said, "made me a fully-fledged pro."[24] So just like Nelson, no exams or application forms were required to turn pro—just a clear statement of intent.

Guldahl's growing reputation led him to become professional at the Oak Grove municipal course, and later at Parkdale, where his duties included operating a floodlit driving range from eight o'clock to midnight. His enhanced status also saw him play an 18-hole exhibition match against Horton Smith, who was already a big star, and who would go on to win the Masters on two occasions. Both players played poorly, with Smith winning the medal-play match with a score of 77 to Guldahl's 79. However, despite losing, the experience of playing against such a star name, and in front of gallery of roughly 500 people, was an integral part of Guldahl's golfing education. Some further education, and one of his early successes as a pro, came when he won a weekly sweepstakes event at the Oakhurst Club in Fort Worth with a score of 73. One of the second-place finishers was Ben Hogan with a score of 78. Guldahl won a number of these keenly contested events, in which Ray Mangrum and Ted Longworth also competed. This was part of the "Texas training" he later spoke of in regard to the state's propensity for producing so much golfing talent.

In the same year of 1930, Guldahl qualified for the U.S. Open at Interlachen—his first. The Minnesota course has a distinguished history, having hosted a number of golf's premier events such as the Walker Cup and the Solheim Cup. However, its place in golfing lore was cemented back in 1930 when it hosted that year's National Open. It was reported: "Eight thousand pushing, shoving, panting persons walked and ran over the grassy hills and valleys of the Interlachen golf course to watch 143 of the nation's greatest golfers play their first round in the National Open tournament. Every one of the eight thousand was in imminent danger of sunstroke or heat prostration as they raced across the course." Ralph Guldahl was among the 143 of the "nation's greatest golfers," but there was really just one name on everyone's lips, and that was Bobby Jones, who was seeking the third leg of the Impregnable Quadrilateral, having already won both British amateur and professional titles. It was also recorded:

> The Open also was broadcast live on radio for the first time. Players were interviewed after their round at the KSTP broadcasting stand west of the clubhouse. There was national radio coverage as well, Ted Husing carried a portable transmitter and micro-

phone while he followed the players and covered the action for CBS, while [O.B.]
Keeler reported for NBC. Motion picture trucks for Pathé, Hearst Metrotone and
Paramount Sound News were on site. Players watched themselves in moving pictures
played at the downtown Radisson Hotel on Friday night. The comprehensive coverage
allowed the entire world to follow Jones' improbable pursuit.[25]

In the end, Jones realized his "improbable pursuit" with a score of 287,
and his adoring fans could now look forward to the U.S. Amateur at
Merion and his final championship journey. Ralph Guldahl's ambitions at
this stage were much more modest; he did complete four rounds, although
his total of 308 left him 21 shots behind Jones, and in these harsh times,
there was no prize money for this. However, as he later recalled, "I may
have been out of the money, but I was in the swim."[26]

His performances at the Texas Open and at Interlachen led Guldahl
to believe that he had a chance to make a living from playing the game.
At this juncture, it is worth briefly looking at the journey that he (and
other young hopefuls) was embarking on. When the Professional Golfers'
Association (PGA) was founded in 1916 by philanthropists Rodman Wanamaker, Walter Hagen, Francis Ouimet, and others, its primary aim was
directed more at the needs of club professionals rather than those in the
"play for pay" ranks. However, holding "meetings and tournaments peri-
odically for the encouragement of the younger members"[27] did come under
its remit. What later became the tour was a series of tournaments which
were loosely organized. Indeed, for a period in the 1920s, it was the wives
of some famous players who drummed up both sponsors and publicity.
This formidable group included Nellie Cruickshank, Estelle Armour and
Josephine Espinosa. During this era, however, there was one thing that
did the talking: money. These were the "Roaring Twenties" and the 1,500
"cool iron men" that Jack O'Brien and John Bredemus promised to the
winner of the first Texas Open in 1922 was matched at other tournament
stops. For example, when Harry Cooper won his first important tournament at the Los Angeles Open of 1926, his first prize was $3,500 from a
total purse of $10,000. It was here that Damon Runyon came up with
Cooper's lifetime nickname, "Lighthorse." Before he wrote classics such
as *Guys and Dolls*, Runyon reported on golf and boxing, and he gave
Cooper that nickname because he played so quickly. In winning at Los
Angeles, Cooper was, said Runyon, "like a cavalryman riding to a charge."
The following year, 1927, Bobby Jones's East Lake hosted the Southern
Open and attracted all the leading players with a purse of $12,000, includ-
ing a first prize of $4,000. Here Jones himself won the tournament by
eight with a score of 281. John Golden collected the $4,000 as leading

"Lighthorse" Harry Cooper, a longtime friend and rival of Ralph Guldahl's (courtesy Tufts Archives).

professional. Purses like ten and twelve thousand dollars, however, would soon be a thing of the past.

By 1930, the country had experienced the Wall Street crash of 1929 and was in the early stages of the Great Depression. And in the world of golf, the late 1920s property crash in the game's unofficial capital, Florida, had seriously damaged the potential earnings of professionals and golf course owners alike. The development of luxury hotel and golf complexes stopped, and with it the large retainers which were paid to professionals, such as Hagen, to attract both tourists and tournament sponsors. In 1923, for example, "Sir Walter" received the enormous sum of $30,000 for a four-month contract at the Pasadena-on-the-Gulf course. And while Florida would recover in the mid–1930s, the early years of the Depression were harsh in the world of professional golf.

Bobby Jones retired in 1930, and it was believed this would lead to a decline in the game's popularity with the public. This fear was realized when attendances at the U.S. Open declined in the immediate aftermath of his departure. On the tour, such as it was, purses were reduced to an average of between $3,000 and $5,000. Indeed, at the Miami Open of 1931, there was an undisclosed purse largely made up of entry fees and gate receipts. Joe Turnesa won the tournament. In addition, there was no safety net, and if a player did not finish in the top ten, there was no chance of coming close to making his expenses, which were roughly $100 per week. There was the occasional exception, such as the Agua Caliente Open in Tijuana, a location known for its gambling tables and racetrack, and for attracting rich tourists as well as celebrities such as Bing Crosby and Charlie Chaplin. Here, for example, the second staging in 1931 boasted a prize fund of $25,000 with a first prize of $10,000. Just as importantly, the purse was not front-loaded, with the prize list stretching down to 25th place. John Golden had the most important win of his career here. The event lasted to the mid–1930s, with the prize fund gradually declining on a year by year basis.

But in the middle of the gloom, the PGA had the foresight to appoint a full-time administrator: Albert Gates. Gates had impressive credentials, as he had served four terms as president of the Western Golf Association; he was a respected lawyer; and he was a director of three banks. And the press welcomed his arrival, declaring, "Baseball has its commissioner. The movie industry has its general director, and now comes the golf dictator."[28] In these unforgiving times, however, Gates's main responsibility lay with the 2,000-plus club professionals, many of whom were struggling to survive. And it was only when Walter Hagen's former manager, Bob Harlow, took up the post in 1933 that the tour had a full-time professional looking after its affairs. Harlow would remain in his role until 1937, when he was replaced by Fred Corcoran.[29] In theory, Harlow was the ideal man for the job, as seen by his ability to "sell" Walter Hagen to promoters, sponsors, and the public. Of course, in Hagen he had a good "product," but Harlow's contribution to "Sir Walter's" commercial success was widely recognized throughout the game. In the 1920s especially, Hagen was by some distance the leading money earner in professional golf, and Harlow was the man who made many of the deals. Unfortunately, Harlow's relationships with his employers, especially PGA president George Jacobus, were often tense, and before his eventual departure, there were many disputes. Notwithstanding this, he was a visionary and his skills gave the tour some badly needed impetus, even if money from sponsors was still in short supply. In this regard, he was particularly adept at persuading local chambers of commerce to underwrite tournaments with the promise that his golfing stars would attract fans, media interest, and therefore cash to the locality. It was a simple but effective formula.

So when Ralph Guldahl set off on tour, it was very much a journey into the unknown, complete with the fact that there were no guarantees. If he did not finish in the top ten, there was little chance of a paycheck at the end of the week. This was certainly the case when he embarked on the long car journey from Dallas to Missouri to play in the St. Louis Open of 1930. Here, he was accompanied by Ted Longworth and a young Ben Hogan from Glen Garden. Jimmy Demaret, a fellow Texan and one whose time would come soon after Guldahl's, later recalled a remark from Longworth. "When the three arrived in St. Louis," Demaret wrote, "a Joplin, Missouri, golf writer, asked Longworth who the two youngsters were. Ben was only 19 at the time."

"They're a couple of real good kids," Ted answered. "Guldahl is ready to go now, but the younger one—this Hogan—might take it all someday."[30] Given where Hogan's career was at this juncture, these words can be retrospectively seen as among the finest pieces of foresight in the history of professional golf.

Ted Longworth was a professional of some standing both as a player and as a club pro at Glen Garden, where he had helped both Ben and Byron develop their games. Indeed, after his "streak" of 1945, Nelson was quick to acknowledge the help he received from Longworth back in Glen Garden. He recalled how Longworth was the first to take a real interest in his development and how having a professional take such an interest in a caddy was considered quite an honor. Recounting the long and loose

A young Ben Hogan with the unfamiliar hat. While he and Guldahl started out on tour together, it was the Dallas man who had the more rapid rise to the top. Then, in 1940, when Hogan first became a prolific winner, Guldahl's slide had begun (courtesy *Fort Worth Star-Telegram* Collection, Special Collections, University of Texas at Arlington Library).

"caddy swing" of his teenage years, Nelson spoke of how Longworth "spent a lot of time with me in an effort to shorten my swing and make it firmer and more compact."[31] Nelson spent hours on the practice ground swinging with a handkerchief under his right arm to help the process along.

Longworth is also credited with persuading Ben Hogan to change from his natural left-handed stance to that of a right-hander, although others recognize Ted's assistant, Jack Grout, as being responsible for this.[32] Guldahl had competed against Longworth in a number of one-day events around the Dallas area and against Hogan in their amateur days. In St. Louis, Guldahl led after a first round of 66 and eventually took home $200 for finishing tied ninth. This was a wonderful start and he was in very good company at St. Louis. The winner was reigning PGA champion Tommy Armour, and the names who finished ahead of Ralph Guldahl included Walter Hagen, Horton Smith and Gene Sarazen.

Later that year Guldahl traveled to California to play some events on the traditional winter swing, which would take in late 1930 and early 1931. By now Guldahl was married to the former Laverne Fields from Dallas, whom he met when giving her a series of golf lessons. Ralph later claimed that "we ran off and got married," which very much sounds like an elopement.[33] Indeed, after an interview with Guldahl, O.B. Keeler reported that they "just slipped over across the Texas border to Durant, Oklahoma, the local Gretna Green, and were married, April 11, 1931." They were 19 years old. Guldahl later admitted Laverne was not a very good player. Laverne agreed with this assessment but added that Ralph "didn't seem to have much patience with me. He was a pretty bum teacher."[34] However, she quickly became his greatest supporter during his tournament career. Traveling with a wife in those days was considered something of a luxury because of the cost involved. And while Olaf and Anna Guldahl had been able to provide for their three sons, financing Ralph on tour was not an option. This was similar to the situation faced by young Ben Hogan, who could only play on tour if he finished in the money, and this was often difficult with many tournaments only paying out on the first ten finishers. The third Texan, however, had a more comfortable start in that Byron Nelson's future father-in-law loaned him $660 to help him get a proper start on tour. On the back of this, Byron put in some fine performances and was able to pay back the money in a matter of weeks. But there was no safety net for the Guldahls, and later Ralph admitted that "we didn't have to watch each dollar, we had to watch each penny."[35] Regardless of the pressure engendered by having little start-up money, the California swing proved to be lucrative for the Guldahls, as Ralph won roughly $2,500 in total. Most significantly, however, he won his first tournament.

In the early 1930s, tournaments attracted in a variety of sponsors, ranging from luxury hotels in Florida, to newspapers, to local chambers of commerce anxious to promote trade and tourism in their area. Guldahl's first success came in the Motion Pictures Open of 1931, which carried a first prize of $1,000 and was held at the famed George Thomas–designed Riviera Country Club. Later, in the 1940s and 1950s, Riviera would be associated with Ben Hogan, for it was here that he won the Los Angeles Open twice, as well as his first National Open title. In addition, it was at Riviera in 1950 that he began his comeback from his near fatal car crash. Hogan and Sam Snead tied in the L.A. Open, but Snead won the play-off. Unsurprisingly, the course was often referred to as "Hogan's Alley."

But back in the 1920s and '30s, Riviera was a second home for many Hollywood silent movie stars such as Charlie Chaplin, Douglas Fairbanks Jr., and Mary Pickford. Greta Garbo lived close by the 14th fairway. Given the tournament's name and location, it was no surprise that it was Fairbanks and another silent movie great, Harold Lloyd, who each put up $500 towards the purse and persuaded other friends to do likewise. In this regard, the two stars were helped by the contribution of Leo Diegel. Diegel was undoubtedly one of the most colorful and popular professionals of this era. Known as a great theorist, he was also a wonderful player who won thirty times on tour, including two PGA Championships. He also had a number of very high finishes in both the U.S. and British Opens. But it was not just the public and his fellow professionals that Diegel was popular with. He was also an insider with many in Hollywood, and he had already starred in an Irving Thalberg comedy short appropriately called *Fore*. And later in his career, the movie mogul Joe Schenck hired him for a year as his private teacher. For the Motion Pictures Open, Leo was instrumental in persuading a number of the rich and famous to make their donations.

"Young Ace Wins Big Tourney" was how one newspaper described the victory.[36] Another said, "Now we have a new 'Kid Wonder' to look at since Horton Smith. The critics are cocking their weather eyes at a kid named Ralph Guldahl, 19 years old."[37] The comparison with Smith was praise indeed, as at the age of 21, Horton won eight times in 1929. And Guldahl's victory did not go unnoticed in his home city of Dallas. One fan wrote to the *Dallas Morning News* to say, "Guldahl has brought valuable advertising to Dallas by his victory and likely will bring it much more in the future."[38] Equally important as the headlines was the level of player Guldahl beat on his way to the title. For example, in the early rounds of this match-play event he beat future U.S. Open and PGA champion Olin Dutra; he also beat multiple tournament winner Joe Kirkwood; and in the semifinal he defeated the vastly experienced and prolific tournament winner MacDonald Smith. In addition, in the 36-hole final, he beat a future National Open Champion, Tony Manero, on the final green. His victory was also significant in that Ralph was three down after 11 holes of the morning round. After his success, Leo Diegel marked him out as one who was "going places in a golfing way."[39] Ralph Guldahl was on his way, and he was only 19 years old. Until Jordan Spieth won the John Deere Classic in 2013, no player under 20 would win a tour event. As noted earlier, Spieth is another "Texas Ranger" who also hails from Dallas.

In these, the early stages of the Great Depression, making a living from tournament golf was hard. Certainly there were a number of significant first prizes such as the $1,000 Guldahl won in California. However, such riches were relatively rare, and the payoff for a successful tour player was that prestigious clubs would offer him a secure club job. In this regard, after his success in California, Guldahl was appointed professional at the Donald Ross–designed Franklin Hills Country Club, Detroit. Here he was indebted to Walter Hagen, who recommended him for the post. The word "secure" can be qualified, however, as even the most distinguished clubs in the 1930s suffered from falling membership and loss of revenue.

In 1932, Guldahl's good form continued with a number of high finishes. For example, early in the year, he came joint 11th in his native Texas Open with a score of 296. Here the winner was Clarence Clark, whose score of 287 won him a first prize of $600. The 1,500 "cool iron men" on offer for the winner of Jack O'Brien's first Texas Open of 1922 was a distant memory as the Great Depression grew. The following week in Houston, Clark won again, with Guldahl finishing a respectable joint ninth and taking home $55. The very tall Clark was one of the lesser-known professionals from this era, but he was good enough to win seven times on tour. His prize in Houston was $500. An even better finish for Guldahl came in the Pasadena Open where he tied joint fourth with Hagen behind Harry Cooper and won $290. At the Los Angeles Open, he finished joint sixth with Sarazen and Abe Espinosa behind Mac Smith and took home $250. And in the lucrative Coral Gables Open in Florida, he won $650 when finishing fifth behind Sarazen. These were good weeks for Guldahl, and a second tournament win was not far away.

On today's PGA tour, the Phoenix Open is one of the best supported, most popular, and loudest tournaments in terms of fan participation. Sponsored by the Waste Management Company, the tournament is now held at the TPC stadium venue at Scottsdale. Phil Mickelson is a three-time winner of the title. Back at the inaugural event in 1932, it was called the Arizona Open and was a much more somber affair. The event was played at the San Marcos course and it marked the second win in Guldahl's professional career. The five-shot win with a three under par score of 285 carried a first prize of $600 from a total purse of $2,500. Apart from the money, the victory was significant because in second place, five shots back, was Johnny Farrell. When his name was mentioned, invariably the word "classy" was used to describe Farrell. This was in reference to his personality, his attire, and his golf game. He was good enough to gain 22 tour victories, including a U.S. Open win in 1928. Here he beat Bobby Jones in a 36-hole play-off, and he was still winning in the early 1930s. He also represented the U.S. teams in the first three Ryder Cup matches. For Guldahl to defeat such a player so comprehensively was a considerable achievement for a 22-year-old.

As a seriously promising player, Guldahl had by now been appointed professional at the extremely prestigious St. Louis Country Club, which had already held the National Men's and Women's Amateur Championships. Furthermore, the previous professionals included U.S. Open winners Jim Foulis, Fred McCleod and Willie Anderson. In fact, Anderson was the first man to win four National Open titles, and to this day he remains the only man to win the title in three consecutive years, 1903, 1904 and 1905. A very young Ralph Guldahl was following in famous footsteps, but he proved to be popular with members and local players alike. His time there had certain advantages and disadvantages. The disadvantages were that during these early Depression years, the club was not open seven days a week, and so the club professional would suffer accordingly. On the other hand, this left Ralph plenty of time to play local events and exhibitions and so hone his game. In this regard, it was reported that his arrival in St. Louis got the Missouri pros "on their toes," as "all the boys started to play and practice." It was also recorded that he played in a number of exhibitions that attracted large crowds.[40] Guldahl was playing well, but regardless of this and his success at the Arizona Open, his performance at the National Open of 1932 might have shaken his confidence. That year's championship was held at the Fresh Meadow Club, New York, and his total of 314 was a full 28 shots behind the winner, Gene Sarazen. There was no money for such a low finish. However, the members at St. Louis would have a more enjoyable U.S. Open the following year.

The disappointment of Fresh Meadow proved to be something of a minor glitch, and in 1933, Guldahl's steady progress continued when he won the St. Louis Open. This was not a recognized tour stop, but it did attract many well-known players because it had a healthy prize fund. In the final of this match-play event at his home club, Guldahl defeated Orville White 8–6 in the final. White was a well-respected player who won many regional events and who would go on to compete in the Masters on numerous occasions. The only major Guldahl played in that year was the National Open, as the Masters had not yet started and he did not qualify for the match-play stages of the PGA. But his form in the majors would change at North Shore, where he came so close to winning his first major title.

The North Shore Country Club was founded in 1900, but by 1924 the club had moved to the Glenview district of North Chicago, and the Harry Colt–designed course quickly became one of the top-rated courses in the region. This was impressive, as the area was home to clubs such as Medinah and Olympia Fields. It also quickly gained tournament pedigree and was awarded the Western Open of 1928, at a time when the Western was deemed a major title. The championship was notable as it largely involved a close contest between the Espinosa brothers, Abe and Al, with the former winning on a score of 291. Espinosa's total was reflective of a challenging course, and by 1933, North Shore was rated as a formidable test for the nation's top golfers.

Guldahl's quest for the 1933 National Open had an inauspicious start. In those days, there was a 36-hole regional qualifier, but rather than try to qualify in the St. Louis region where he was based, Guldahl opted for the Chicago district. His logic was that he should qualify comfortably regardless of *where*, but being in the vicinity of the North Shore Club would make it easier for him to play practice rounds over the championship venue. Even at this early stage of his career, lengthy preparation for the U.S. Open was deemed to be essential. However, he almost came unstuck, as he barely qualified with rounds of 81 and 76. Indeed, he was so discouraged that Laverne suggested they pack their bags and return to St. Louis. But he stayed and became part of a championship which would be memorable in his career and in the history of American golf.

In the days of Bobby Jones, golf fans were used to an amateur winning the U.S. Open. But the amateur on everyone's lips at North Shore—Johnny Goodman—was a meatpacker's son from Nebraska. Goodman's parents were Lithuanian immigrants, like 1931 U.S. Open champion Billy Burke. Goodman was orphaned at 14 when his mother died giving birth to her thirteenth child. Her husband, unable to cope, left home. There were certain similarities between Ralph Guldahl and Johnny Goodman in that both learned the game as caddies and were self-taught. And like Guldahl, Goodman had some local success, as when he won the Omaha City title at age 16—with borrowed clubs. At this time, however, notwithstanding Francis Ouimet's achievements, amateur championship golf in America was predominantly for players from the right side of the tracks. In one article, Johnny was described as the "Hobo of the Links," and while that may seem a little far-fetched, it was revealed that for the Trans-Mississippi Championship of 1927, Johnny "bummed" his way to the tournament on a freight car.[41] He won the event, but Johnny first came to national prominence by beating Jones in the first round of the National Amateur at Pebble Beach in 1929.

After that surprise victory, however, it would be fair to say that Goodman's career and his fortunes were mixed. Indeed, in 1930, he officially announced his retirement from the game, deeming it a "rich man's game."[42] Fortunately, the retirement was short-lived and he came back to win the amateur medal when Gene Sarazen won the U.S. Open in 1932. However, his score of 302 was decidedly average when compared to the winning total of 288. Furthermore, he was not deemed worthy of a place in the U.S. Walker Cup team for the same year even though he had been runner-up in the National Amateur. Socially, however, his growing golfing reputation proved advantageous, and by 1933, he had the respectable profession of an insurance salesman. This was a long way from his impoverished background, but not everyone was impressed; the USGA had its suspicions that Goodman was using his golfing reputation to enhance his business career. Back then, there was no blurring of the lines between amateurism and professionalism, and any question of using golf to enhance an occupation was either frowned upon or could lead to suspension. There was a certain irony in the fact that Ralph Guldahl would turn to the insurance business when he quit the tour in the early 1950s.

In more recent times, coverage of the four majors is distributed on a relatively even basis. During the Depression era, however, of the three majors played in America,[43] there is little doubt that the National Open stood head and shoulders above the Masters and the PGA Championships in terms of public interest. This was even more so in regard to radio and, especially, press coverage. Days ahead of the opening round, the nation's top golf writers converged on the venue to assess the playing conditions and the form of the leading players. And on the day following the championship, it was not unusual to find a significant reference to the victor on the front page of the national newspapers, never mind the headlines which dominated the sports pages. The National Open was, to quote one writer from that period, comparable to "The World Series of baseball; the heavyweight championship of boxing and the derby of horse racing."[44]

The chosen course always received a great deal of coverage in the lead-in to the championship. Usually this involved just how tough a test it would be for the leading players. North Shore was no different in this regard. For example, it was reported that "North Shore stretched a full

6,927 yards and appeared to be a long-hitter's course but the sun-baked track was as hard as asphalt.... However, North Shore was also dangerously tight." And wire service reporter Davis Walsh told readers, "The fairways start out narrow and then sharpen to a mere footpath, so that only the perfect tee shot avoids the rough. The rough is like a matted beard. Some say it needs a niblick. Perhaps, I'd prefer a scythe."[45] In addition, at the start of the championship, temperatures soared to over 100 degrees, ensuring that the 1933 National Open would be a serious examination of both mind and body.

And a further and integral part of the newspaper build-up focused on practice scores, which were of particular importance to the bookies and their odds. In general, players were very open about exactly what they shot during practice. In this regard, in the lead-in to North Shore, Johnny got some favorable publicity as he recorded some good practice scores. But much of the attention was focused on the title holder, Gene Sarazen, whom some bookies had at odds as low as 4–1. Gene had also won the British Open in 1932. In one of his practice rounds, Sarazen played with Guldahl's old Dallas rival, Gus Moreland, and was so impressed that he somewhat prophetically claimed, "There ought to be a great battle between him and Johnny Goodman for the top amateur honors."[46] The other favorites included Olin Dutra, Craig Wood (the year's leading money winner), and Tommy Armour. There was certainly no mention of Ralph Guldahl.

In the first round, it was Tommy Armour who set the pace in the sweltering heat. His round of 68 was a new course record, beating Al Espinosa's record by one. He led by five from a group including Hagen, Wood and Revolta. The holder, Sarazen had a 74 while Johnny Goodman had a 75. Ralph Guldahl was well back on 76. For the second round, everything changed. Armour slipped back with a 75 and Sarazen played himself out of contention with a 77. The story of the day was Goodman, who shot a record 66, which saw him start with three birdies; hole a chip at number 15 for an eagle three; and birdie the treacherous par four 18th hole. In total, he had only 25 putts. Crucially, Goodman's round contained many par-saving putts, and it was this ability to scramble when necessary that was a feature of his victory. Guldahl shot 71 and played himself back into respectability, although he was still six shots behind Goodman.

The final day, with 36 holes facing the players, began with rain and a softer course. This, however, would change in the afternoon when the rain disappeared and the course firmed up again. And on the final morning, both spectators and fans were greeted by the views of Gene Sarazen in his syndicated column when he said, "Given a few breaks today we may see another Francis Ouimet pop up and amaze the country with a triumph over the professionals."[47] The draw for playing partners on the final day of a major is crucial, especially for a player who is leading for the first time. In this regard, Goodman was fortunate that his partner for his final examination was MacDonald Smith, who was not only a wonderful player, but who was also from the gentleman's school of golf. As it turned out, Goodman had a seventy on Saturday morning in a round which contained only 26 putts. Surely he was now home and dry, and as one of his biographers put it, "To some observers the real question now was whether Johnny would break the U.S. Open record, held jointly by Sarazen and Chick Evans. Two over would do the trick, child's play the way Goodman was performing."[48] Ralph Guldahl continued his quiet move up the leaderboard and matched Goodman's round of 70.

At the start of the final round it seemed as if Goodman would smash Evans's record; after a par, eagle, birdie start to his final 18, his lead was

The victor and the vanquished: Johnny Goodman, left, and Ralph Guldahl after the 1933 U.S. Open (courtesy North Shore Country Club).

increased to nine. However, he faltered as the pressure intensified, and a series of dropped shots saw him reach the turn in 39. On the back of this, Charles Bartlett of the *Chicago Tribune* reported, "Johnny acted as though he had been hit by a left hook when he was in front on points. There were traps and rough, rough and traps and more of the same."[49] Goodman, however, responded like a champion and settled down with pars at ten and eleven. After the event, Johnny told George Trevor of *Golf Illustrated*, "I don't deserve to win after such a gutless finish."[50] A look at the last four holes tells a different story. Goodman came up 30 yards short of the 511-yard, par five 15th hole. However, he managed to get up and down for a vital birdie four. At the 16th hole he came out of a bunker and holed the putt for a par, but he dropped a shot at the 17th. He now faced the daunting final hope and he played it like a champion: a perfect drive followed by a long iron to six feet. A birdie here would put the title beyond reach of anyone else, but his cautious putt ensured his par and a final round of 76. Playing the demanding final four holes in level par was not by any means a "gutless finish," given the circumstances.

Goodman was finished well ahead of Guldahl and could only wait, but for a time, another player came into the picture: Walter Hagen. "The Haig" was, at age 40, "titillating the gallery,"[51] and at one stage looked as if he might shoot a 61 or 62. In the end, however, he shot 66 and so equaled the course record Goodman set the day before. Eventually, he tied for fourth place with Tommy Armour, five behind the winner. Perhaps the fact that after Goodman's finish, the huge crowds focused on Hagen and so took some of the pressure off Guldahl. Whatever the reason, he played steadily and made up Goodman's lead by the time he reached the 15th hole. Here, however, where Goodman earlier had a birdie four, Guldahl took three from the edge with a costly missed five-foot putt. He reclaimed this shot as he played the next two in par, in contrast to Goodman's one over, and as he stood on the 437-yard 18th, he needed a par to achieve just that. He also needed a birdie for outright victory.

Charles Bartlett of the *Chicago Tribune* described Guldahl's final and dramatic moments after a perfect drive:

Without spending too much time over the shot, he whipped out an iron. His aim was a trifle to the right and his ball landed on the slope of a bunker guarding the left-hand side of the green bouncing into the sand. He didn't have much green to work with between the edge of the green and the flag stick. Silence reigned around the green as he went down into the bunker to look over the lie. The young pro, apparently unnerved by the mishap, wiped his hands with a towel. He seemed to regain his pose as he took his stance to play the shot on which so much was at stake. Finally he flicked the ball out onto the green, and it started for the hole. For a moment it appeared as if it would roll dead to the hole but finally it stopped, and Guldahl was left with a putt of not more than four feet.... Taking his stance, Guldahl gave the ball a little tap, but he had not figured the slope of the green quite accurately. The ball started for the hole, then curled off. It missed the cup by a slight margin on the left-hand side, inches away.[52]

"I guess I had the jitters," was Ralph Guldahl's more than honest assessment of his second to last stroke.[53]

Johnny Goodman's place in golfing history was now assured as he became the eighth and last amateur to win the U.S. Open title. He also joined an elite group of players who won both National amateur and professional golf titles. This list includes Woods, Nicklaus, Palmer, Little and Jones. As for his finish at North Shore, Grantland Rice summed it up perfectly when writing of the burden Goodman carried on the final day and of losing such a big lead: "Few can come back against such a hostile turn of events. Panic usually sets in. But under this strain, Goodman played the last four holes in par, and he got his four where it counted most, on the final green."[54]

A further disappointment for Ralph Guldahl was that his narrow loss cost him a place on the Ryder Cup team for the upcoming matches to be played in Southport, England. In the 1930s, selection was based on votes cast by both national and regional PGA committees. After North Shore, it was reported that as well as his $1,000 prize, "Guldahl may also be given a place on the Ryder Cup team.... There is one place open on the team and it is believed that it was held open for the professional leading the field in this tournament."[55] As Guldahl finished as the leading professional, he understandably had hopes of being selected, but it seems as if nobody had entertained thoughts of an amateur winning the title. In the end, after considerable lobbying by Gene Sarazen, Billy Burke, U.S. Open winner in 1931, was given the tenth and final place. The matches were played at Southport, England, and the U.S. team lost by one point.

After the missed putt, and even when he had won two back to back National Open titles, it was hard to find an article on Ralph Guldahl that did not refer to the 72nd hole at North Shore. The fact that he was just 22 was not mentioned, and yet Sam Snead did not start winning majors until he was 29, and with Ben Hogan it was 34. Nor was it mentioned that he had no real Open form and was rated a 100–1 outsider by the bookies. (His performance in the qualifying rounds backed up these odds.) And his remarkable comeback during the final round, when he made up nine shots in 15 holes, was just a footnote. In addition, it went almost unnoticed that his four-round total of 288 was only two shots shy of the all-time U.S.

Open record. Grantland Rice, as was often the case, attempted to put Guldahl's performance into context. In reference to the two missed putts and numbers 15 and 18 he wrote, "These memories leave their poison behind." And he went on, "Guldahl's frantic pursuit, his recovery of nine strokes in eleven holes must remain one of the greatest chapters in golf when you consider that it was the final round of an open championship and that the pursuing challenger was only twenty-one years old and making his first bid."[56]

These sympathetic but perfectly sensible words, however, were rare at the time. Guldahl was a loser and that was what counted. Indeed, one journalist claimed that at the back of the 18th green at North Shore, one professional was heard to say, "Once a runner up, always a runner up. Golfers never come back after one bust like that."[57] Other locker-room sages were reported as commenting, "It's too bad. He's a nice boy but he's all through."[58] These quotes (more than likely) may have been pieces of imaginative journalism, but Herb Graffis, who was editor of *Golfing* and who authored many books on the game, was perhaps a more authoritative voice. In 1937 he recalled how a famous old-time pro passed the following judgment on Guldahl as the pair stood around the final green at North Shore: "He's just shot himself through the heart. As a star golfer, this boy is dead from now on." In addition, Graffis claimed, "Bar room authorities [were] already predicting that his putting was going the same way as Hagen."[59] At this stage of his career, many believed that "The Haig" had a touch of the "whiskey fingers" or "yips" on the greens. Regardless of how many of these comments were authentic, there is little doubt that not too many present would have expected Guldahl to become a double U.S. Open winner within the matter of a few years.

If the media was clear on its view of Guldahl's performance, it was not certain then if Ralph took his narrow loss as badly as the newspapers suggested he might. He was now under contract to Wilson Sporting Goods, and in a clever piece of marketing, he wrote an open letter to the firm in the aftermath of North Shore. Essentially the letter was to tell the readers of *Golf Illustrated* magazine that the new Wilson "Ogg-Mented" irons were so good that having tried them out just two weeks before the "off," Guldahl was quite happy to use them in the championship. (The irons were named after Wilson designer, Willie Ogg, and featured the then novel idea of placing the weight more in the center of the club-head rather than in the heel.) Some might have queried the wisdom of Guldahl's playing in the National Open with such an untested set of clubs, but fellow Wilson player Gene Sarazen was not among them. Speaking of Guldahl,

Sarazen wrote, "I admire him greatly for daring to play a new set of clubs just because they appealed to him which he hardly tried out before the tournament.... I am a firm believer in a man not becoming a slave to any club in his bag."[60] The facts supported Sarazen's view, for as Guldahl later said, "72 holes in even fours. It was the best tournament golf I ever played."[61] As noted, the letter's primary aim was to boost the sales of Wilson equipment, but there was also truth in the level of golf Guldahl played, especially on "Open Saturday" when he shot 70–71. And with Goodman being an amateur, there was the $1,000 first money, which would be useful to him and his young wife, Laverne.

And, if anyone was trying to find further positives, there was also the often-asked question to consider: does a golfer need to *lose* a "big one" before he can win one? Tom Watson, for example, missed wonderful opportunities to win the U.S. Open in both 1974 and 1975 before going on to dominate the game within a few years. More recently, Rory McIlroy admitted that his final day "Masters Meltdown" in 2011 was the making of him. This was when he took a four-shot lead into the final round and shot an 80. In an interview before the 2015 Masters, McIlroy said, "I've always said that the last round at Augusta in '11 was a huge learning curve for me and I took a lot from that day." In the same interview, when asked if he could have gone on to win the U.S. Open a few weeks later at Congressional without the Masters experience, he responded, "No way."[62] And when reflecting on North Shore, some years later, Byron Nelson was in no doubt that missing out in 1933 was a major factor in the development of Ralph Guldahl. He was, said Nelson, "the perfect example of a golfer who lost a championship and became a better golfer as a result."[63] Maybe Nelson's analysis was correct, but at the time it must have been difficult for Guldahl to appreciate this. Certainly he put a brave face on matters, but the loss of a Ryder Cup place, not to mention the endorsements and guaranteed exhibition tour, must have been harsh medicine for a young professional and his wife in the early 1930s. Just as importantly, a judgment was made on the career of Ralph Guldahl, and history judged that the 18th green at North Shore, 1933, saw him *lose* the National Open title and enter into a seemingly irreversible slump.

2

The Comeback

There was a general consensus that Ralph Guldahl's game went into decline after the missed final green putt at the 1933 National Open that saw him lose out to Johnny Goodman by a single shot. His fall from grace, however, did not happen immediately, as after North Shore, there were some strong performances. For example, at the Canadian Open won by Joe Kirkwood, Guldahl finished fourth, and at the Western Open, he came fifth behind winner Mac Smith. Top five finishes in these prestigious tournaments were hardly indicators of a golfer who was "washed up." Then, the following year, 1934, there were some bright spots, such as a win at the relatively minor Westwood Open in Los Angeles. Here he beat Willie Hunter, another transplanted British golfer, who won the British Amateur Championship before he emigrated to America and turned pro. For almost thirty years, Willie served as pro at Riviera, scene of Guldahl's first tour victory. There was also the matter of the National Open, played that year at the Merion Club in Philadelphia.

Merion was already seen as one of the most prestigious clubs in the land, but without doubt, this reputation was very much amateur-centered. Merion had hosted the U.S. Amateur of 1916, 1924 and 1930. The 1930 Amateur, more than any other event, cemented the club's place in American golfing lore, as it was here that Bobby Jones won the final leg of his Grand Slam. Merion also hosted the Women's Amateur Championship in 1904, 1909 and 1926. But changes were about to take place, and in 1934, it was decided that the "wholesale presence of the professional golfers and their attendants at the Golf House would not be objectionable."[1] This hardly represented a fulsome welcome for the professionals, but it was a start, and Merion subsequently hosted the National Open on numerous occasions.

Whatever may be said about the stuffiness of the club, there was no doubting the quality of the course, and 1934 saw the pros face a brutal examination. Merion, at just under 6,700 yards, was not long by National Open standards, but it was tight, and in theory, the premium on accuracy from the tee should have suited Guldahl. On the par 70 course, Bobby Cruickshank led after two rounds with a score of 142, Gene Sarazen was on 145 with Guldahl on 151, one behind Olin Dutra. The Saturday morning was windy, and this saw the slick greens become even faster. With Cruickshank slipping to a 77, Guldahl made his move with the best round of the week, a par-equaling 70, thirty-five shots for each nine. Along with Dutra, he was now on 221, just three behind leader Sarazen and two behind Cruickshank. This was a far better position than he was in a year earlier at North Shore. However, the conditions finally caught up with him on the Saturday afternoon as he faded to a 78. Dutra, meanwhile, played steadily for a 72 and won the title by one over Sarazen. His total was 293, thirteen over par. While Merion was not nearly as big a blow for Guldahl as North Shore, it did raise serious questions about his ability to finish the job in major championships. Johnny Goodman, incidentally, never featured in his title defense, and the amateur prize was won by Lawson Little, who was about to become the "world's best amateur."

After the U.S. Open, Guldahl tied with Jimmy Thomson for the Santa Monica Open with a score of 271 on the Clover Field Country Club. Thomson won the play-off with a 70 to Guldahl's 74 and took home the modest prize of $300. Guldahl received just $200 but his performance over five rounds of medal play was encouraging. Furthermore, there was a creditable joint fourth place at the Pasadena Open. Here, his score of 288 was seven shots behind winner Jug McSpaden. For 1935, however, his form was considerably worse. An example of this was his score of 300 at Phoenix, where he finished 19 shots behind Ky Laffoon and won $12.50. There were also a number of tournaments in which he either could not afford to play or in which he did compete and won nothing. And if he was hoping for any form of U.S. Open redemption at Oakmont, he was to be disappointed. Here Guldahl finished a full 19 shots behind the winner, Sam Parks, who won with 299. Guldahl later described his performance as "the worst I ever played in the Open."[2] Form like that ensured that Ralph Guldahl would not feature among the select sixty invitees to Augusta.

If Guldahl did not make any noise on the course at Oakmont, he had plenty to say after the championship. And this was an early display of the outspokenness which marked his career. This was something of a paradox, as on one hand he was described in the newspapers as being soft-spoken and without color. And then on the other, he was capable of outbursts which could be seen as arrogant or certainly controversial. His comments after Oakmont fell into the latter category. It would not be unreasonable to suggest that Sam Parks was one of the most unlikely National Open winners in a list that includes Cyril Walker, Jack Fleck and Orville Moody. It was the only tournament of note he ever won, although he did make the Ryder Cup team of 1935. Ralph Guldahl, however, believed that his win had been unfairly received by many of the established professionals, and at the relatively tender age of 23, he was not afraid to voice his opinion. "I don't know what our profession is coming to," he said. "The Americans are letting them foreigners crowd them out ... yes, they stepped up and congratulated him ... [and then] ... detracted from his achievement as much as they could.... In my book he was the best golfer in the tournament. But he showed up the would-be stars of the profession and they can't take it." And he did not stop there, claiming that "these birds who won the open several years ago with scores that soared several strokes higher when the competition wasn't so tough, give me a pain with their attitude towards Parks' 1935 triumph."[3]

All the evidence suggests that Guldahl was correct in his assessment of Parks's victory, as Oakmont in 1935 was regarded as being one of the most brutal tests in U.S. Open history. Lightning-fast greens, severe rough, and the famous Oakmont bunkers saw to this. The par of 72 was bettered on only two occasions, which puts Parks's final round of 73 into context. Only a champion would come out on top there. But the reference to the "foreigners" must refer to the Scottish or British-Americans who dominated the American game in the early decades of the twentieth century and who were perceived as having a level of knowledge superior to that of the home pros. What these comments do suggest is that even at this early stage, and despite the 72nd green at North Shore, Ralph Guldahl had self-confidence, an inner resolve, and a strength of mind that would stand to him well in the coming years. But for 1935, and with virtually no tour earnings, he returned to Texas for a time and gave lessons at the beautifully named Mockingbird Driving Range.

The slump lasted until 1936, and when he began his comeback, the press gave it the full "Hollywood" treatment. For example, one scribe wrote, "The story of Guldahl, his troubles and comeback comprise one of the brightest chapters in the history of the game. It is a story of progress and poverty, of a kid who missed his greatest chance, fell to the brink of despair with a wife and young baby in his arms and then came back a winner."[4] The "missed his greatest chance" was a reminder of the 72nd hole loss at North Shore, but notwithstanding the colorful language, it was a remarkable achievement for such a young man. The reference to his baby is important, for by now the Guldahls were parents to young Ralph Jr., or "Buddy." However, because of the baby's poor health, Ralph and Laverne took him from Dallas to the warmer weather in California, and it was here that the comeback began in earnest. Later, Guldahl recalled that trip so vividly that he even remembered the exact cost. "That trip," he told O.B. Keeler, "from Dallas to Los Angeles cost exactly $27.45 for the three of us. But we had nothing to use for money when I got there and I was playing badly.... I couldn't scrape up the funds to reach Sacramento and San Francisco for the tourneys there."[5]

Theories on how far down he was and what brought about the comeback have varied, with one version suggesting that Guldahl sold cars for a time after giving up the game. This account appears to be true, and for years, headlines such as "Great Finish Gives Auto Salesman $1,000 first place prize"[6] were plentiful. That the Guldahls were far down is not in doubt. PGA tournament director Bob Harlow recalls Laverne telling him that they were in "deep poverty" and that "she would not wish any struggling family to endure such tough times as the Guldahls experienced."[7] Bob Harlow also recounted another occasion when money was so scarce that Laverne and three other professionals' wives had to remain in Florida while their husbands traveled to a tournament in California in a "broken-down flivver."[8] Later, Guldahl admitted that for a period he was not an official member of the PGA, as he could not afford the annual dues of $25.[9] There were also stories that he wore the same suit for almost three years because he could not afford a new one. And some reports have suggested that he designed Kilgore, a nine-hole course in Texas, and so earned himself and Laverne a few dollars.

Guldahl's parents, however, had a slightly different recollection. After his son's first National Open victory, Olaf told reporters that "he only once wired for money ... and he got it. He always, except for one year, has won enough prize money to get along."[10] What was not in doubt is that for a time, Ralph Guldahl gave up the game and took up work as a carpenter on a Hollywood lot. However, the reason he moved to the movie capital was not simply a random choice. "I heard," he later said, "that a pro could pick up some money teaching movie stars. We were going to sleep in the car if need be. But I was lucky. I ran into Rex Bell and the late Robert Woolsey. I taught them and played with them and made a hit."[11] The tuition he gave Bell and Woolsey was accompanied by a number of money matches on a nine-hole course in Palm Springs. The stakes were not high but Guldahl made enough to help pay some bills. Guldahl also spent a lot of time, according to Keeler, practicing four-foot putts: just the length he missed on the final green at North Shore.[12]

Rex Bell was an actor who specialized in B Westerns such as *Law and Lead* and *The Tonto Kid*. His last appearance on screen was a cameo role in Clark Gable's final movie, *The Misfits*, which also starred Marilyn Monroe and Montgomery Clift. Bell was also married to the "It Girl," Clara Bow. Woolsey was a comedian with several movie credits to his name, and he and Bell, having seen Guldahl regularly shoot a 30 or 31 on the nine-hole course, encouraged him to try his luck on tour again. It has been suggested that at this stage, Guldahl's clubs were in hock, and Guldahl himself confirmed that he borrowed clubs when he returned to the big time. A further part of the encouragement from Bell and Woolsey was a stake of $100 to help in play in the U.S. Open qualifier in Chicago. Guldahl was also helped in another way, as *en route* to Chicago, he was invited to play in an exhibition match in St. Louis with Jimmy Manion, a local professional, and Orville White, whom he beat for the St. Louis title in 1933. The appearance fee was $45, and while this may seem an insignificant sum for a day's work, it was important for the Guldahls just then. With this modest sum behind him, he went on to lead the National Open qualifiers and was then able to play in the next tour stop in Detroit.

When the move from hickory to steel shafts came about at the beginning of the 1930s, True Temper, "The Choice of Champions," quickly established itself as brand leaders, and for a time sponsored a tournament. In the 1936 event, Guldahl played well, finishing in sixth place behind winner Olin Dutra. He won $275, which was a lot of money considering where he was a few weeks earlier. Further help came in the shape of what Guldahl described as "two new friends and one old pal," who "lifted me from the financial and mental depths I wallowed in for several years."[13] The "old pal," and a gift to the golf writers who loved such stories, was "an ancient rusty putter which I found in the attic of my parents' home in Dallas."[14] That putter, according to Guldahl, helped him lead the qualifiers for the 1936 National Open.

After 1936, his performances ensured that he was exempt from the qualifying ordeal. The championship that year was played on the famed upper course at Baltusrol. Not for the first time would Ralph's friend, Harry Cooper, be proclaimed the winner, only for the prize to be snatched from his grasp. In a preview of what would happen to Sam Snead the following year at Oakmont, Cooper had to wait and watch as Tony Manero set a new championship record of 282 and so beat him by two shots. Ironically, Manero only gained entry to the U.S. Open by virtue of a final hole chip-in in his prequalifying rounds. Guldahl played steadily for an eighth-place finish with a score of 290. This finish was worth $137.50, but despite this relatively modest sum, Ralph Guldahl believed he was on his way back.

The two new friends Guldahl referred to were from the giant sports manufacturer, Wilson Sporting Goods: Chick Gance, an executive who loaned Guldahl a new set of clubs; and energetic president Lawrence Blaine (L.B.) Icely. Wilson dated back to 1913 when it was named the Ashland Manufacturing Company, whose core business was meatpacking. A sideline for the firm was making violin and tennis racket strings from meat leftovers. In 1914, Ashland's parent company, Sulzberger, went into receivership and the bank appointed meatpacker Thomas E. Wilson as boss. It was the bank's decision to name the new enterprise Wilson & Co. but not after the meatpacking Wilson. The firm was named after President Woodrow Wilson, who was very popular at this time, and who would soon take America into World War I. It was a smart business move. As Wilson's sporting goods empire expanded, L.B. Icely was appointed president, and under his stewardship, sales and profits grew even faster. Wilson, along with Spalding and MacGregor, was one of the three giants who dominated the sports equipment market during this era. And while baseball and football provided millions in revenue for the firm, golf was becoming an increasingly important market. In this regard, Gene Sarazen, Walter Hagen, and later Sam Snead, were among the players to endorse Wilson products. It was estimated that when the revolutionary Gene Sarazen sand wedge was marketed in 1933, the firm sold 50,000 models that year.

As we saw above in regard to North Shore, Guldahl had used Wilson equipment since his early days on tour, and as Guldahl attempted his comeback, Icely advanced him the substantial sum of $4,000, which took care "of various bills that had mounted."[15] Perhaps Icely retained a sense of loyalty to him, or perhaps he was taking a chance on what Guldahl might achieve in the coming years. Whatever the reason, it was a sound business decision and it was seen by Guldahl as a career-saving moment. There were other stories from this era of dead-broke golfers having their careers turned around by an offer of financial backing. Certainly Henry Picard's offer to back a young Ben Hogan gave the Texan a tremendous boost, even if the offer was never availed of. And Guldahl often acknowledged that it was the show of faith by Icely, as much as the financial backing, that was instrumental in his comeback. Overall, as he colorfully recalled, "I was like a snowball rolling downhill. I had been prized [sic] loose by the putter and given a shove by two benefactors."[16]

Guldahl signing his card after a round (courtesy *Fort Worth Star-Telegram* Collection, Special Collections, University of Texas at Arlington Library).

Later, in 1939, and as a three-time major winner, Ralph Guldahl shed some further insight into what caused his slump and what helped him come back. Throughout the history of the game, there have been various instances of famous players experimenting with their games and as a result losing their form. Gene Sarazen, for example, despite having won the National Open and the PGA in the early 1920s, experimented with his swing a few years later. "I tore my swing apart at least once a year," he wrote, "and reassembled it to incorporate the slower pivot or the more upright backswing or the firmer left-side or whatever it was that my doctor of the moment was prescribing for a sick and dispirited patient. I remained a dispirited golfer."[17] Sarazen even abandoned his regular interlocking grip and adopted the more popular Vardon model. A key part of his recovery was a return to the interlocking grip he had used since he was a boy.

Guldahl admitted to making the same mistake as Sarazen when reflecting on his fall. He admitted, "I learned a lesson back in those days and every young golfer would do well to remember. Develop a free natural swing at the very beginning and never tamper with it. If you do you're a goner. In my case, I lost a lot of time and money looking for something I had all along but had forgotten."[18] Guldahl, however, did make one significant change. On the advice of two-time major winner Olin Dutra, he began to grip the club more in his fingers rather than in the palm of his hand, and this was an important factor in his recovery. In his book, *Groove Your Golf*, he placed particular emphasis on the "finger" grip.[19]

Apart from leading the U.S. Open qualifiers and a strong performance in the championship itself at Baltusrol, Guldahl showed other signs of a comeback in 1936. Guldahl placed joint second with Roland MacKenzie behind Ed Dudley at the Shawnee Open and won $450, and he also finished joint runner-up in the 54-hole Centennial Open at Wheeling in West Virginia. Here he tied with former British Amateur Champion Phil Perkins on 207, one shot behind 1931 U.S. Open winner Billy Burke. And he came fourth behind Craig Wood at the General Brock Open, just across the border in Canada. At this stage of his career, Wood was the "nearly man" of the majors, with four second places to his name. This, however, would change in 1941 when he won both the National Open and Masters' titles. At the General Brock Open, Guldahl's prize was $360. The checks from Shawnee and Canada may appear modest, but for the Depression era and considering where Ralph and his family were a year earlier, this level of money was significant.

Canada would also be good to Guldahl a little later on that summer. The far-sighted PGA tournament director, Bob Harlow, had long sought to expand the emerging tour from the sunshine states of Florida and California and make it a national journey, just as it is today. In this regard, he came up with the idea of "The Evergreen Trail" and persuaded local clubs and chambers of commerce to sponsor a series of tournaments which would include stops at Portland, Seattle, and up as far as Vancouver. One of these events was the Seattle Open, held at the Inglewood Country Club, where a crowd of over 6,000 attended the event and got a rare glimpse of the stars. Admission was $1.10 including tax. Here Guldahl gave further evidence of his growing confidence. Trailing leader MacDonald Smith by two heading into the final nine holes, he forced a play-off on 285. Both men had birdie fours at the final hole in regulation play. "Mac" Smith, as he was often known, came from a celebrated golfing family in Carnoustie. Two of his brothers, Alex and Willie, would win the U.S. Open title, and Smith himself had many "near misses" in the majors. His most famous loss was at the Open Championship of 1925 at Prestwick, when in front of his own Scottish people, he shot a last round of 82 to lose by three. The winner was another transplanted British golfer, Jim Barnes. In total, he won twenty-four tour events. In 1936, Smith, at age 44, was in the veteran category, but in the 18-hole play-off, he won the first prize of $1,200 with a wonderful 65. Guldahl shot a steady 71 and won $750. Overall, the trip to America's Northwest and Canada was lucrative, as apart from this tie at Inglewood, Guldahl had top-ten finishes at Vancouver, Victoria and Portland.

The hard evidence of the comeback, however, would come in the shape of tournament victories at the Augusta Open (not to be confused with the Masters), the Miami Biltmore Open, and the Western Open. The first of these events carried a $1,000 first prize; Guldahl won despite incurring a two-stroke penalty for playing the wrong ball. The event was played at the Donald Ross–designed Forest Hills course, and with a score of 283, Guldahl beat Henry Picard and Denny Shute by two shots. He again showed his finishing power by closing with a 67. The win pushed him ahead of Harry Cooper in the Radix Cup race for best scoring average. Coming in November, this was a crucial win for Guldahl.

There was a further rules incident at the end of year Miami-Biltmore Open, where the first prize was the significant sum of $2,500. Going into the final round, Guldahl held a commanding lead over the chasing pack, which included Lawson Little and Denny Shute, his playing partners for the final eighteen. However, after a shaky start, Guldahl hit into the bank of a canal on the seventh hole, which was inside the hazard stakes. Believing he was entitled to identify his ball, Guldahl parted the grass for inspection, and this brought objections from Little and Shute. In the event, after the round and following long deliberations between PGA officials, a two-stroke penalty was imposed which changed Guldahl's final score from 74 to 76. With a score of 283, he still won by two shots from Horton Smith, but there were also some parting comments from his rivals. Lawson Little, for example said, "Next tournament we're going to start you five of the first tee. Then you can do anything you want to."[20] Regardless of the incident, the matter was quickly forgotten, and certainly no damage was done to Guldahl or his reputation. Despite the first prize of $2,500, it was not the Miami-Biltmore victory which fully confirmed Ralph Guldahl's comeback. Instead it was his win at the Western Open, which carried the significantly smaller first prize of $500.

The question of whether or not golf should have a fifth major is alive and well today, with the Players Championship regularly touted as being worthy of joining the "Big Four." However, the issue is not new, for back in the 1920s and 1930s, "The Western" was seen as just this before the Masters formally assumed the mantle of the game's fourth major. Indeed, in 1938, four years after the first Masters, *Time Magazine* referred to it as the nation's "second ranked tournament"[21] (behind the U.S. Open but ahead of the PGA). This owed much to history, the quality of the fields the tournament attracted, and the venues. For example, the Western was first held in 1899 and was the second oldest U.S. championship after the National Open. The event continued until it was renamed the BMW Championship in 2007 and became one of the four Fed-Ex play-off events.

The first winner was Willie Smith, who was part of the aforementioned

Smith golfing dynasty from Carnoustie. Other Western winners included Hagen, Barnes, Armour and Sarazen, and the event was often held at America's most prestigious courses such as Interlachen, Oakland Hills and Olympia Fields. In addition, the Western gained extra prestige from the enthusiasm of J.K. Wadley. Wadley was a successful and wealthy businessman who discovered golf relatively late in life. He became a fine player and was taught by two-time Western winner and major champion Jim Barnes. Wadley also became a director of the Western Golf Association, and in 1923, he donated the J.B. Wadley Trophy, which added even more luster to the already celebrated Western Open. Even when the name was changed to the BMW Championship in 2007, the Wadley Trophy endured and continues to be presented to the winner. Wadley is also recognized as being the first person to use a golf cart.

So the 1936 Western at the Davenport Country Club, Iowa, was a target for the game's leading players. The Davenport club was founded in 1924 and the course was designed by the noted British firm of Harry Colt and Charles Alison. Davenport quickly established itself as one of the leading clubs in the Midwest and managed to survive the early Depression years when many other clubs did not. Here it was helped by placing slot machines in the clubhouse, a practice which was not uncommon during this era. It was here at Davenport that Ralph Guldahl announced that he really was back.

Guldahl opened with rounds of 68 and 67, but his chances seemed to have disappeared after a final morning third round of 75, which saw him fall three shots behind fellow Texan Ray Mangrum, his teenage rival from the days of Randall Park in Dallas. However, in his last round Guldahl produced one of the finishes for which he would become famous over the coming years: he closed with a 64, which included a back nine of 31. Key to his victory was three consecutive birdies from the twelfth to fourteenth holes, followed by a fifty-foot birdie putt for a two on the 71st hole. He then had an escape on the final hole when his approach hit a cameraman's equipment and came to rest where Guldahl could chip and putt for a closing par. In his final round, he did not have a single five on his card on a course where there were four holes featuring par of that figure. His 64 tied the course record held by Gene Sarazen, who had accomplished this feat a few years earlier in an exhibition match with Babe Zaharias. The course, however, was lengthened by 1936. The 64 was also a record for the Western Open at that time and gave him a ten under total of 274. And his victory was further enhanced by the quality of player he beat. Apart from Mangrum, who was second, the next three places were filled by Byron

Nelson, Harry Cooper and Horton Smith. So, apart from Smith, four of the first five finishers were products of Texas.

The first prize was $500 and this sum was matched by the same figure from Wilson Sporting Goods. This form of manufacturer's bonus was not uncommon during the Great Depression and, apart from exhibitions, was one of the few ways a successful player could earn some extra money. Guldahl's comeback was now almost complete and the scribes were quick to recognize this. One report read, "The golfing trade can forget all about that little putt Ralph Guldahl 'blew' in the 1933 national open ... and remember instead a spectacular round of sixty-four that made him the 1936 western open champion."[22] Understandably, perhaps, the missed putt at North Shore was not forgotten, as just about every report on his victory made some reference to it. However, the image of Ralph Guldahl was fast becoming that of a golfer who could play his best when the chips were down.

The culmination of Guldahl's comeback year was twofold. First, his achievements saw him finish second in a national poll for "Greatest Comeback of the Year." Ralph Guldahl was in good company. The winner was the baseball pitcher Vernon Gomez, and in third place was boxing legend Joe Louis. And second, he won the Radix Cup for the lowest scoring average of the year. The Radix Cup was the forerunner of the Vardon Trophy and was first presented in 1934 by Harry Radix. Radix was a golfing enthusiast who served as president of the Chicago Golf Association on a number of occasions. He was also an all-round sportsman who captained the U.S. Olympic ice-skating team. The first two winners of his trophy were Ky Laffoon and Harry Cooper.

Since its inception, ongoing tensions between PGA President George Jacobus and tournament director Bob Harlow had led to disputes regarding who should "own" the trophy. In the event, even though the award was announced in December 1936, the trophy was not presented until the summer of 1937 due to these PGA politics. Regardless of this, it was a prestigious and much sought-after award. Ralph's scoring average for 1936 was 71.64. In addition to these awards, Guldahl finished second leading money winner to Horton Smith. His total of $7,682 was only $202 behind the "Joplin Ghost." Evidence of the comeback was there for all to see in the tangible forms of money, trophies and awards. But there was still the matter of 1933 at North Shore, and only a convincing display in the National Open would convince many (perhaps Guldahl too) that he really was back.

3

Oakland Hills

For 1937, the perception of Ralph Guldahl and his prospects for the coming year were very different from twelve months previously. He was now one of "those to watch" and early on he did not disappoint. In January that year, for example, part of the "California Swing" was the inaugural Oakland Open, which was played at the Alister MacKenzie–designed Claremont Country Club. At just under 6,000 yards, the course was short by tour standards, but as would be expected from the man who designed Augusta National, it was a good test of golf with its tight fairways and heavy bunkering. Guldahl opened with a 64 and his total of 272 looked a certainty to win. However, his party was spoiled when a relatively unknown ex-caddie from Virginia passed him with 270 to win the $1,200 first prize. Sam Snead had a birdie four on the final hole to claim the title. This was Samuel Jackson Snead's first tour victory and he was so unknown that he later claimed that the scoreboard spelling for his name read "Sneed."

In fact, the seeds of Snead's first big win were sown a few weeks earlier at the Los Angeles Open. First, Sam got an Izett driver from Henry Picard. The club was made by a Philadelphia club maker, the Scots-born George Izett. Izett learned his trade from the famed club-maker Ben Sayers, in North Berwick, Scotland. When he emigrated to America he spent time at the Merion Club, where his reputation as a club designer grew. With its stiffer shaft and extra weight, the Izett driver helped cure Snead's tendency to hook. Picard, in another example of his generosity, charged Snead $5.50, which was exactly what he paid for the club. Sam would go on to use the stiff-shafted club for much of his career.

And second, also at Los Angeles, Snead bought a $3.50 putter from Leo Walper, a colorful pro from the 1930s who at one stage almost teamed up with Snead so they could share expenses. Sam later admitted that he and Johnny Bulla, with whom he was sharing expenses, were just about broke when they arrived at the tournament. Bulla later played an important part in the career of Ralph Guldahl. Before Oakland, things were so bad that, to quote Snead, "we went on a chicken-salad sandwich and soup diet and lived in a fleabag hotel."[1] But after his meetings with Picard and Walper, he told Bulla that "he now had the two most important clubs in the bag, driver and putter, and that he was very confident of his chances."[2] Retrospectively, this victory can be seen as one of the seminal moments in American golf, as it launched one of the greatest ever careers in the professional game: a career which saw Snead win seven majors in a total of 82 official PGA tournaments. It is estimated that when Seniors and regional events are taken into account, Snead won over 150 professional tournaments.

The Oakland tournament also marked the start of the Snead-Guldahl rivalry, which would dominate the tour for the next four years. Despite his losing out to Snead, this was an important part of the year for Guldahl. At Oakland he won $750 for second place, and in the Los Angeles Open, he led during the final round only for Harry Cooper to pass him with a closing 66. Purses were improving by now, and the Los Angeles stop saw Cooper win $2,500 and Guldahl receive $1,250 for his second-place tie with Horton Smith. In total, for the four tournaments on the west coast, he picked up $2,141. In those days, there was a mini order of merit for the California "swing," and Guldahl finished second to Harry Cooper, who won $3,740. Once again the two Dallasites were making the headlines *and* a tidy amount of money.

And, when looking at the bigger picture, it was possible to see a slight upturn in the fortunes of the tour. Largely thanks to the pioneering work of tournament director Bob Harlow, sponsors were gradually becoming easier to attract and the purses were benefiting accordingly. Fred Corcoran, who succeeded Harlow that year, built on his predecessor's work and if anything, proved to be a more able salesman. Fred's annual salary was $5,000 plus $5 per day expenses. Some of this remuneration was funded by equipment manufacturers, such as Spalding. Fred took over as PGA tournament director after Harlow and George Jacobus had quarreled once too often. Not everyone was happy about the change, and a number of players, led by the highly articulate Horton Smith, signed a petition demanding that Harlow remain as tournament director. Among this group was Ralph Guldahl. Jacobus, however, had his way, and Corcoran went on to do an excellent job for the tour and its players.

In addition, despite serious lapses in private club membership in the early 1930s, there were many new converts to the game. It was one of the paradoxes of the Depression era that despite great hardship for millions, participation in sport was seen as a release and golf benefited accordingly. That it did was in no small way due to the thousands of public courses which were built as part of Franklin Roosevelt's recovery program. New converts meant growing sales in equipment and greater galleries at the latest stop on tour. When the drawing power of Snead was added in, things were looking up.

Guldahl's good form continued into April, when he placed second to Byron Nelson at Augusta. This was the year Nelson picked up six shots on Guldahl at the 12th and 13th holes: a birdie/eagle burst which led him to his first major title. (See chapter 5, "The Masters.") The PGA Championship, which was very much a moveable feast back then, was played in May at the Pittsburgh Field Club, and here Guldahl made little impact as he lost to Jimmy Thomson in the early rounds. Denny Shute retained his title in thrilling fashion when he beat "Jug" McSpaden in the final at the 37th hole. So Guldahl's form could be classed as just reasonable by the time the players assembled at Oakland Hills, Chicago, and he was also having a certain amount of trouble with the trajectory of his irons, which he felt was too high and therefore lacking in penetration. Back in the 1930s there were no traveling swing coaches, and if a player had a problem he either rectified it himself or he might have a word with a fellow pro. In this regard, Ralph was lucky as the head professional at Oakland Hills was Al Watrous. Al was another professional who came from golf's "melting pot": in his case he was of Polish descent. He played on the first two Ryder Cups of 1927 and 1929, and he won eight times on tour. But he is perhaps best remembered as the man who finished runner-up in the British Open of 1926 at Lytham, when Jones hit his miracle shot from a fairway bunker at the 71st hole and so gained a decisive two-shot advantage over Watrous. This was Jones's first Open title. Watrous was also a fine teacher who would look after the members at Oakland Hills for thirty-seven years. He suggested that Ralph cut down on his backswing and so achieve the lower trajectory he had been seeking. Despite this advice, Ralph admitted that in six practice rounds, not once did he break par. Once the championship started, however, the medicine began to work, and Ralph was more than ready to praise Watrous after the championship.[3]

The venue for the 1937 National Open was a Donald Ross–designed course. It was reported that when he first surveyed a stretch of land some eighteen miles northwest of Detroit in 1916 Ross said, "The Lord intended this for a golf links."[4] Ross then built two courses, but it was the South Course which would host the U.S. Open many times. The club was the brainchild of a Ford sales executive, Norval Hawkins, and his accountant friend Joseph Mack, who had invested in this real estate venture and thought about building houses there. But as the game of golf became more popular, they decided to create a country club where carmakers working in the Motor City could socialize in style. Ross was hired and the club opened in 1917.[5]

Even at this relatively early stage in the nation's golfing history, Oakland Hills was part of the game's royalty. It had already hosted the U.S. Open and the Women's Amateur Championship and would host many more majors in the future. In addition, "Sir" Walter Hagen was the club's first professional. Walter would later be made an honorary member of the club. Apart from its glittering history, Oakland Hills was also known as one of the toughest courses in the country. Back in 1924 when it first staged the National Open, it was reported after the event that "the tournament probably was the most trying contest ever participated in by contenders for the national championship, many stars running into the eighties and a score of the 85 starters dropping out before the finish."[6] Cyril Walker from England was the surprise winner with a total of 297, three better than Bobby Jones. The lowest score for the week was a 71 by Abe Espinosa.

Thirteen years later, in 1937, the course certainly lived up to its fearsome reputation. One report read, "The course, longest ever used for the national open, has been given a face lift since the same tournament was staged here in 1924. Tee shots are blind on six holes, fairways are narrow, and roughs are deep and full of trouble."[7] The changes implemented included new tees having been built on hole numbers 2, 4, 8, 15 and 18. The eighth hole in particular was radically changed, as it was lengthened from 430 yards to a 491-yard par five. It would play a pivotal role in the final round. To compensate for this increased severity, some bunkers were removed. The course, at 7,037 yards, was certainly long, and the rough was a foot deep and made even more treacherous by the rain which fell in the lead-up to the opening Thursday. Experienced Leo Diegel was sure that nobody would beat 290.

In more recent years, two of the U.S. Open's most successful players, Ben Hogan and Jack Nicklaus, were noted for their intense preparation ahead of the National Open. Each man would achieve four victories with many other near misses. Both before and after these illustrious names, however, Ralph Guldahl equaled any player in history in terms of assiduous planning ahead of the National Open. Even at a time when chasing every dollar was vital, Guldahl would miss out on a tour stop close to the start of the championship and head for the Open venue instead. Certainly for the 1937 championship, he was ahead of the field when it came to knowing the demanding Detroit course. Roughly three weeks before the start, Ralph, Laverne and Buddy took rooms in a house in nearby Pontiac, from where Ralph commuted on a daily basis to make sure nothing was left to chance. The strategy worked.

After his comeback year of 1936, and his strong start to 1937, Ralph Guldahl might have expected to be favorite for the event, but the name on everyone's lips was the 25-year-old Snead. It was Snead's introductory year, and apart from his win at Oakland, he won four more times and finished leading money winner. Furthermore, Sam had a wonderful golf swing and was almost as long as the "Big Blaster," Jimmy Thomson. These qualities, allied to his homespun wit, made him a draw for fans and scribes alike. Stories of learning to play barefoot in a cow pasture with a maple stick were plentiful, as were (later on) stories of how he kept his money in cans buried in the back yard. This was food and drink to his manager and salesman, Fred Corcoran. As Fred recalled, "I promptly drafted an agreement which Sam signed and which stated that I was his sole representative in exhibitions and other matters. This piece of paper marked the start of a business relationship with Sam which has continued down through the years."[8] Fred's reference to "this piece of paper" that "I drafted" is instructive, as neither man was particularly fond of lawyers. In fact it was at the Oakland Open, scene of Snead's first tour victory, that the pair initially met. At this stage, both men were relative novices, certainly as far as the tour was concerned. However, when Fred saw the enormous potential of this newcomer, he immediately took on the role of promoting Sam. In time, some professionals took exception to the amount of publicity Snead was getting, with the newspapers already referring to him as the "Fairway Moses." But there was no disputing his drawing power.

It was also clear that it was not just Corcoran who promoted Snead, as Sam himself was more than able in this regard. Sam later admitted that he "resented being portrayed as an ignorant hayseed," but at the time he was happy to play the part.[9] As Judy Corcoran later recalled, "He came down out of the mountains of West Virginia, but he was a quick study and had a keen, shrewd mind. He discovered the pockets of that hillbilly costume were lined with gold and he wore it with relish…. His own fertile imagination kept pace and he contributed a few gems to the growing file of Sneadisms."[10]

So as well as promoting the tour, Fred now had the added responsibility and pleasure of arranging deals for Snead. The logic was simple: if

Fred could get lots of good publicity for Sam, it would help the game, and the tour needed all the good P.R. it could get to continue attracting sponsors in these difficult times. So even though this was his first U.S. Open, Snead was favorite, and two-time winner Gene Sarazen said, "I don't see how anyone can beat Snead at Oakland Hills. That kid has everything and the Birmingham course is made for him."[11] Bobby Jones disagreed and later said, "It was stupidity to make the boy betting favorite in his first Open. He is unquestionably a great player—anyone who knows a golf swing could see that. But winning an Open Championship requires more than a swing."[12] Harry Cooper, who was pipped at the death at Baltusrol by Tony Manero the previous year, was next in the betting to Snead, along with Ralph Guldahl.

In all, 170 of the nation's top professionals and amateurs teed it up, and what was surprising was how many good first-round scores were produced on the brutal Oakland Hills course. The reason for the good scoring may have owed something to an unusual decision taken by the USGA on the eve of the championship. Traditionally, the USGA was known as erring on the side of penal when setting up U.S. Open courses. However, on this occasion, the committee ordered that the rough, saturated by the aforementioned rain, be cut. USGA President John G. Jackson said, "The rough will be shortened in a half a dozen places where the fairways have been narrowed."[13] The Oakland Hills Club was not pleased by the decision, as a softer course, with less punishing rough, meant a slightly easier examination for the stars. And it was not just Oakland Hills which disagreed with the USGA's decision. Journalist H.G. Salsinger of the local *Detroit News* had this to say: "Oakland Hills was made an easier course by moving up the markers on a majority of tees and placing the cups in the most accessible spots on the greens. It was an easier one than the course over which the 1924 tournament was played."

However, the final word, as was often the case, was left to intrepid reporter Henry McLemore. In a scene which is unimaginable today, McLemore somehow managed to persuade the USGA to allow him play nine holes on the eve of the championship and so challenge any ideas that the course might not be a true National Open test. McLemore, as ever, wanted to give his readers the "real story," which in this case meant providing a firsthand report on what the players would face. In his report he painted a picture of the Oakland Hills rough which he claimed was "the toughest ever faced by a National Open field." And to add a touch of color, he began by recording how he "made a safari into the rough of the Oakland Hills golf course," and he followed by claiming that on the first tee, "Gene

Sarazen presented me with a snake kit."[14] That McLemore was a writer who was prone to hyperbole was not in doubt, but from his highly personal account, it was clear that Oakland Hills, despite the USGA decision on the rough, *and* the concerns of Oakland Hills, would be no pushover.

After the first round, Snead and Denny Shute led with 69s. The highlight for Snead was an eagle three on the 18th hole. These scores were not unexpected, as Snead was favorite, while the cerebral Shute was an excellent player in the major championships. He had never won the National Open, with his best finish to date being a tie for third place in 1929. However, he won the Open Championship at St. Andrews in 1993 and a few weeks before Oakland Hills, he won the PGA Championship for the second successive year. He was clearly a man in form. Guldahl was well placed on 71. By Friday night, the field was tightly bunched with three shots covering the first ten players. Guldahl was among the leading group on 140 after a 69. The basis for his score was a fine outward half of 32. Guldahl was joined on 140 by Frank Walsh, who, although not one of the game's big names, was good enough to finish runner-up to Olin Dutra in the 1932 PGA Championship. Walsh had two very impressive rounds of 70. Also on this total was Jimmy Thomson, who had a 66. Thomson did a great deal to attract fans to the game in the 1930s, as he was seen as the biggest hitter on tour. Back then, the scribes loved nicknames, and Thomson had plenty such as "The Big Blaster." He was also one of the "Spalding Fourball," whose exhibition tours did so much to spread the golfing gospel during the Depression years. Admission was free to these matches, and as well as an 18-hole four-ball, the fans were treated to a clinic. The other Spalding-affiliated members were Horton Smith, Lawson Little and Harry Cooper.

Thomson was another of the Scots-born professionals so numerous and so prominent in American golf in the early decades of the twentieth century. In Thomson's case, he came from North Berwick and was from vintage golfing stock, as his uncle, Jack White, won the Open Championship in 1904. Although Thomson was not a prolific winner on tour, he was used to being in contention at the U.S. Open, having lost out to Sam Parks by two shots in 1935, only because of a closing run of bogeys. He was also runner-up to Denny Shute in the previous year's PGA Championship at Pinehurst. Snead lay two shots back alongside perennial contender Harry Cooper. Denny Shute slipped down the leader board with a second-round 76.

In those days (and up to 1964) the USGA had its "Open Saturday" with the final 36 holes being played on the same day. Going into the final round, Guldahl and Snead matched each other at 212 and trailed Ed Dudley by one shot. Dudley had three steady rounds of 70–70–71. Thomson had dropped out of contention with a third-round 78. Ed Dudley faded in the last round, but Guldahl and Snead played out one of the most thrilling finales in U.S. Open history. Gene Sarazen, who had tipped Sam to win, believed nobody would beat 288 because of the brutal Oakland Hills course. However, Guldahl would beat this figure by seven shots and Snead bettered it by five.

Snead played ahead of Guldahl and finished off his round in style by holing a curling 30-foot eagle putt on the 18th to seemingly win the National Open at his first attempt with a closing 71 and a record score of 283. He later recalled the words of Tommy Armour, who told him, "Laddie, you've just won yourself a championship worth more than a seat on the stock exchange." And Sam also recollected that "the radio boys pushed mikes in my face and everybody toasted the smiling winner. In a few minutes, I was due to collect money for endorsing everything from corn plasters to flea powder." The teetotal Snead also admitted later that he wished he were a drinking man, but instead he settled for a gun and a fishing rod and headed "for the mountaintops back home ... that's the best remedy for anyone who is ready to smash his clubs and take up liquor and strange women."[15]

An interested observer to all of this commotion was Laverne Guldahl, who recalled being in the clubhouse when Snead came in and saw "all those people congratulating him. It was a funny sensation but I kinda had a hunch Ralph would beat him."[16] And 1,200 miles away in Dallas, the drama at Oakland Hills was unfolding in the front room of the Guldahl home at 419 South Glasgow Drive. Back then communication was very different from what it later became. Television sets were rare and certainly there was no televised golf. And, like many other families, the Guldahls had no telephone in their home. So Anna and Olaf Guldahl listened to the day's events from Birmingham on the radio. In a post-tournament interview with the Guldahls, it was reported, "Mother Guldahl fairly camped on the radio all day Saturday. To the exact minute she can call the time various announcements were made covering the progress of the players at Birmingham."[17] Like most people at Oakland Hills, Anna also believed Snead would win. She heard the commentator say that Sam's score would almost certainly hold up and she hoped that her son might claim second or third place.[18] After the news came through, Anna told a reporter that when the commentator said, "'Folks, here comes the new national champion Ralph Guldahl,' I thought Papa was going to tear up the chair he was

sitting in. Tears streamed down his cheeks. He almost broke me in two
with a hug and began pacing the floor, walking all over the house." Olaf
had followed his sons on the course but only once attempted to play the
game himself.[19] Anna also remembered North Shore and how "I could just
see him again in the movies of that 1933 tournament at Chicago and that
look of disgust on his face as he missed a four-foot putt to tie Johnny
Goodman on the seventy-second green."[20] She was also quick to give praise
to Bill McConnell, who was professional at the Cedar Crest club in Dallas
when Guldahl was emerging as a player. Guldahl played a lot at Cedar
Crest in his amateur days, and it was McConnell, Anna suggested, who
gave the new champion a great deal of sound advice.

The loss at Oakland Hills was the first of many for Snead, and he was
not the only one to feel disappointed. A Snead victory would certainly
have gone down well with the fans who had taken to the new golfing sensation and to the media whom Sam provided with story line after story
line. Fred Corcoran would also have been pleased both for the deals that
would come his and his protégé's way and for the boost it would give the
tour. It appeared that just about everyone would get their wish. Fred, many
years later, said, "I always thought that Sam, if he could have won that
1937 Open title on his first shot at it, might have gone on to win it four
or five times."[21] But, despite four second-place finishes, it was never to be.

On the first nine on Saturday afternoon, Guldahl had comfortable
pars at the first four holes. In fact, he had a few birdie chances, notably
at the 512-yard, par-five second, where he was bunkered in two, splashed
out to ten feet, and narrowly missed for a four. He did, however, birdie
the difficult par-four fifth when a long putt dropped for a birdie three. He
gave this shot back immediately, though, when he missed from six feet for
his par at the 351-yard, par-four sixth. A par four followed at the 416-
yard, par-four seventh hole before one of the first of a number of seminal
moments in his final round. The eighth hole was a reachable par five of
491 yards, and here he hit a wonderful fairway wood to forty feet and
made the putt for an eagle three. He then had a birdie two at the 215-yard
ninth hole, where he hit a superb two iron to ten feet and holed the putt.
This eagle, birdie run saw him out in 33 shots. And by the time Ralph
Guldahl reached the 10th tee, he knew what was required to win. There
was, however, still the brutal back nine to play, and knowing exactly what
he had to do could create unbearable pressure and bring back memories
of his 1933 loss to Johnny Goodman. However, it was on the 10th tee that
he uttered one of the most often quoted lines in U.S. Open history. When
told that he could play the final nine in 37 or one over par and still win,

Guldahl said, "If I can't do it, I'm a bum and don't deserve to win the Open."[22] In the event, he managed a 36 to win by two shots, but not without some skirmishes. For example, he was in the rough three times at the par-four 10th hole and his fourth shot was a blind chip shot from tangled rough. One report claimed that Guldahl remarked that "I'll shoot for that cloud,"[23] before playing the shot. If he did say this, it worked, as he pitched to four feet and made the putt for a "good" bogey. However, there were more problems at the 413-yard 11th hole, where he three-putted for another bogey five.

These two successive bogeys meant that his cushion was gone, and according to *Sports Illustrated*, the tension was building not only on the course, but in the clubhouse also. "'Guldahl's started to crack!' The word spreads like wildfire around the course and reaches the locker room where Sam Snead is receiving congratulations.... A slight blond [*sic*] woman waiting on the terrace hears the ominous whispers. 'I don't believe it—Mrs. Guldahl knows how much is at stake.... She and her husband need the money.'"[24] During these years, the question of money was never far away in reports on the Guldahls. However, as was becoming the norm, the champion-to-be responded immediately. At the dogleg 555-yard 12th hole, he had a birdie four, and his third shot here was described by Bobby Jones as "the greatest shot of the tournament and the one which made his great finish possible." Jones explained his reasoning: "He had started home 5–5. He needed exact par to tie—and on some of the last few holes this was not easy. If he was to pick up anything it almost had to be on the par-5 twelfth or the relatively easy par-3 thirteenth." After two shots he was thirty yards short and Jones continued, "Confronting him was a wide expanse of putting surface, finally mounting a bold contour and sloping down to the hole. The cup was placed at the base of the downslope, not over a dozen feet from the crest and about the same distance from the troublesome short rough around the green's edge.... The shot was an exquisite knock-down pitch which bit twice, barely topped the slope and slid down a yard past the hole. The resulting 4 was the tonic needed."[25] In those pre-televised golf days, writers invariably saw events unfold and we can be sure that Jones witnessed the pitch firsthand. Jones might have added that just before playing this pitch, Guldahl was interrupted by a swarm of bees that descended on the 12th fairway, and that the champion-elect's calm reaction was the sign of a man who was in complete control of his emotions.

Guldahl followed this with a five iron to 12 inches at the short 13th. These two successive birdies meant he was back in control, and as

Grantland Rice put it, "In place of weakening and flinching in the face of trouble he met the issue with a cool head and a stout heart with his finest golf. And once back in the lead he never slipped again."[26] There were, however, a few more scares, such as at the 15th when his approach was headed for the rough but hit a spectator's foot and bounced into a bunker. Guldahl got up and down to save his par. Then came the treacherous 16th. Over the years this became the signature hole at Oakland Hills with its slight dogleg right and its shallow green guarded by a large pond ready to catch the slightest mis-hit or misjudgment. The hole has seen seminal moments in the history of major championships. For example, it was here in 1972 that Gary Player hit a "miracle" shot from the right-hand rough, over trees and over water, to within a few feet of the hole. The resultant birdie was crucial in his two-shot victory. More recently in the 2008 PGA Championship, Sergio Garcia led Padraig Harrington by one when the pair approached this hole. Garcia found the water with his second and took five, whereas Harrington got his par from a greenside bunker. The one shot swing was a massive psychological blow for Harrington on his way to the title.

Another vital moment in championship history came in 1937 as it was here, according to one writer, that there was another contender for "shot of the championship," when Guldahl faced a seven or eight iron approach across the water to the tight landing area. "I can't recall," said the writer, "ever having seen such a display of down-right valor, plus composure, at a time when most men's knees and stomachs would be curling up in utter fear. To me that approach on the sixteenth ... stamped Guldahl, for years a wandering giant of the fairways, as a man possessed of great courage and steely nerves and one who is doomed to be a very big factor in the golfing years ahead of us."[27] The approach across the water was played to the heart of the green, and two putts later, the champion-to-be had his par. A safe par three followed at the 17th hole, and then at the par-five 18th, he was in the rough from the tee, just short of the dogleg. From there, he played safe with a seven iron before an eight iron set him up for a two-putt par from twenty-five feet. On that final stretch, it seemed that every time he was tested, he came up with the answer. This was particularly true in regard to his putting. It will be recalled that at North Shore, he missed two short putts in the closing holes, notably a four-footer on the 72nd hole. Here his putting was consistent throughout, something Guldahl later attributed to an eve-of-tournament session on the practice green with Lloyd Mangrum, who was one of the game's outstanding putters. A match which started as a one-dollar Nassau led to Guldahl's taking two hours to get even with Mangrum, in the process finding "something" which gave him confidence for the three days ahead.

Guldahl was also helped by the fact that his playing partner for the final round was his old sparring partner from Dallas, Harry Cooper. In all the excitement about Guldahl's closing round and because of their friendship from the days back at Tenison Park, it was easy to forget that Cooper was also in contention to win his first major title after a number of near misses. Starting the final day, he was on 142, only two shots behind Guldahl. Cooper certainly thought he was in with a chance, and when reminiscing in 1990, he said, "At Oakland Hills ... I was playing with him the last 36 holes, and he drove me nuts. I mean he was—I'm a fast player, and he was a very slow player, and uh, it—it really hurt me."[28] The words "it really hurt me" were not those of a man who was there to play a supporting role. In the end he was not too far away with a score of 286, adding to an already outstanding record in the National Open.

However, knowing he could not win, by all accounts Harry kept Guldahl calm during the demanding final nine holes. For example, on the tough par-three 17th, Guldahl hit a beautiful long iron shot into ten feet but missed the putt. However, instead of going straight to the next tee, Cooper suggested he try the putt a few times, just to break the tension.[29] And when, on the final tee, Guldahl asked Cooper what he needed to win, five or six, the reply was, "Just don't drop dead. That's the only way you can miss."[30] By this stage, Cooper clearly wanted Guldahl to win, and in the same 1990 interview referred to above, he referred to his old Dallas pal as a "helluva nice guy." Then, on the final green, Guldahl was responsible for one of the most curious incidents in the history of the U.S. Open. Before holing his final putt, he stopped to comb his hair, explaining later, "Before an important shot I try to steady my nerves and slow down my breathing before I take my stance. That little comb has saved me many a stabbed putt."[31] Whether or not it was aiding his concentration, the gesture was seen as further evidence of his aloofness and the perception that "he had no idea of what the galleries wanted in a champion."[32] It should be noted that later, Guldahl said that the hair combing was so he might look good for the cameras. A further performance of note in Detroit was that of Johnny Goodman who, on 215, was only three shots behind Guldahl after the third round. Goodman slipped a little in the last round with a 75 but his very creditable score of 290 brought him the amateur medal.

Regardless of whether or not he had an "image" problem, the media was quick to play up Ralph Guldahl's comeback from North Shore and its aftermath. "Horatio Alger," read one report, "in his most imaginative days, never wrote a more thrilling story than the one Ralph Guldahl has scribbled in bold capital letters over the fairways and greens of the Nation's golf courses."[33] Alger was a nineteenth-century American novelist whose specialty was writing stories in which the hero was invariably a teenage boy who rose from the slums and abject poverty to middle-class respectability through hard work and determination. The analogy may have been a little far-fetched, but the story line read well, and certainly there was no doubting the determination and courage shown by the new National Open champion.

For Guldahl, the ghost of North Shore had been laid to rest, and despite putting a brave face on matters at the time, he subsequently explained the impact that the missed four-foot putt in 1933 had on him in. "That's why my victory ... was doubly sweet," he recalled. "It wiped out the memory of that awful afternoon in 1933 when I stood on the threshold of national fame and stumbled. For four years that putt haunted me ... for four years I could see the look in the eyes of the crowd that rimmed the home green that day."[34] And now that the "wrong" of 1933 had been "righted," Ralph Guldahl was keen to cash in on his win, and the question of what a U.S. Open champion could make from such a victory was always a hot topic among players and the media alike. The first prize for 1937 was $1,000, and as we saw with the previous year's Western victory, players' equipment sponsors such as Wilson and Spalding often matched this sum by way of a bonus. Guldahl reckoned to make roughly $25,000 a year for five years, mostly from exhibitions. It was, he claimed, the "gravy." And Laverne had her say on how the "gravy" was the driving force behind her husband's victory. Holding Buddy in her arms, she told reporters, "Ralph wanted to win because of what it meant financially to him and me and Buddy here." She too had a figure of $25,000 in her mind and added, "How Buddy and I can use some of that."[35] The figure of $25,000 was widely quoted after a National Open victory, but it is not clear if this sum was ever realized. One thing that could be guaranteed was that whatever money came to a new National Open champion would be hard earned through a series of day-on-day exhibition tours which involved driving thousands of miles.

For his win at Oakland Hills, however, it is not clear how much the "gravy" amounted to. The following week he set off for England for the 1937 Ryder Cup, and so there was little time left for arranging exhibitions immediately after his Oakland Hills victory. As the new U.S. Open champion said, "Shucks, I wish we weren't going so soon. I won't have much time to line up testimonials, ads, and that soft side dough."[36] There was, however, time for some of that "soft side dough" in the form of Guldahl's collaborating on a series of six articles with well-respected journalist and cartoonist Art Krenz. These ranged from the influence of competition in Texas on his career, to the need for good equipment, to the importance of a good grip in golf. This final tip was a theme which would feature strongly when Guldahl wrote his own instructional book a few years later. The series was called "The Cinderella Man of Golf," and was a clear play on the name given by Damon Runyon to the Depression-era fighter, James J. Braddock. (*Cinderella Man* was the title of an award-winning 2005 screen biography of Braddock, with Russell Crowe playing the fighter.) Fittingly, Braddock was universally known as a boxer who fought back against adversity, notably in 1935 when he defied odds of ten to one to overcome Max Baer and win the world heavyweight title. Ralph Guldahl was keeping good company on the sports pages.

There was an unofficial Ryder Cup match at Wentworth in 1926 between a team of Americans, led by Hagen, and a team of British pro-

The 1937 U.S. Ryder Cup team, suitably attired at a send-off in New York. As the new National Open winner, Guldahl is seated in the center flanked by Snead (seated left) and Shute (right) (courtesy Tufts Archives).

fessionals led by Ted Ray. The home side thrashed the U.S. team by thirteen matches to one. However, officially the Ryder Cup began in 1927 at Worcester, Massachusetts, and since then, the Ryder Cup spoils had been divided on a 3–2 home and away basis. And while the U.S. winning margins were higher than those of their British counterparts, another close encounter was expected in 1937. This was especially true in regard to the Southport venue, where in 1933 the British team scored a famous one-point victory. In a contest witnessed by the Prince of Wales, Syd Easterbrook defeated Denny Shute on the final green to clinch a six-and-a-half to five-and-a-half point win for the home team. Guldahl joined a team that was awash with major winners such as Sarazen, Shute, Smith, Nelson, Manero and Revolta, and American confidence was high. There was also another rookie in the shape of Snead. Hagen as usual was captain and Fred Corcoran was installed as team manager. Regardless of this talent, however, the vastly experienced Grantland Rice tipped Britain to win. This opinion was based largely on the difficulty the Americans would have in adapting to British links conditions, especially the weather.

The American team was given a rousing send-off before it left New York on June 16. A lavish dinner was held at the Hotel New Yorker, and the team, suitably attired in blue slacks and white blazers, walked in to the function room to the strains of "The Star Spangled Banner." All were present except Hagen, who was in the middle of a world tour with Joe Kirkwood. The captain would meet up with his team in London. In more contemporary times, Ryder Cup sides are supplied with lavish wardrobes containing clothes for every occasion. The same principle applied back then, even if the range on offer was more modest. For example, each man received a pair of golf shoes and black and white dress footwear, three pairs of wool socks, and a number of matching ties. The U.S. PGA believed that "it will be a smartly attired as well as a powerful playing aggregation that will meet the British."[37] The latest in rain gear was also presented and this proved to be important in the wet British conditions.

The trip, which included the Open Championship at Carnoustie, lasted almost six weeks and came at a time when Ralph Guldahl's name was "hot." In addition, the PGA allowed the players just $1,000 expenses, and so unless a player won the Open, it was likely the trip would see him take a loss. So with no time to bask in (or cash in on) his National Open win, Ralph and Laverne and Buddy set off for Southport and the Ryder Cup which no "away team" had ever won, but not before Laverne had a few words to say on the matter. If Guldahl was sometimes seen as lacking color, Laverne was often sought out by the scribes for a quote or two. And, as we saw earlier, she rarely disappointed. In advance of traveling to Southport, she seemed rather underwhelmed by the prospect and told one reporter, "It's funny, but I don't care about making the trip to England any more than Ralph does. Do you think the baby will get seasick? Babies never do? Anyhow I don't think they have anything over there we haven't got here. A King? Oh well. Every American woman has her king and Ralph's mine."[38] Laverne's devotion to Ralph was well known, as was her view that he was the "handsomest man in the world."

Regardless of the prospect of seasickness or thoughts of loss of

Ralph Guldahl's greatest supporter, Laverne, who attended most tournaments, but who was not allowed get too close to the action because she might jinx her husband (courtesy *Fort Worth Star-Telegram* Collection, Special Collections, University of Texas at Arlington Library).

earnings after Oakland Hills, Guldahl was very much in business mode when he got to England. The James Braid–designed Southport and Ainsdale venue was in the middle of one of the richest stretches of links in Britain. Across the railway track which bordered the 16th hole lay Hillside, and a little further on was Birkdale. As in 1933, it was sure to provide a real test for the teams, especially in the anticipated bad weather. Practice rounds were carefully watched by both fans and golf writers during this era, and players were generally quick to divulge exactly what they shot, at the back of the 18th green. At Southport and Ainsdale, Guldahl played well in practice, and along with fellow rookie Ed Dudley shot an impressive 67 in the lead-up to the main event. Guldahl's score was particularly impressive as it contained eight birdies, with six of these coming in the last seven holes. His U.S. Open form had clearly traveled with him across the Atlantic. However, with Henry Cotton posting a 64 in practice, and with others among the home team also playing well, there no overwhelming sense that an away team would win for the first time. Captain Hagen, however, was in confident mood and in an eve-of-the-match interview with the *Glasgow Herald*, he declared, "You can forget all about this business of visiting teams never winning. We have a team over this year that can and will win. It's the best team we have ever had and I've captained them all."[39]

In these days, there was just one series of foursomes and one of singles and all matches were played over 36 holes. In his foursomes, Guldahl teamed up with the previous year's U.S. Open winner, Tony Manero, and they combined to beat Bill Cox and Arthur Lacey, 2–1. This was a creditable performance by the American team as the rookies were up against

Commdr. R.C.T. Roe, W.J. Cox, A. H. Padgham, T. H. Cotton, A. Perry, R. Burton
(P.G.A. Secretary)
A.J. Lacey, S.L. King, C.A. Whitcombe, D.J. Rees, P. Alliss

The British Ryder cup team of 1937 (courtesy Southport & Ainsdale Golf Club).

two players with Ryder Cup experience. Lacey featured on the victorious British team of 1933, when he lost to Hagen in the singles by a margin of 2–1. And Cox gained a half point against Horton Smith at Ridgewood, New Jersey, in 1935 when the U.S. team overwhelmed the visitors by a score of 9–3. Given the conditions, the golf was of a high standard, with the British pair being round in 72 in the morning and one up. The afternoon round continued in a similar close vein, with the British two up after six holes, only for the Americans to square thanks to Manero's putt for a two at the short eight. With four holes to play, the sides were all square. The match was decided on the 16th and 17th holes. A hooked tee shot by Lacey on the first of these, followed by a loose approach on the next, saw Guldahl and Manero win both holes and gain a 2–1 victory. The other victory for the American team was surprising in that Hagen was accused by the local press of sacrificing the rookie Nelson and Ed Dudley when he paired them against the "invincible" British duo of Cotton and Open champion Padgham. Hagen, however, knew what he was doing and his selection of the pairing was not a random choice, as Nelson later recalled. Before the matches the captain told the Masters champion, "Byron, you've got a lot of steam, a lot of get-up-and-go. And Dudley needs someone to push him. So I'm going to put you two together. You can get him fired up."[40] In the event, Nelson and Dudley had a relatively comfortable 4–2 victory with the 16th hole playing a seminal role in both morning and afternoon rounds.

The par-five 16th was the signature hole at Southport and Ainsdale. On the right, from the tee, was the railway line which separated the course from Hillside, and in the middle of the fairway, roughly 100 yards from the green, was a cavernous bunker fortified by railway sleepers. The hole was called Gumbley's, reportedly as a certain Mr. Gumbley once used a large number of strokes trying to extricate himself from the hazard. In the morning round, Dudley and Nelson were one down playing the hole, but a birdie four helped them to square the match and finish the first 18 all even. In the afternoon, the Americans took command and by the time the match reached Gumbley's, they were dormie three. Any chance of a recovery was dashed when Cotton's second shot found the famous bunker and Dudley and Nelson won by a margin of 4–2. It was a significant psychological blow for Hagen's men, and after the foursomes, the Americans led by two and a half points to one and a half.

For the singles next day, the *Times* described the challenge faced by the players: "More deplorable conditions than those of the morning are hardly conceivable." And the report continued, "The sky was black with never

Guldahl in action at the 1937 Ryder Cup in Southport & Ainsdale (courtesy Southport & Ainsdale Golf Club).

a break; the light was bad; the ground was rapidly getting water-logged, although it stood up to its trial nobly."[41] It was against this background, at 10 a.m., that Guldahl faced reigning Open Champion Alf Padgham. There was a precedent for the U.S. Open champion facing the Open title holder, as in 1935, Sam Parks had squared off against Alf Perry. There were a number of doubts expressed about Padgham's form since his great 1936, but the captain insisted he play lead-off. And he was a man with a serious golfing pedigree. For example, in 1934, Padgham finished third in the Open, and in 1935 he placed second before winning the title at Hoylake in 1936. He also won four other tournaments that year, including the Dunlop tournament which was played at Southport and so local knowledge would be to his advantage.

The golf correspondent of the *Times* newspaper of London (also known as Bernard Darwin) was on hand to see the match. "Padgham began well enough against Guldahl," Darwin wrote, "and this match was all even at the fifth. Then Guldahl holed a huge putt at the sixth and away he went."[42] The "away he went" comment was significant, as during this period, once Guldahl got his nose in front he was rarely beaten. Darwin also observed Guldahl's style. The golf correspondent of the *Times* was worth listening to on this topic, as without doubt he was the foremost golf writer of his, or some would say, any generation. His first article for the *Times* appeared in 1907 and he did not retire from his post until 1953, by which time he had seen Ben Hogan's definitive Open triumph at Carnoustie. He saw the Great Triumvirate at close quarters over their vintage years and he had the privilege of being a marker for Francis Ouimet at the historic play-off for the U.S. Open at Brookline in 1913 when the young Bostonian beat Vardon and Ray. Darwin had also reported on the great triumphs of Hagen and Sarazen and Jones. And he played amateur golf at a high standard and featured (as a reserve) in the first Walker Cup match of 1922, when he won his singles match.

When writing of golfers' methods, Darwin wrote descriptively and with a certain flourish. He believed that Jones's swing had a "certain drowsy beauty" to it and contained a "strain of poetry." However, of Guldahl, he wrote, "He is a big strong man, with a not very engaging swing. He has something of a 'duck' in it but he is very good and very accurate."[43] This appraisal may not seem complimentary, especially the part about "the duck." It may have been the case that some tall players, who grew up on hickory shafts, had a slight dip in their swings, as Byron Nelson appeared to have the same feature.[44] However, the "very accurate" comment was not the first time Darwin used this term to describe Guldahl, as before the contest he referred to the new U.S. Open champion as a man of "appalling accuracy." Darwin, while a great admirer of American golf, was also known as being fiercely partisan when it came to British golf. And so his comment can be taken as a real compliment. Accuracy was very much in keeping with Guldahl's form in 1937—not necessarily very spectacular, but someone who made few mistakes and who had the capacity to come up with big shots at the right time.

In the end, Guldahl did "go away" from Padgham and beat him 8–7. As National Open champion, he was first out to meet his British counterpart and was six up after the morning round. It is worth recording that in three Ryder Cup matches, Padgham never won a point, but this should not take away from Guldahl's fine golf, which saw him only four over par when the game ended on the 29th green. This was excellent golf in the foul conditions, as most victors had scored roughly 73 or 74 for their morning rounds, and Byron Nelson shot 81 for his first 18. Unsurprisingly, Nelson lost his match to a British rookie: the 24-year-old Welshman, Dai

SUPPLEMENT TO THE

Ryder Cup Official Souvenir Programme

Order of Play and Starting Times:

FOURSOMES, TUESDAY, JUNE 29th, 1937

End of 18 holes	Result	Points	U.S.A. GT. BRITAIN	End of 18 holes	Result	Points
			MATCH NO. 1			
1 up	4/3	1.	E. DUDLEY and B. NELSON v. A. H. PADGHAM & T. H. COTTON Times of Starting: 10 a.m. & 2 p.m.	—	—	0.
			MATCH NO. 2			
	2/1	1.	R. GULDAHL and T. MANERO v. A. J. LACEY and W. J. COX Times of Starting: 10-20 a.m. & 2-20 p.m.	1 up	—	0.
			MATCH NO. 3			
Square	Square	1/2	G. SARAZEN and D. SHUTE v. C. A. WHITCOMBE and D. J. REES Times of Starting: 10-40 a.m. & 2-40 p.m.	Square	Square	1/2
			MATCH NO. 4			
·	·	0.	H. PICARD and J. REVOLTA v. P. ALLISS and R. BURTON Times of Starting: 11 a.m. & 3 p.m.	3 up	2/1	1.
Total	2½			Total	1½	

End of 18 holes	Result	Points	U.S.A. GT. BRITAIN	End of 18 holes	Result	Points
6 up	8/7	1.	**MATCH NO. 1** R. GULDAHL v. A. H. PADGHAM Times of Starting: 10 a.m. & 2 p.m.	·	·	0.
Square	Square	1/2	**MATCH NO. 2** D. SHUTE v. S. L. KING Times of Starting: 10-10 a.m. & 2-10 p.m.	Square	Square	1/2
·	·	0.	**MATCH NO. 3** B. NELSON v. D. J. REES Times of Starting: 10-20 a.m. & 2-20 p.m.	1 up	3/1	1.
·	·	0	**MATCH NO. 4** T. MANERO v. T. H. COTTON Times of Starting: 10-30 a.m. & 2-30 p.m.	2 up	5/3	1.
	1 up	1.	**MATCH NO. 5** G. SARAZEN v. P. ALLISS Times of Starting: 10-40 a.m. & 2-40 p.m.	1 up	—	0.
2 up	5/4	1.	**MATCH NO. 6** S. SNEAD v. R. BURTON Times of Starting: 10-50 a.m. & 2-50 p.m.	·	·	0.
1 up	2/1	1.	**MATCH NO. 7** E. DUDLEY v. A. PERRY Times of Starting: 11 a.m. & 3 p.m.	·	·	0.
1 up	2/1	1.	**MATCH NO. 8** H. PICARD v. A. J. LACEY Times of Starting: 11-10 a.m. & 3-10 p.m.	·	·	0.
Total	5½			Total	2½	

IDENTIFICATION OF PLAYERS

Taken from the official souvenir program, the results from the 1937 Ryder Cup matches (courtesy Southport & Ainsdale Golf Club).

Rees. Rees surprised Nelson with his 3–1 win and went on to play in nine Ryder Cups, captaining the team on five occasions. "Guldahl Trounces British Open King," read one headline.[45] And in a somewhat understandable display of chauvinism, the *Dallas Morning News* reported how "Dallas product beats British Open Ruler 8 and 7."[46] It was estimated that 12,000 people braved the elements to watch the final day's play and that overall gate receipts of £4,000 broke all previous records for the contest.

Overall, the U.S. team became the first away team to win, by a margin of 8–4. Hagen, incidentally, had predicted this exact score before the matches began on the basis of America's greater strength in depth. And after the matches he claimed the victory was "the greatest thrill of my golfing career."[47] For a man who had four Open titles to his name, this may seem excessive, but there was no doubt "Sir Walter" was excited by the result, and in his acceptance speech, he even managed to say how delighted he was to become the first captain to win on "home" soil. When his error was pointed out to him, being Hagen, he recovered and explained that he had always been so well received in Britain that it felt like home. Sadly, Samuel Ryder was not present to witness the first away in his contest, having passed away the previous year.

In terms of *why* the American team had such an impressive victory, many reasons were advanced. American journalist Gayle Talbot claimed it was a matter of the superior mental strength of the U.S. team. "The Britishers," Talbot wrote, "individually showed they had every shot in the Americans' bag. But ... when the going got really tough and for a time looked as though any of half a dozen matches be decided, they folded their tents."[48] And there were other opinions voiced, with one in particular catching the eye, this time from the British side of the Atlantic. *Golf Monthly* wrote of the Americans how "the deportment of every man cannot be over-praised. Quiet and reserved, tailored in the best taste, well groomed, in perfect physical condition, they presented a splendid spectacle of athletic youth. They were much more impressive in all those respects than the British team as a whole." And, with the awful weather conditions in which the matches were played, the journal also noted the "slackly fitting oilskins which did not incommode or restrict the swing."[49] It will be recalled that in the rain-sodden 2010 Ryder Cup at Celtic Manor in Wales, Corey Pavin and his team had serious difficulties with the quality of their official rain gear, and so it is interesting to note that roughly seventy years earlier, this aspect of golf clothing was seen as being crucial in an American victory.

After the contest, the prominent golf writer Louis T. Stanley concluded,

"The British team dressed like workmen and played at the game; the Americans dressed like golfers and worked at the game."[50] Bernard Darwin, however, opted for a more incisive view of the matches under the heading of an article titled "Yankee Foozle." "Never shall I set up in business as a golfing prophet," Darwin wrote. "It was not a role in which I greatly fancied myself, but I have never been so wrong as this time, and the only consolation is that a good many people were wrong with me. I thought we might win the Ryder Cup match at Southport, because we always managed to win at home and because the Americans had not had long to get acclimated.... Moreover, they not only won, but they looked the better golfers man for man and were obviously the better putters." In addition to these comments, Darwin had some words for the British captain, Charles Whitcombe, and wrote, "I do not think that they would have won by such a margin if the British captaincy had been better. It was a mistake to put Cotton and Padgham together: they did not fit in and when they were well and truly beaten by Nelson and Dudley, we lost a vital point hardly to be recovered." But he did conclude, "The Americans would have won in any case."[51]

Perhaps Robert Browning, writing in *Golfing*, put the defeat most neatly and sportingly into its correct context. "The result is the most serious blow to the prestige of the British professionals that they have yet sustained," Browning wrote.

> Everything was in favour of the home team. The Americans were short of practice, and handicapped by having to play with a ball of unfamiliar size. The weather, too, was in our favour. The foursomes on the first day were played with a stiff sea-breeze blowing directly across the course—the very conditions calculated to test the newcomers to the American team. And even the swift change to the rain-sodden depression of the second day might be said to favour our men, long grown familiar with Southport and Ainsdale course under every aspect. And yet we could only win three matches out of ten! It is the proper thing to say on these occasions that we were beaten by a better team. In this case it goes without saying.[52]

As for Ralph Guldahl, if his Ryder Cup debut was impressive, his skill at public relations was not, and this made more headlines than his outstanding golf. In more recent years, the question of spectator partisanship has been a live one at Ryder Cup matches, with Brookline in 1999 being the most infamous example of all. However, like many other things in golf, this issue is not new. Certainly in the aftermath of the 1937 matches, accusations followed by counter-accusations were plentiful, and Guldahl was at the center of this storm. On departing Britain he had this to say: "If the British golf customers are sportsmen then I hope I never see the tight little isle again.... They're quite the nuts taken at Southport or

Carnoustie."[53] And on returning to America in late July, he was quoted as saying, "As far as I'm concerned, I wouldn't swap a Texas cactus plant for the whole of England.... I don't care for British sportsmanship." According to Ralph, after his victory over Alf Padgham, he went out to watch Tony Manero play Henry Cotton and saw the crowd refuse to give Tony six or seven feet so he could swing his club. And finally Guldahl added, "I noticed they'd never cheer until we made a mistake."[54] Ed Dudley did not hold back either. Despite the fact that he beat Alf Perry 2–1 in his singles match, "Big Ed" claimed that on one occasion, a spectator had bumped his opponent's ball closer to the hole. Unsurprisingly, Perry refuted this and called the allegation "a lie" saying that the ball hit a ridge.[55]

Guldahl was backed up by some but not all of his teammates. Rookie Byron Nelson, for example, thought the British fans were just passionate and had every right to cheer their team. However, Guldahl's words brought a strong response from across the Atlantic. Henry Cotton said he was astounded, and Alf Padgham, whom Ralph had thrashed in the singles, said his comments were "disgusting." The strongest words, however, came from Arthur Lacey, whom Guldahl and Tony Manero had beaten in the foursomes. He said of Guldahl, "Perhaps it would be a good thing if he doesn't come back. I thought he was a rather difficult fellow, especially when things were going against him."[56]

Fred Corcoran, who had traveled to Britain as team manager, tried to present an entirely positive spin on the trip. As well as being golf's greatest salesman, Corcoran was the game's leading diplomat. In the 1950s, and for years after, he ran the Canada Cup (later the World Cup), which was designed "to promote international goodwill through golf." The skills required for this job were certainly necessary after Southport, and he wrote, "Contributing to the enjoyment of our boys were many features too numerous to set down or catalogue, but best of all was the outstanding warmth and good fellowship of our hosts, the British PGA, the Ryder Cup players, their galleries and last if not least, the British press, which from first to last hailed and applauded our players with unlimited courtesies and acclaim."[57] It should be noted that these words appeared in the official PGA journal and so it was understandable that Corcoran would accentuate the positives from the trip. However, there was no doubting the fact that golfing relations between Britain and the USA were at a low ebb, and so it was that PGA President George Jacobus intervened.

Jacobus was a highly influential figure in the world of professional golf. A professional himself, he took a young Byron Nelson on as his assistant at the Ridgewood Club and later recommended him for the head

professional's position at Reading. He also had several disputes with Bob
Harlow before removing him as tournament director in favor of Fred Corcoran. Although Jacobus had remained in America during the Ryder Cup
matches, he kept in close touch with events at Southport and initially his
delight at the outcome was unbounded. In this regard, he sent a telegram
to Captain Hagen reading, "To the greatest general in the world congratulations for leading the greatest golfers in the world to a wonderful victory
which brings great honor to your country, the PGA, and your fellow professionals who are proud of you. Your achievement will go down in golfing
history as the greatest of all time: we salute you, admire your courage and
honor you as our champions and heroes. Out of the happiness of my heart
I send my personal congratulations and fondest regards to each man."[58]
The "greatest [achievement] of all time" accolade may have been a little
far-fetched but there is no doubt that the American PGA saw this first
"away" victory as a considerable achievement. And in a sportsmanlike gesture, he sent a telegram to Charles Whitcombe saying we "congratulate
the finest losing team ever to play in the Ryder Cup Matches."[59]

In view of this euphoria and of his extending the hand of goodwill
across the Atlantic, Jacobus prompted Guldahl and others to clear the air
in the form of an apology. And it was not just British-American golfing
relations which concerned Jacobus. He was also in danger of finding himself in an embarrassing situation with the White House. In this bout of
telegrams, Jacobus also sent one to the White House which began, "As
President of the United States you will be happy to learn that the American
Ryder Cup Team of golf professionals today brought honor and glory to
our great country by winning the International Cup Matches ... the first
time that an invading team has won these international matches since
their inception ten years ago." And he continued to tell the president of
how proud we can be "to have [the golf team] represent our country not
only as sportsmen but as ambassadors of good-will.... These matches contribute greatly to the promotion of friendly relations between ... our two
great English speaking countries."[60] As a former golfer, FDR would appreciate the victory, and as commander-in-chief, he would be very pleased
with the diplomatic success with his greatest ally on which Jacobus had
reported. In view of this extravagant language, the last thing the PGA
chief needed was a diplomatic *faux pas*. In the end, Guldahl did issue a
form of apology, but its heading in the *Glasgow Herald* suggested that his
words owed more to Jacobus than his own true feelings. "Guldahl And
His Alibi" read the headline, and the piece in the newspaper went on to
quote Ralph as saying he had "a swell time in Britain and the galleries were

enthusiastic, the same as in our country. But I'm the same as other golfers and reserve the privilege of an alibi when I don't beat anyone."[61]

Byron Nelson and Johnny Revolta also went on the record to say how "graciously" they had been treated in England. Nelson in particular had good reason to have fond memories of Southport. He later recalled that in the custom of the times, professionals were hardly let into clubhouses and that their wives certainly weren't. In fact, after the matches, Britain's *Golf Monthly* magazine carried an article titled, "Should Wives Attend Championships?"[62] The magazine cited the example of how "Australia, most experienced of national teams on tour, decline to allow their cricketers when visiting England to be accompanied by their wives. Gene Sarazen is all for barring golfers' wives from the course." Sarazen's views on the place of women in the life of the professional golfer were well known, although his own wife Mary was known to accompany him to some tournaments. Regardless of these more conservative views, on the final day of wind and rain, the mayor of Southport's wife saw the American wives "huddled together trying to stay out of the wind. She had enough compassion to invite them all into the clubhouse and because she was the mayor's wife, no one could say no to her. Then she served them some 200-year old port, and they warmed up quickly after that. They said later they'd never tasted anything as good as that port in all their lives."[63] And Byron went on to single out the experience of his wife Louise, whom he said had a "delightful adventure, she made friends with the British wives and soaked up the local customs."[64]

Guldahl's words about "a swell time" under the "alibi" heading had a hollow ring to them because he did not need an excuse. He won both his matches and the U.S. team had a commanding victory. As alluded to above, it would appear that the players, notably the extremely vocal Guldahl, had been instructed by Jacobus to calm the waters. Jacobus was clearly angered by Ralph and went as far as to say, "I am not going to say whether Guldahl will be invited to represent America again.... I won't be President of the PGA then." Jacobus also said, "I have done everything I can to rectify this deplorable breach of etiquette."[65] These strong words left nobody in doubt as to where Jacobus felt the blame lay for the Ryder Cup incident. However, Guldahl's quasi-apology seemed to work, and in the event, no lasting damage was done to U.S.-British relations.

With the Ryder Cup won, the American team traveled north to Carnoustie for the Open Championship. The last time the Open was held at Carnoustie was in 1931 when Tommy Armour won. Officially Armour was American, as he took citizenship when he came to the United States in the early 1920s. However, since he was an Edinburgh man, his victory was warmly welcomed by the locals, who saw him as "one of our own." After the loss in the 1937 Ryder Cup match, "The Open" assumed even greater importance than usual, as the full might of American golf would be represented and it was a matter of national pride that "Britain" won the claret jug. However, the signs for the home effort were not good and the *Chicago Tribune* declared, "So strong is the field it appears impossible for Great Britain relying almost entirely on Henry Cotton to withstand the threat of the American professionals who as a group are quoted at even money to win."[66] It appeared that the locals agreed with this assessment, with Ralph being singled out for particular mention. "Canny Scotchmen," it was reported, "watching the big Texan's play hastened to cut his odds from 10 to 1 to 7 to 1 alongside Hilarious Henry Cotton whom they considered is good 'even if he is an English man.'"[67] The reference to Cotton's hilarity was laced with sarcasm, as it was no secret that Henry was regarded by some as being aloof and even arrogant. A story by Jim Ferrier backs up this assessment.

In the mid to late 1930s, Ferrier was Australia's outstanding amateur golfer, with multiple wins in both the Australian Amateur and Open titles on his résumé. He would later turn professional and win the U.S. PGA title as well as numerous other tournaments. As an amateur he also worked as a journalist and wrote syndicated articles for a number of publications. When covering the 1937 Open, he recorded in the *Sydney Morning Herald* how he "summed up the courage to ask [Cotton] for a game. He refused. He said he always played alone because the watching of other styles put him off his own swing." Ferrier concluded by writing, "I thought this was taking the extreme view of practice."[68] There were other similar stories about Cotton, but his many supporters claimed that this was part of the dedication and single-mindedness which helped make him a triple Open champion. In Carnoustie, both his personality and the question of his being English were quickly put to one side by the locals. For the purpose of the championship he was most definitely representing Britain.

Guldahl's short price in the betting was not surprising given that he was reigning U.S. Open champion and that he had played so well in the Ryder Cup. Furthermore, wasn't this an era of American golfing dominance, and frankly, one of Britain's sense of inferiority? American victories in the shape of Hagen, Jones and Sarazen were the norm, and on the most recent occasion when the American Ryder Cup team competed at the Open (St. Andrews, 1933), Denny Shute and Craig Wood tied first. Indeed five Americans filled the first six places. Shute won the 36-hole play-off by five shots the following day with a score of 149.

The home mood was not helped by scores in the pre-qualifying rounds. In this era (and for some time after) all players had to endure a 36-hole qualifying ordeal before the championship proper began. In 1937, this involved 18 holes at Carnoustie and another 18 at the nearby Burnside course with the leading 140 players playing in the Open. At the end of these qualifying rounds, Americans filled the first five places, with Horton Smith leading the way, followed by Sarazen, Hagen, Snead and Nelson. Their scores ranged from 138 to 142. Guldahl was on a respectable 144. Losing Ryder Cup captain Charles Whitcombe admitted he was close to "throwing in the sponge" on the back of the qualifying scores. "One of these American kids is bound to win the championship," he said, "and I wouldn't be surprised to see them take the first five or six places. The only man we have with any chance of stopping you is Henry Cotton, and he isn't playing well enough right now. Our other Ryder Cup players are still suffering from the shock they got at Southport."[69] Whitcombe's view was that the gulf in ability between the two sides was due to the greater number of tournaments played in America which, he claimed, made for producing tougher competitors. "These American boys," he said, "are shooting for money almost twelve months of the year while we have only a couple of money events worth entering."[70] Whitcombe may have exaggerated with his "almost twelve months of the year" comment, as the all-year-round tour, while evolving, was still some way off. However, his basic point was correct, as Britain then, and for some years after, held very few professional tournaments.

He also believed that the smaller greens in the United States, compared to the traditionally larger British links-land surfaces, led to greater accuracy with approach shots. As it turned out, however, Whitcombe's pessimism was misplaced, as in the championship itself the home players fared very well and at the halfway stage, one headline read, "Britain Takes the Lead."[71] This was in reference to his brother Reg Whitcombe's showing the way on 142. Charles himself was two back along with Ed Dudley who was flying the American flag. And on 146 were Cotton, Shute, and Alf Padgham who seemed to have recovered from his Ryder Cup thrashing.

As for Guldahl, along with most of his Ryder Cup teammates, he fared poorly at Carnoustie. He began with a 77, part of which was witnessed by Bernard Darwin, who commented on Guldahl's finish of 5–5–4–5–5, and an inward nine of 41, as follows: "He seemed to be trying to force long seconds with irons where other people wanted all they could do with wood and he was never in sight of getting up."[72] Considering the 14th and 18th were par fives, and conceivably holes where a shot or two might be picked up, this closing stretch was ruinous to Guldahl's chances. He followed up his poor start with a steady 72, but he finished with a final score of 300, which was a full ten shots behind the winner, Henry Cotton, whose victory was without doubt the greatest of his career. To be fair to Guldahl, only ten players finished ahead of him, and for a first attempt, this could be seen as a reasonable effort. However, there was no doubt that as U.S. Open champion, he had set his sights much higher. The best golf on the final day was played by British-born but nationalized American Charles Lacey, whose rounds of 70 and 72 were exceptional in the circumstances but still two short of the winning total. Byron Nelson was best of the Americans with a score of 296, which gained him fifth place. For the Ryder Cup captain, this was his last appearance in a championship he had won four times. "The Haig" finished with a total of 309. The scores overall may appear high but there were two reasons for this. First, Carnoustie, at over 7,000 yards, was the toughest course on the British Open roster. In the 1931 Open at Carnoustie, for example, a score of 296 was good enough to win for Tommy Armour. And second, the weather was appalling. Indeed, at one stage on the final afternoon, there was a concern that play might be abandoned, such was the number of pools which appeared on the course. Several holes had to be recut on the flatter parts of the green to ensure the championship would finish on time.

Regarding the severity of Carnoustie, Guldahl had his views, and when safely on board the ship home, he voiced his opinions. "Carnoustie wasn't fair. They had traps in the center of the fairway 230 yards out that would catch a perfect shot. We had to play safely by playing to the right or left. Can you imagine that?"[73] The question of these newly installed bunkers on certain holes (such as the par-five sixth) was the subject of much discussion before the Open began. And it should be said that even certain local commentators questioned their fairness. Essentially, a golfer either played short or aimed for a narrow pathway on either side of the bunkers. Typically, Bernard Darwin laid his cards firmly on the table: "The player had to drive down those narrow ways, almost like the eye of a needle, or he had to take a spoon or iron and play short. To my mind, these bunkers made for good, interesting golf, thoughtful golf, but I do not think the players enjoyed them very much."[74] This lack of enjoyment was especially true of the visitors, but in earlier years, Jones, Hagen, Shute and Sarazen learned how to deal with such "unfairness," and maybe Ralph needed a few more Open Championships before he got used to links golf. But this was to be his only experience of the Open.

As for the bad weather, this was also the case at Southport, and in the aftermath of America's win, British captain Charles Whitcombe said, "Surely this must dispel the notion that the Americans cannot play well under our weather conditions."[75] And Hagen, who had played and won in the difficult British conditions, was thoroughly honest in his appraisal. "It's no good talking about the weather," Hagen said. "Golf is an all-weather game and if you cannot play in the rain, you do not deserve to be champion. Henry has done well. In fact, so has Great Britain as a whole."

At Carnoustie, it appeared that Guldahl and his Ryder Cup colleagues were just outplayed by Henry Cotton, whose final round of 71 was regarded by Reg Whitcombe as probably "the greatest round of golf ever played under similar circumstances."[76] Whitcombe's was a formidable voice as he finished second to Cotton and won the Open the following year at Sandwich. But Cotton's victory did not come by chance, as several weeks before the championship, he traveled north for a ten-day visit and played a number of practice rounds at Carnoustie. In this he gained a distinct advantage over the Americans and perhaps over his British colleagues as well. It is also worth looking in a little detail at his play in his last round of 71 and in particular the wizardry of his short game. As Bernard Darwin reported, "Such chipping and putting have seldom been seen even from the best of Americans. Nine times in the round he did it."[77] Comparing his short game to the Americans was the highest compliment Darwin could have paid Cotton, and the nine single putts when the pressure was at its most intense was the mark of a man in complete control of his game and his nerves.

After the Open Championship, Henry Cotton summed up his own and the national mood perfectly: "I feel more proud than at any moment in my life—not so much because I won the cup again but because I was able to win for Britain against so great and representative a field."[78] Britain's golfing honor had been restored, and as if to celebrate, the *Times*, which usually placed cricket and even croquet ahead of golf on the sports pages, placed Darwin's report on Cotton's triumph on page four of the newspaper, alongside reports from the courts and ahead of every other sport. This was quite a tribute.

And Darwin's summation of events at Carnoustie was both accurate and magnanimous. "That the Americans as a team failed," he wrote, "is unquestionable and I gladly own myself as bad prophet. They made a bad start and never recovered from it." But he went on, "Let us never forget in the moment of triumph what our visitors have taught us."[79] Like many others, Darwin was pessimistic before the Open and was quick to admit this. However, as well as celebrating Cotton's victory, he was suggesting that the British players were already learning from the defeat at Southport and from America's golfing prowess, which Darwin was never slow to acknowledge. Perhaps there was something equitable about how the summer of 1937 worked out with the United States winning the Ryder Cup and "Britain" holding on to the claret jug.

The following week, Cotton restored Britain's pride even further when he beat Denny Shute in an unofficial world championship match. The venue was Walton Heath near London and, over 72 holes, Cotton won by 6–5 and collected $2,500. While not comparing the Open Championship to a sponsored match, this sum of money was significant for Cotton when compared to the £100 he received at Carnoustie. Who should represent America was a bone of contention, but as the contest was over match-play, PGA President George Jacobus decided it should be PGA champion Shute, rather than the new National Open winner, Ralph Guldahl. In view of his comments on Britain and British sportsmanship, perhaps Guldahl was happy to miss out on the match against Cotton.

The fallout from the trip continued when the team returned home, with some members of the American team happy to feed the media with their views on the trip to Britain. John Lardner, son of the illustrious and sardonic Ring, wrote one tongue-in-cheek piece about the latest complaints from the U.S. team which partially explained the American failure to win the Open championship. It was, according to Lardner, because "they couldn't get enough to eat in England. In their boundless turpitude, the English buried all the mutton pies and bubble-and-squeak and scones and crumpets and Yorkshire pudding many feet under the ground and won the British Open by siege and starvation."[80] When making due allowances for the fact that the Open that year was played in Scotland and not England, and that Yorkshire pudding and the rest may not have been quite as popular north of the border, Lardner's deliberately satirical words indicate that it was time to accept that Cotton had won the title because he was the best player. And in fairness to Lardner, he did go on to report on how a number of the American players, such as Shute and Smith, were fulsome in their praise for Cotton and his swing.

Guldahl's only appearance in Britain was in 1937. Like most Americans, he did not travel to Sandwich in 1938 when Reg Whitcombe won the Open in a gale. And in 1939, the only Americans of note to make the journey to St. Andrews were Lawson Little and Johnny Bulla. Bulla finished second to Dick Burton. There is little doubt that the costs involved were prohibitive, but this was also the case when Hagen and Sarazen regularly made the trip across the Atlantic in "non-Ryder Cup Years." It seemed that both men's desire to win golf's oldest major championship was greater than some of their contemporaries. However, there was the possibility that Guldahl's and Henry Cotton's paths might cross again. This was in 1939 when the Ryder Cup matches were scheduled for America. There was considerable speculation regarding a possible match between America's number one and the man who had beaten the full might of America's Ryder Cup team at Carnoustie. In fact, Guldahl had sown the seeds of a possible match-up with Cotton in America when traveling back from Britain in 1937. Of Cotton he said, "He's good but maybe he wouldn't go much better than we did in the British Open. Courses are different you know."[81] In 1939, with the help of the newspapers, it was Guldahl who threw down the challenge when saying, "I'd jump at the chance to play this Cotton. I've only seen him two or three shots but I know he must be a grand shot maker. I'd like him at 72 holes. Just anywhere he cares to play."[82] There was more than a hint of boxing language in these words and it seems that Cotton was keen to meet him as part of a brief American tour built around his Ryder Cup duties. However, in 1939, the Ryder Cup matches were canceled due to the outbreak of the Second World War, and that was the end of a possible Guldahl-Cotton meeting.

After the Ryder Cup and Carnoustie, Guldahl returned to golf in the shape of some strong performances at home. For example, at the Chicago Open in Medinah he finished joint eighth behind winner Gene Sarazen; in Hershey he came second to Henry Picard and won $750; and in the Belmont match-play event he lost in the semifinals to Picard and won $700. Byron Nelson took home the substantial first prize of the tournament of $3,000. As the country entered the latter stages of the Great Depression, the tour was getting stronger. Guldahl's main interest, however, was earning some of the "gravy" which came to all National Open winners. In this regard, he embarked on an exhibition tour of the Southern states with Sam Snead.

Exhibition matches had long been a vital component in the life of a successful professional golfer. In the days of small tournament purses, guaranteed appearance fees were indeed welcome. Harry Vardon's tours of America were hugely successful commercial enterprises for the six-time Open champion, and in the 1920s Walter Hagen, often accompanied by Joe Kirkwood, toured both domestically and globally earning guaranteed dollars. As Stephen Lowe recorded, "Hagen and Kirkwood were making too much money to stop and play in formal tournaments, where they

might or might not collect a pay check."[83] Sarazen also toured with Kirkwood, and in 1934, the pair were touring South America when the inaugural Masters was held. "The Squire" estimated that for the 22-match tour,
he and Kirkwood each came out $3,500 "on the right side of the ledger."[84]
This came to approximately $160 per appearance.

In a less exotic vein, domestic exhibitions were a very important part
of a professional's life during the Depression era. Even so, it was something
of a grind because of the travel involved. Harry Cooper recalled an exhibition match when he traveled to the Mississauga Club, which hosted the
Canadian Open in 1938. After the Saturday finish, Cooper and Snead were
tied and a play-off was scheduled for the following Monday. Cooper took
up the story. "And I had to play an exhibition," he said. "Drive 75 miles
from Toronto at the time on the Sunday, give a 45-minute shot-making
demonstration, and then play 18 holes in a driving rain, and then drive
back and be ready to play off with Sam Snead on the Monday morning at
10 o'clock." Eventually Cooper lost the play-off, which went to 27 holes
since the players were tied after the regulation 18 holes.

But the players rarely complained because these matches were a
chance to cash in while one's name was "hot," particularly for the National
Open champion. Sam Parks, for example, the 100–1 shot who won at Oakmont in 1935, claimed he made $17,000 from his victory, "mostly for exhi-
bitions."[85] Typically two big names would team up against two local
amateurs or professionals in an 18-hole match. A clinic would be held
either before or after the match. Sometimes there would be a guaranteed
fee of a few hundred dollars, or the big names would play for a percentage
of the gate receipts. As the matches were usually attended by good crowds,
the stars were guaranteed a decent payday either way. On one occasion
at the Holston Hills Club in Tennessee, Snead and Guldahl turned down
an exhibition fee of $200 each in favor of the entire gate receipts. The
gallery was estimated at 500, and with a usual charge of one dollar admission for these matches, the Wilson pair did just marginally better than the
guaranteed fee. The post–Ryder Cup trip would be one of a series of tours
with Snead that were orchestrated by Wilson, to whom both players were
contracted. This was a smart business move by L.B. Icely and his staff, as
having the two hottest properties in the game promoting the Wilson brand
was good for business. That the two were rivals was not in dispute, with
Guldahl usually coming out on top in the clutch finishes. However, if their
appearances in exhibitions or in the four-ball tournaments that were so
popular in this era were the product of the Wilson marketing department,
there is also evidence of a friendship between the pair.

Guldahl with the Western Open trophy of 1937 (courtesy Western Golf Association).

In the Depression era, with money so tight, players often saved on expenses by driving to tournaments together or even sharing rooms. At a time when playing the tour cost roughly $100 per week and when to make money a golfer often had to finish in the top ten, this made sense. As we know, the Guldahls usually traveled together, but nonetheless, one of Snead's biographers, Al Barkow, recalled how Ralph "remembered the long drives, sometimes with Sam Snead sprawled in the back seat playing a banjo and singing songs and telling Ralph how he ought to leave his wife at home."[86] It is not recorded if Laverne was in the car at the time, but the story suggests that Guldahl and Snead got along well.

After the exhibition tour, in September 1937 it was back to tournament golf, and Guldahl continued his good form when tied second behind Henry Picard at the Hershey Open. Picard was the host professional at Hershey and he was also the defending champion. However, for once, Guldahl's finish let him down. Leading on 207 going into the final round, he had three sixes in the first four holes and shot a 76 for 283. Picard beat him by three with 280. The disappointment did not last long, as there was a more important tournament coming up in the shape of the Western Open. There was also the chance to make a little history by becoming the first-ever player to win the U.S. Open and the Western in the same year.

The tournament was held at the Canterbury Club in Cleveland, which was founded in 1921. The original design was done by Herbert Strong, but in the late 1920s, alterations were completed by Jack H. Way. It was then Canterbury became known as one of the nation's toughest challenges, with a particularly tough finishing stretch. By 1937, it had already hosted the Western Open of 1932 when Hagen achieved one of the final victories of his glittering career. It would go on to host many more majors in the

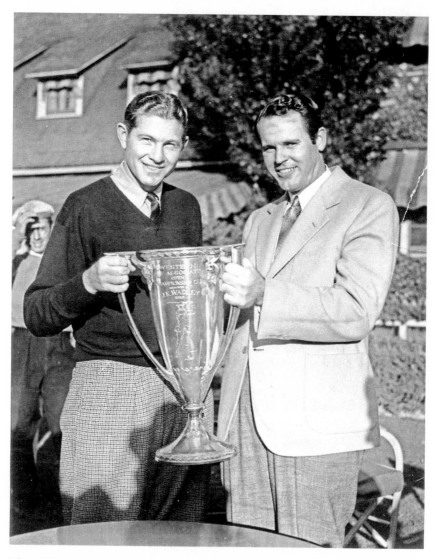

The 1937 Western Open, where Guldahl beat Horton Smith in a play-off (courtesy Western Golf Association).

future, both amateur and professional. For the 1937 Western, the course had been considerably lengthened, and experts were predicting a winning total of 290. This proved to be quite an accurate forecast. Guldahl was one of the favorites, but this was a very tight affair. He went into the final round with a one-shot lead; he was level with Snead after the first nine; and when Sam faded, he ended up in a tie with double Masters winner Horton Smith on 288. That he achieved a tie was due to a holed 16-footer for a bogey six on the 615-yard 16th hole. Here he went out of bounds, which in those days incurred just a one-shot penalty. The play-off was much more comfortable than the tournament itself, as Guldahl won with a 72 to Smith's 76. His prize was $500 plus half of the crowd receipts for the play-off, which amounted to $300. When adding in the "like for like" winner's bonus from Wilson's, this was a good week for the Guldahls. Winning the Western of 1937 saw him become the first man to hold this title and the U.S. Open in the same year. He also joined an illustrious group of repeat Western winners, which included names such as Jim Barnes and Walter Hagen.

A further performance of note for Guldahl came in the Canadian Open. And here again the strength of golf in Texas was demonstrated as he went toe to toe with Harry Cooper. The two were paired together on the final day, and with many scores in the low 80s, each shot a 72 on the Saturday morning. In the afternoon, however, Cooper had a 74 to Guldahl's 75 and won by two with a score of 285. And the good golf continued to the very end of the calendar year when in the Miami Open, played in Christmas week, Guldahl tied second on 272 with Horton Smith and split the second- and third-place prize money of $700. Both, however, were five shots behind Snead, who closed with a pair of 66s on the final day and took home the $700 first-place money.

Harry Cooper would feature again in what was the final honor left for Guldahl in his memorable year of 1937. As National Open champion, he got to pick the ten members of the All American golf team. Tradition determined that the champion did not pick himself, and as his number one, Guldahl selected Harry Cooper ahead of Henry Picard and Sam Snead. The two teenagers from Tenison Park in Dallas had come a long way.

So, in terms of results, the change in fortune was there for all to see. But off the course there was also evidence of Guldahl's enhanced reputation when he was appointed winter professional at the exclusive Miami Biltmore Hotel complex. His co-professional was Denny Shute, and so the Biltmore had both the National Open and PGA champions as its star attractions. The practice of engaging the services of leading professionals for the winter months was not unusual during this era. Walter Hagen started the trend in the 1920s and other pros, such as Gene Sarazen, followed accordingly. Tommy Armour also made serious money from playing and especially teaching at Boca Raton, and then retiring to his duties at Medinah for the spring and summer. For predominantly tour professionals, like Denny Shute and Ralph Guldahl, this arrangement was ideal: they had their retainer from the resort and they could play the tour, as a number of tournaments were played in Florida during the winter and early spring. And all of this in return for giving some lessons and playing with the guests in a series of pro-am events or inter-club matches. Such a prestigious position was further confirmation that Ralph Guldahl was now very much part of golf's elite.

4

Cherry Hills

A talking point among the pros at the start of 1938 was the introduction of a fourteen-club maximum rule. It was believed that this new regulation would place greater emphasis on skill and ease the burden on caddies. Before this, a player could carry as many clubs as he liked, and some brought this to extreme lengths. Harry Cooper, for example, was known to carry as many as 29. The response to this rule from the professionals was generally positive. Indeed, Harry believed it would bring the more skilled golfer to the fore. And Sam Snead agreed—"I think golfers could get along with ten clubs after he got accustomed to it."[1] Tommy Armour concurred when saying, "Fourteen clubs are plenty. More than that usually duplicates."[2] But there were some dissenting voices, and Ralph Guldahl was one of these. When he won at Oakland Hills the previous year, he carried nineteen clubs: four woods, 13 irons and two putters. As ever, unafraid to voice his opinion, he declared the new rule to be "silly,"[3] and he was not alone. Henry Picard and "Wild Bill" Mehlhorn, two recognized shot-makers, also shared Guldahl's view, as did golf's great theorist, Leo Diegel. Denny Shute felt that a compromise of sixteen clubs should be reached, and Tony Manero claimed that in his 1936 National Open victory at Baltusrol, all nineteen of his clubs were used.[4]

Across the Atlantic, Henry Cotton, who carried up to twenty-two clubs, disagreed with the new rule even though Vardon, Braid and Taylor were in favor of the change. In fact, even though the official rule change was to take effect on January 1, 1938, the fourteen-club maximum had its first tryout at the Miami Biltmore Open in December 1937. Guldahl just happened to be resident winter professional at the Henry Doherty–owned Biltmore resort. The event was won by Johnny Revolta, who favored the new rule. What Revolta did was "play to his strength," which was his short game. He continued to carry at least three wedges and discarded some of the longer clubs, such as his two iron. In the end, the fourteen club limit passed without a great deal of fuss and endures to this day.

Unlike 1937, Guldahl did not take part in the "California Swing" at the start of the year. Being based in Florida, he played in some exhibition matches and some tournaments as a way of keeping his game sharp and pocketing some cash. But he was building up to the majors, and just before the Masters, he finished third in the inaugural Greensboro Open behind Johnny Revolta and the winner, Sam Snead. For a man who was sometimes perceived as being a little aloof or even arrogant, it is worth recording part of a letter which Guldahl wrote to one of the Greensboro tournament organizers, Laurence Leonard, that January. Having opened by saying how he hoped that 1938 would be as successful as 1937, he went on to say, "[S]o why [should I] not start the year right by resolving to participate in your $5,000 tournament." And he continued, "I wish to extend the appreciation of the professionals to those instrumental in putting on the Greensboro Open. Certainly this is going to be one of the outstanding tournaments of the New Year. Cordially yours, Ralph Guldahl."[5] As it turned out, the Greensboro Open would be good to Guldahl, and especially Snead, in the coming years.

The performance at Greensboro showed Ralph Guldahl was in good form in the lead-up to the Masters. This good form continued at Augusta, where he finished a close second to Henry Picard. (See next chapter.) The disappointment did not appear to damage Guldahl's confidence, and he got ready for the task of defending his National Open title in early June at the new venue of Cherry Hills. Holding the 1938 U.S. Open at Cherry Hills, Denver, was a milestone in American golf, as it was the first time the championship was held west of the Mississippi. For this reason, a concentrated effort was made by the organizers to promote not just Cherry Hills, but also the region. "Denver and June," said the program notes, "a matchless combination, unite in inviting National Open Championship officials, contestants and visitors at the tournament, to make the most of their sojourn in the Colorado Capital." The committee was particularly keen to advertise the Rocky Mountain region as the "PlayGround of America" for winter or summer sports.[6] Even the governor of Colorado, Teller Ammons, took time to extend a welcome to all visitors to the region, and he also highlighted the many attractions of "the West."

As surprising as it was that the National Open was moving west, it was also interesting in that the club was only sixteen years old. It was designed by William Flynn, who would go on to redesign Shinnecock Hills in 1931, and who, earlier in his career, came up with the idea of wicker baskets rather than flags at the famed East Course at Merion. The club would go on to host many more majors, perhaps most famously Arnold Palmer's only National Open win in 1960. For the United States Golf Association (USGA), part of the attraction of Cherry Hills was its space both for parking and for practice facilities. The first of these was very important; despite the Depression, motoring was a growing pastime in America. Awarding the National Open to Cherry Hills came with a demand for a $10,000 bond to ensure the event would be profitable for the USGA. During the Great Depression, when many clubs had to close due to falling membership, this was a significant sum. Objections were raised to this demand, notably by Will F. Nicholson, who was a leading member of Cherry Hills and also on the USGA executive committee. "There's never been a guarantee before," Nicholson had observed. The Open had never been held west of the Mississippi, the USGA retorted. "$10,000?" screamed Nicholson. "Hell, we don't have enough in our treasury to buy a case of ketchup!"[7] Nicholson, however, gave them the guarantee and persuaded some business friends to come up with $500 each to help close the deal. And revenues for the week totaled $23,000, which was no small sum, for, like many other clubs during the Depression era, Cherry Hills had experienced financial difficulties.

The city of Denver contributed greatly, and as well as a press tent on the course, the Shirley-Savoy Hotel housed a downtown press center in an effort to make life easier for the many sports reporters who converged on the city. These included big hitters such as Grantland Rice, Alan Gould of the Associated Press, and Charles Bartlett of the *Chicago Tribune.* In addition, the club itself and many of its members hosted numerous parties. Overall, the charm offensive worked, and it was recorded that largely due to Pathé News, "Millions of Americans who had but a hazy idea of Denver and its surroundings saw the Queen City of the Plains with new clarity as a result of the National Open."[8] In every way the event was a great success, with crowds for practice rounds reaching 10,000 and a similar figure recorded for the final day's play. The Cherry Hills committee, in addition to local businesses and politicians, had every reason to be happy, as had the USGA.

As far as the golf was concerned, Guldahl went into the week as one of the favorites, but beforehand, all the talk was of how tough Cherry Hills was. In this regard, in order to make par harder to achieve, the USGA lowered par from 72 to 71. In order to do this, the treacherous 18th hole, guarded by water on the left, was changed from a par five to a four. One newspaper ran a headline that said it was "Complaint Time In The Rockies"[9] as a way of describing the number of grievances among the pros. And Henry McLemore called it the "finest jungle in North America." Ten holes had been lengthened by anything from 15 to 60 yards, but Alan Gould saw this as a positive development. He wrote, "The officials have made a championship course since March. The new tees, adding length to several holes, are in excellent shape, the rough is plenty tough and the fairways are narrowed."[10]

The players, however, did not agree, and the high rough, narrow fairways and small greens provoked much controversy. The rough in particular came under fire, with eventual runner-up Dick Metz saying, "They'd better station three or four caddies on every hole or there will be so many balls lost we'll never get through here."[11] Even the fact that being a mile above sea level would allow the ball to fly much further than usual was not seen as any form of "equalizer." The course was also different from many other venues in that it had no parallel fairways. The always quotable Gene Sarazen said 290 would win and had these words for the many professionals who were complaining about the severity of the Denver test: "They haven't played a course like this for years. Some of them want a polo field to work on. You have to control the ball here."[12] And Guldahl himself said before the tournament, "Give me a 286 right now and I wouldn't shoot a strike."[13]

In contrast, Lawson Little, who had won the Colorado State Amateur title at Cherry Hills during his amateur days, believed the scoring would be low because of the high altitude. Guldahl concurred with Sarazen's prediction before setting out his strategy for tackling the par 71 course. He was also quietly confident, as he explained the eve of the first round. "No, I'm not the one that has the heat on him," he said. "The real pressure is on the fellow who never has won the Open. My name is on the cup and never can be erased. I know I'm good enough to win because I have proved it and I might be good enough to win again."[14] And he backed this calm assurance up by placing an $80 bet on himself which netted him $360.[15] It was a feature of Guldahl's career that he was not afraid to publicly express confidence in his own abilities. Sometimes this was misplaced, but the facts backed him up in that he was a good "repeater," as evidenced by his successive wins at the National Open and his "hat-trick" of victories at the Western. He saw winning a big championship as a springboard for further success rather than a reason to become defensive. At Cherry Hills, however, not everyone shared his confidence, and Francis J. Powers, a respected writer and once a part-time tournament director of the PGA, while telling his readers that it would be difficult to pick a winner because of the severity of the course, also told them, "About the only thing I am sure about is that Guldahl will not repeat."[16]

As we know, during the Depression era, one of the features of golf coverage in the press was that the U.S. Open dominated. Days in advance, scribes were searching for quotes from the leading contenders. Similarly, the championship gained considerable coverage after the event, usually in the form of a series of lucrative articles loosely titled, "How I Won The Open." After his victory, Ralph Guldahl let golf enthusiasts into the secrets behind his success at Cherry Hills, and much of this referred to preparation and strategy. In terms of his preparation, Guldahl arrived in Denver early, having skipped the previous week's Kansas City Open to make sure he was ready for the challenge of Cherry Hills. As for his strategy, much of this was explained in the fighting vernacular which was so popular in that era.

"I decided to come out here days in advance and work out against my opponent," he said, in reference to the treacherous Cherry Hills course. Guldahl then went on to explain the advantage the golfer had over a professional boxer. "A Schmeling or a Louis can't work out against his opponent.... But the golfer has his opponent in front of him for as many workouts as he cares to make." This simple logic had been employed by Guldahl the previous year at Oakland Hills, when "many workouts" were also an integral part of his preparations. And he further explained, "I had to find out whether it would be wise to box him or fight him. And I soon reached the conclusion the best thing to do was go in for finesse in the Tunney manner." The reference to Gene Tunney was apposite, as the great heavyweight champion of the 1920s was well known for his cerebral approach to boxing, certainly in comparison to the more violent style of his fierce rival, Jack Dempsey. And Guldahl went on, "After I had three work-outs I was satisfied this was no place for a driver."[17] The final workout was what really convinced Guldahl, as on that day, he missed eight fairways. Instead, for most of the championship he drove with either a brassie (no. 2 wood) or a three wood. And with the high altitude at Cherry Hills, he lost very little in distance in comparison to his usual drives. Some of his workouts were in the company of Sam Snead, whom Guldahl had pipped the previous year at Oakland Hills. Cherry Hills, however, would not see the anticipated repeat of the previous year's dramatic finale, as Snead never featured. His best score was a 76.

Ralph Guldahl began the defense of his title at 10:20 a.m. on the opening Thursday in the shadow of the snow-covered Rocky Mountains. He was partnered by his fellow Wilson player, and occasional exhibition partner,

Johnny Revolta. At that stage in the season, Revolta was the leading money winner on tour. Partnering a familiar opponent, and one who was in good form, was a good draw for the defending champion. However, despite his careful planning, Guldahl did not dominate at Cherry Hills. In his first round he shot 74 and was four behind Henry Picard and Jimmy Hines. Picard was the Masters champion and one of the pre–Open favorites, but Hines's presence at the top of the field was less expected. The big-hitting Hines had learned the game as a caddie on Long Island, and that he was a formidable player was not in doubt. His record shows a total of nine wins in his tournament career. He was also good enough to gain a place on the 1939 U.S. Ryder Cup team, but the matches were canceled due to the outbreak of war. But, along with Jimmy Thomson, Hines was one of the game's big hitters and, as we saw, this was not necessarily an advantage at Cherry Hills. Some of the casualties of the first round included Jimmy Thomson on 82 and Horton Smith on 80—evidence that Cherry Hills could punish both a power hitter like Thomson, and a methodical player like Smith. Snead shot 77, along with Nelson and Shute, and was never a factor in the championship. As for Guldahl, his game was generally sound and his slow start was due to a poor day on the small greens when he missed seven putts of five feet or less. And overall, 74 was not such a bad start: scoring was high, with approximately half the field of 160 failing to break 80. Apart from the severity of the course, the players also had to deal with swirling winds for much of the day.

Guldahl's putting improved in a second round of 70, and at the halfway stage he was four behind Picard on 144. Picard also had a 70, but Dick Metz, who had a brilliant 68 for 141, was just one shot back. Perennial U.S. Open favorite Harry Cooper played himself into contention with a 69 for a halfway total of 145. "Open Saturday," however, would see Picard fade. "The Hershey Hurricane" took three putts from ten feet on the first hole of his morning round and reached the turn in 40. His final rounds were 77 and 78. As the players started the final round, Guldahl, with a morning round of 71, was at 215, four shots behind Dick Metz's 211. And it was only four because of a chip-in by Guldahl at the final hole of the Saturday morning round. Jimmy Hines was one ahead of Guldahl on 214. The leader was often referred to as "Handsome" Dick Metz because of his Hollywood looks and because he was linked with movie star Jean Chatburn, whom he would marry in 1939. He was also called a "Golfing Adonis." The "Hollywood" image was certainly noticed by a famous bandleader from that era, Ben Bernie. Bernie, who appeared in a number of movies, believed Metz was star material and suggested that he should do some tests in Hollywood. He also claimed that if Metz could ever win the National Open title, he (Bernie) would guarantee that Dick would make $50,000 from the movie contracts which would flow his way. This was an added incentive for Metz, as $25,000 was the accepted figure that would come to a U.S. Open winner, and much of that was hard earned through long journeys on the exhibition route.

Metz, however, was much more than a man with Hollywood looks or movie-star aspirations. He was yet another pro from the Texas production line; though he was born in Oklahoma, his formative golfing years were in the Lone Star State, mostly at the San Angelo Club. Back in 1932, Metz arrived on the tour with a flourish, and a number of top-ten finishes saw him being referred to as the next "sensation." He was also a courageous player, as evidenced by his comeback from a very serious auto accident in early 1937. Just prior to this, Metz had won his first two tournaments at the Thomasville and Hollywood Opens. It is likely that the accident cost him a place on the Ryder Cup team of that year, as he was in such good form at the time. Overall, his record shows that he was a very accomplished golfer who won ten times on tour. However, Cherry Hills was Metz's first time in contention at the National Open. In truth, carrying this burden *and* having the defending champion breathing down his neck in the final round was too much for him.

Dick Metz began by holing a long par-saving putt on the short par four, first hole, but that was as good as it got for him on the opening nine, and it was here that the championship was really decided. The fourth hole was a dogleg of 418 yards; the fifth a long par five of 535 yards; the sixth a relatively straightforward par three of 164 yards; the seventh a severe dogleg left of 395 yards; and the seventh a very tough par three of 225 yards. Metz had bogeys at all five holes. In contrast, Guldahl had pars at his first four holes, birdies at the fifth and sixth, and while he dropped a shot at the difficult par-three eight, he was out in 34 and in control of the championship. After this, his strategy, allied to some fine putting (seven single putts in the closing round), paid off in style and saw him finish with an outstanding 69. Metz, in contrast, stumbled from one disaster to another and he finished with a 79. Jimmy Hines, who was one ahead of Ralph after 54 holes, shot 83 in a final round when the punishing rough eventually caught up with him. These scores of Metz and Hines help put into context the quality of Guldahl's final round. In the end the winning score was a level par 284 with Metz finishing second on 290. And third place was shared by Harry Cooper and Italian-American Toney Penna, a further two shots back. On the tough Cherry Hills course, Guldahl had nothing worse than a five for the 72 holes, and given what was at stake and the severity of the course, he believed this was his finest performance ever.

In a post-victory interview, Guldahl was modest, and in reference to Metz and the others who faded, he commented, "They certainly made it easy for me." However, his main cheerleader, Laverne, who was too nervous to watch the last 36 holes, retorted, "They did nothing of the sort. You made it tough on them. They could have played their own game and you still would have won."[18] These words may appear to be just those to be expected from a supportive wife. However, Laverne was perceptive in that Ralph's final round once again demonstrated his ability to finish the job when he was in contention. As one writer commented, "The champion is establishing himself as a stretch runner of the Man O'War type."[19] The reference to one of the nation's most successful racehorses would not be lost on American sports fans and it was a tag which was well earned. Apart from Cherry Hills, Guldahl showed his ability to finish the previous year at Oakland Hills, and with his closing 64 to deny Ray Mangrum at the 1936 Western Open.

Guldahl's status as the game's best finisher was also recognized by his peers. Leonard Dodson was a renowned gambler who learned from Titanic Thompson. But he could also play tournament golf, as evidenced by his eight wins on tour. And he was a reliable witness, as he had personal experience of Ralph Guldahl's ability to play under pressure. "Stroke by stroke and hole by hole," Leonard said, "Guldahl was the hardest worker that I had ever seen. I played him once for $100 when neither of us could afford to lose $5. I had a 67. All Ralph had was a 63. Most of us get upset by this or that. Guldahl doesn't."[20] And he reflected on Ralph's win at Cherry Hills by saying, "The guy doesn't think he can lose.... I know that fellow. He can save more strokes in a pinch than anyone I ever saw. And that's what you have to do in the last round of an open." And he went on, "The last nine holes are the killers at Cherry Hills. They were saying, wait until he hits the hot spot. Guldahl's answer in the midst of this narrow, water-guarded span of destruction was 3333—four in a row. That's how much the finishing pressure affected the big Texan."[21] The "hot spot" Dodson referred to was holes no. 12 to 15, and their severity is worth recording in a little detail.

No. 12 was a par three of 205 yards with a parallel creek bed all the way down the left-hand side. Back in 1938, the hole required either a long iron, or more than likely a wood, to a green guarded by penal rough. No. 13 was a par four of 385 yards which was lengthened for the championship by 35 yards. Out of bounds on the right faced the player from the tee and

Ralph and Laverne holding the U.S. Open trophy after his victory at Cherry Hills in 1938 (courtesy Cherry Hills Country Club).

again a creek came into play in front of the green. No. 14 was probably the toughest hole on the course and at 470 yards was very long for a par four. There was out of bounds down the right and a creek on the left. In addition, the hole featured a dogleg to the left, which tempted players to play towards the creek with their second shots. And No. 16 was a 160-yard par three to a tiny green guarded by large bunkers and a creek on the left-hand side. The praise bestowed on Guldahl by a fellow professional was well deserved, as to play this treacherous stretch in 12 shots when a National Open was on the line was a remarkable achievement.

Grantland Rice, who closely followed the leaders in the last round, followed up on the "stroke by stroke" assessment of Leonard Dodson's. He suggested, "Guldahl is not bothered by the curse of imagination." He based this view on an interview after the final round when Ralph told him, "I never bother about the ones I've missed. They are already gone. Golf isn't a game

During his great years, putting was one of Ralph Guldahl's strengths. Here he demonstrates his style complete with a reverse overlap grip (courtesy *Fort Worth Star-Telegram* Collection, Special Collections, University of Texas at Arlington Library).

of 18 holes or 36 holes or 72 holes. It is a game of one stroke after another."[22] In an era when golf psychologists and mind gurus play an increasingly important role in the professional game, many golfers have paid a great deal of money in trying to acquire the thought process of "one shot at a time," especially when the pressure is at its highest. Arguably the prince of modern-day golf psychologists is Dr. Bob Rotella, and one of his dictums is "playing one shot at a time and trusting yourself, it's a darn hard challenge."[23] Yet in the formative days of the PGA tour, Guldahl (and many others) figured this out for themselves. After the championship, Grantland Rice concluded, "Cherry Hills attacked the nervous system more than any other Open championship course I've seen. It had no effect on Guldahl's nerves."[24] And in a further tribute to the new champion, Rice added, "His faith in his swing remained unshaken."[25] Ralph Guldahl may not have had a classical golf swing *à la* Snead, but there is no doubt that for a period in the mid-late 1930s, his temperament was superior to that of anyone else in the game, something that was recognized by peers and critics alike.

In two successive National Open Championships and on two contrasting but equally demanding courses, Ralph Guldahl had produced scores of 71–69–72–69 at Oakland Hills and scores of 74–70–71–69 at Cherry Hills. These scores constituted an average over 144 holes of 70.6 per round. Furthermore, on both occasions he had to come from behind to win, and each time, he shot a final round of 69 to accomplish his goal. He had also achieved what (up to then) only three golfers had done in the forty-one-year history of the U.S. Open: win back to back titles. These were Willie Anderson in 1904–05; John McDermott in 1911¬–12; and Bobby Jones in 1929–30. Later, in his wonderful book, *Golf Is My Game*, Bobby Jones wrote of how golf had changed over the decades. Using an athletics analogy, he complimented Roger Bannister for breaking down one barrier by becoming the first man to run the mile in under four minutes. For golf he said, "I award to Ralph Guldahl the credit for breaking the barrier in golf. First at Oakland Hills, and again at Cherry Hills in 1938, Ralph made it clear that in order to win, you had to play four good rounds, not just three."[26] This may seem a little unfair to Tony Manero who shot 73–69–73–67 the previous year when winning the title at Baltusrol. Arguably, however, what Jones had in mind was that Guldahl was the first to achieve this level of scoring in the majors on a regular basis. Coming from the man who, at that time, was the greatest to have ever played the game, this was an enormous compliment. However, the words were genuine and a measure of how Ralph Guldahl had raised the bar in championship golf.

One of the more unusual features of the 1938 season was that when the National Open finished on Open Saturday, the "fifth major" started the following Tuesday. In fact, there was some speculation as to whether or not Guldahl would compete in the Western, considering his exertions in Denver. As it was, Ralph caught a Chicago-bound train at 6 o'clock on the Sunday morning in order to make sure he was in St. Louis on time. He was "hot" and there was no reason why his form should not hold up the following week. In between, Guldahl had time for a little celebration as L.B. Icely held a dinner for him at Cherry Hills. He was very much Wilson's "favorite son" now. Almost all the top pros who competed at Cherry Hills followed Ralph to the Western Open to see if they could stop him from completing a hat-trick of wins. Unsurprisingly, Guldahl went into the Western as 6–1 favorite. The tournament this year was held at the Westwood Club, St. Louis, and with such a short interval, there was little time for Guldahl to celebrate his second successive U.S. Open triumph as he had to prepare for the Western. However, despite just one practice round, his confidence was as high as ever, and he declared that Westwood "is made for me and I anticipate no difficulty with it."[27] He also had the advantage of knowing the Westwood course from his time as a professional in St. Louis in the early 1930s.

On a very windy day, Guldahl led after a first round of 71, and if this showed that his form was not in doubt, so too did his ability to finish. After three rounds on the tough Westwood course, he and Sam Snead were tied at 214, but the final round saw the defending champion pull away. "The greatest finisher in golf," read one report, "painted his masterpiece today as big Ralph Guldahl left a birdie and eagle trail along the final 18 holes.... Par, tradition and the spirit of his rivals were shattered as the big Madison N.J. pro, well-rounded from his shoulders to his golf game, methodically tore to shreds a course which for the first two rounds ... had successfully withstood every assault."[28] Yet again, Guldahl outplayed Snead down the stretch as he closed with a 65 and gained a seven-shot win. His chip-in on the 72nd hole was the perfect finish to a perfect ten days. In winning the Western of 1938, Ralph Guldahl became the first man in the thirty-eight-year holding of the tournament to win the trophy in three successive years. His prize at Westwood was $750 to go with the $1,000 winner's check from Cherry Hills, and the manufacturer's bonuses. These were heady times and his triumph was best summed up by Charles Bartlett of the *Chicago Tribune*. In an era of journalistic heavyweights such as Grantland Rice and W.D. Richardson, Bartlett enjoyed a seat at the top table. And apart from his writing prowess, he was also someone who sought to develop the game in Chicago, as evidenced by his co-founding of the *Chicago Tribune* golf school. This initiative saw many local courses make their facilities available to offer free tuition to groups of all ages. Bartlett was a seriously respected figure in the world of golf.

Of Guldahl's latest victory, he wrote:

> The king of golf, Ralph Guldahl, today proved his right to the throne by winning the Western Open Golf Championship at the Country Club for the third consecutive year, five days after he had won the National Open title for the second year in a row. The twenty-six-year-old Madison, New Jersey, professional, reared on the public fee courses of Dallas, Texas, today brought

Guldahl completes his hat-trick of Western Open wins in 1938 (courtesy Western Golf Association).

> off the most remarkable golf achievement since Robert Jones's 1930 grand slam.... So it was this afternoon that the game's new monarch decided to assert himself in the fashion of kings. Within a space of five days he has accomplished a feat hitherto unmatched by any golfer in the history of the country's two ranking medal-play shows.

The reference to Jones was the greatest compliment a golfer could receive, and given how the Masters had quickly been given the mantle of "major championship" since its inception in 1934, it is interesting to note how Bartlett classed the Western (not the Masters) as the other "ranking medal play show" apart from the National Open. He was not alone in this regard. For the 144 holes of the U.S. Open and the Western, Guldahl never took more than five. Given the challenges he faced at Cherry Hills and at Westwood, and in regard to what was at stake, this achievement was a tribute to all aspects of his game.

The following month, July, saw Guldahl and Snead act out another chapter in their keen rivalry. This was in the Chicago Open, played at the illustrious Olympia Fields, which had hosted (and would continue to host) so many important championships, such as the National Open. The event was shortened to 54 holes, and on this occasion, despite a closing last round of 68, Guldahl came up one short of Snead's winning total of 207. His prize for second place was $750. Later that month, the PGA Championship was held at Shawnee on Delaware, and unsurprisingly, Guldahl was installed as an 8–1 favorite. Based on his preparation for the National Open, it could have been expected that Guldahl would devote a similar amount of groundwork to the season's final major. In fact, the opposite was the case, and his approach did not find favor with his fellow professionals. In an article titled "Guldahl Irks Rivals," it was recorded that "it will be not only a feather in the cap of the man who defeats the twice Open winner, it will be a new head dress too. The boys are a bit peeved at the light manner in which Guldahl has taken this tournament." The report went on to tell the readers how Guldahl had played the Shawnee course a few years back and knew all he needed to know. Furthermore, readers were informed, the National Open champion would stay at his home in New Jersey, fifty miles away, rather than locate "on site."[29] His rivals had a point, as Guldahl's approach smacked of either overconfidence or casualness.

As for the championship, it will be recalled that in his recent National Open win, Guldahl easily overtook Dick Metz on the final day. Here, however, it was Metz's turn to win as he beat Guldahl in the last 32, one up. The defeat to Metz, however, showed Ralph Guldahl in a less than favorable light and again demonstrated the unease he sometimes felt in the match-play format. During this era and up to the end of 1951, the stymie was part of match-play golf. On the green, if you were within six inches of your opponent's ball and were impeded by it, you had to play it. Many players thought this was unfair, but Bobby Jones believed the stymie was an integral part of golf and even called for its reinstatement as late as 1960. It was always a "gray" area as to whether or not stymies were deliberately laid (as in billiards) or by accident. Regardless of *how* it came about, however, coping with a stymie, by lofting the ball over one's opponent's, was a skill which players had to master.

Three times in the match with Metz, when laid stymies by his opponent, Guldahl displayed flashes of temper, and on the second occasion, it was reported that he had thrown his club on the green. This account was later refuted by Guldahl, who claimed that after the third stymie, his frustration got the better of him and he "unconsciously rapped Dick's ball away intending to bat it so his caddie could pick it up." And he admitted that he "was burning with disappointment and my disgusting bad luck at being stymied on three holes. In my fever, I hit Dick's ball too hard."[30] The report on Guldahl's temper was the work of Henry McLemore, who appeared to take a particular interest in Guldahl's career. This was an era of highly respected golf writers such as O.B. Keeler, confidante and biographer of Bobby Jones; Charles Bartlett of the *Chicago Tribune*; and W.D. Richardson of the *New York Times*. Perhaps the most revered was Grantland Rice, who had a very high regard for McLemore and his abilities, and in fact had adopted him as something of a protégé. However, the writing styles of the two men were different, with Rice often bursting into self-written verse to help capture an important golfing moment, while McLemore had a more colloquial style and was something of a maverick who enjoyed attracting or even creating controversy. The 1935 National Open winner Sam Parks, for example, referred to him as a "dirty writer."[31] This was because McLemore referred to Parks as "Lonesome Sam" in a reference to Parks's never winning anything of note before or after his victory at Oakmont. It was a deliberate "put-down," and as we know, one that would have found no support from Ralph Guldahl. However, a point in McLemore's favor was the fact that he was always on the spot for the big golf tournaments. He did not rely on the words of others, but instead, as we saw at Oakmont when he personally inspected the rough, his reports were invariably firsthand.[32] In addition, he had the ear of all the top golfers, including Ralph Guldahl.

At Shawnee, McLemore reported that "Dale Carnegie, the 'how to win friends and influence people' man, would have been horrified at the conduct of Ralph Guldahl, national Open champion, when he was losing to Dick Metz." McLemore went on to claim that Guldahl's antics had turned the crowd against him and suggested that the U.S. Open champion was in danger of becoming the "Jack Sharkey" of golf.[33] The reference to Sharkey was pointed and would certainly resonate with sports fans, as the heavyweight boxer was seen as being arrogant and unpopular, certainly when compared to his much-loved rival, Jack Dempsey. Perhaps McLemore exercised some license in his report, but having played in match-play events since he was a boy (including the Ryder Cup, where he had plenty to say about British sportsmanship), Guldahl was well used to the stymie, and so his behavior at Shawnee deserved a certain amount of criticism. In the event, however, the incident did him no lasting damage. As for the championship itself, it was one of the most memorable in history as "Little Poison" Paul Runyan beat big-hitting Sam Snead 8–7 in the final.

In the closing months of the year, Guldahl again took to the exhibition circuit. This time it was not in the company of Sam Snead, but rather a series of local amateurs and professionals who played a number of better-

Guldahl may have had issues with the stymie, but here he demonstrates a perfect technique for the shot (courtesy Tufts Archives).

ball, four-ball matches. Most of these were on the west coast with stops in, for example, Portland and Seattle. And there was also a heavily publicized match at the Rancho Santa Fe club in California, where Ralph partnered Bing Crosby against local professional Glenn Gibbon and English-born pro Charles Lacey. Rancho Santa Fe was where Bing hosted his "Clambake" from its inception in 1937 up to 1942. The match attracted 2,000 spectators and Guldahl lived up to his billing by shooting a 67 as he and Crosby won the match. Ralph was Bing's guest for his stay.

A slightly less than perfect footnote to the 1938 season was a loss to Denny Shute. Challenge matches were big in the 1930s, ever since Florida hotel magnate Henry L. Doherty had come up with an unofficial "World Championship" a few years earlier. The match, in 1932, was between reigning U.S. and British Open champion Gene Sarazen and PGA champion Olin Dutra. Sarazen won the 72-hole affair easily and the event was seen as a good way of boosting both the game and Doherty's hotel interests in Florida, where the match was held. The Guldahl-Shute match was different in that Ralph was the instigator when he challenged Denny to show who was America's "real champion": Guldahl, the National Open title holder, or Shute, winner of the PGA. Many of Ralph's fellow pros warned him off the idea, suggesting he had much to lose and very little to gain. However, Guldahl was determined, and the match was played over 36 holes match-play: 18 at Denny's home course of Brae Burn and 18 at South Shore, which neither player had seen before. In the end, local knowledge was the difference as Denny won the first round three up and the match by 2–1. The prize was a winner takes all the gate receipts. Guldahl complained that the South Shore was too short, as was the match itself, and challenged Shute to a rematch. Denny accepted, but the idea appeared to die a quiet death.

The defeat to Shute, however, was just a blip. Guldahl could look back on a wonderful year and, if he cared to, reflect on the words of longtime golf writer for the *Cleveland Plain Dealer*, John Dietrich: "Golf's No. 1 gate attraction ... is Ralph Guldahl. He is the big champ the game has been looking for since Bobby Jones quit competition.... He has become as indispensable to big tournaments as elephants to a circus."[34] Lofty words, especially the comparison to Jones, but at the time, not unreasonable. And the reference to being the biggest gate attraction was praise indeed, considering the impact Sam Snead had made since his arrival on tour. The influential *National Golf Review* also weighed in on a similar theme: "Selecting the top man of the year among the professionals is a comparatively simple task. When the same player wins the U.S and the

Western Open in the same year he is entitled to be No.1 rating in anybody's list and when he repeats in one as Ralph Guldahl did in the National Open and wins the other for the third successive year, as he did in the Western, this man becomes an outstanding figure of the game. Beyond question, Guldahl's performances in 1938 entitle him to a place among the great golfers of all time."[35]

And there was one final imprimatur for Ralph. Apart from hosting his own tournament and playing exhibitions, Bing Crosby enjoyed mixing in golf circles and played regularly with the game's top players—often at the Lakeside club in Los Angeles. Crosby was club champion there on five occasions. In this regard, Grantland Rice recalled sitting in the Lakewood locker room at the end of 1938 and posing the question to a group which included Leo Diegel, George Von Elm and Bing Crosby—"Who deserves the golfing high spot of 1938, Ralph Guldahl or Sam Snead?" The answer was unanimous in favor of Guldahl, on the basis that *the* "high spot" in American golf was the U.S. Open, and Ralph's performance in Denver left little room for argument.[36]

Whether it was contemporaries, celebrities, or a cross section of the print media, the verdict was unanimous: Ralph Guldahl was *the* top golfer and was on his way to becoming one of the all-time greats. Further major titles would serve to confirm this.

5

The Masters

At the start of 1939, Walter Hagen was asked if Sam Snead was the best golfer in the country. His reply was instructive: "The boy who deserves more of a break in the papers—the real master—is Ralph Guldahl. The mental outlook that Guldahl has taken on the Open title is simply amazing. He won because he knew that he was going to win before play began. In my estimation, the second best player in the country is Snead."[1] There are a number of issues raised here. First, the reference to "more of a break in the papers" suggests that Walter was well aware of the fact that while "Slammin Sam" gained all the headlines, Guldahl's perceived lack of charisma determined that he received far less coverage from the press. Second, the words "real master" were quite a compliment coming from the old master himself. And third, "The Haig" was not among those who saw Ralph's supreme confidence as arrogance, but rather as a vital weapon when it came to championship golf. And after 1938, there is little doubt that Ralph's confidence was high for 1939, with his eyes firmly set on the first major of the year, the Masters, where he had been so close the previous two years.

But before Augusta, there was the matter of preparation and making a living. In this regard, Guldahl's early season form was average, as seen at the Crescent City Open in New Orleans, where he finished 12th behind winner Henry Picard. The month of March, however, would see him in much better form. First, he teamed up with Sam Snead in the Miami International four-ball tournament. As we saw earlier, much of the tournament trail was centered on Florida because of the weather, and it was largely because of this that the term "the Grapefruit Circuit" became a pseudonym for the tour. Another reason was that during the "Roaring Twenties," numerous lavish hotel and golf course complexes were built, and despite the Florida property crash of 1928, many survived and provided ideal amenities for professional golf tournaments in the 1930s. And for those who could afford it, Florida was the ideal holiday destination, especially for golfers. This helped swell the galleries when the pros came to town. This event was held in Miami, where Ralph had a contract for the winter months, and was one of the favored stops on tour. The pros and their wives got to stay in a luxury hotel that offered special rates for those competing. For the 1939 tournament, it was no surprise when Ralph and Sam won the $1,000 each for first prize. In the 36-hole final of this match-play event, they beat Horton Smith and Paul Runyan by 7–6 with reports suggesting that Ralph was the "strong" man of the team. He later claimed that the week of the Miami International saw him enjoy his best-ever putting streak.

The second indicator of Guldahl's form came at the Greensboro Open in North Carolina. It will be recalled that before the inaugural event in 1938, Ralph wrote to Laurence Leonard assuring him of his presence in North Carolina and congratulating the tournament organizers on their vision. The Greensboro Open was a novel event as it was played at two venues: the Sedgefield Country Club and the Starmount Forest Club. And the Greensboro was yet another example of how tournaments were sponsored in the Depression years. The Starmount Forest Club was developed and run by the wealthy Ed Benjamin. His head professional there was Fred Corcoran's brother, George. Like Fred, George was innovative and was one of the earliest promoters of more women professionals and more female caddies. He became Benjamin's right-hand man, and the pair also enlisted the help of Laurence Leonard, who was sports editor of the local *Greensboro News*. Combined, the men approached local businesses and pitched the idea that the tournament should be a civic project that would promote both golf and the town. Their idea worked, with members of both clubs coming on board as well as many business outlets in the town of Greensboro. A group of hotels, for example, contributed $1,000. Today the tournament is called the Wyndham Championship, but the tournament's success and longevity are very much down to the vision of the aforementioned men of Greensboro.

In 1939, Guldahl won the Greensboro Open when he outplayed Lawson Little and Clayton Heafner down the stretch and claimed the first prize of $1,200 with a score of 280. Little, by now, had cemented his reputation, but at this stage, Heafner was an emerging pro. He would, however, go on to achieve seven victories on tour and play in two successful Ryder Cup teams. True to the aims of its founders, the last day at Greensboro was watched by a crowd of 10,000 fans. And as a postscript to the tournament, Laurence Leonard, to whom Ralph Guldahl wrote a letter of gratitude in 1938, invited him to act as guest golf writer on the *Greensboro News* when he (Leonard) was on vacation in July. Ralph accepted and wrote some "bird's eye view" reports of the U.S. Open held at Spring Mill in June. But before that, there was the Masters, and it was clear that both mentally and physically, Guldahl was in the best of form when he headed for Augusta and the now well-established Masters.

The Masters began in 1934 and was originally known as the Augusta National Invitation Tournament. Some journalists used the term "Masters," but originally this was frowned on by the ever-modest host, Bobby Jones, who deemed this title a little arrogant. Grantland Rice, however, was in no doubt about the tournament's "Masters" status, and after the inaugural event he claimed, "There is one point you can gamble on.... The Masters tournament is on its way to becoming one of the big fixtures on golf presenting Bobby Jones again next spring in his second start since 1930."[2] As far as Rice and many others were concerned, the presence of Jones would ensure crowds, prestige and media attention. Later Rice would reflect, "The opening act was an amazing success. There were automobiles parked around the club from thirty-eight states and Canada. Eighteen thousand more words were telegraphed from the Augusta battlefield than from the last United States Open. Thousands of people came from all over the country to see what the mop-up star of 1930 could do against a fast moving field of young stars and veterans, after four years of rest from wars." And he added with some foresight, "The Augusta National happens to be the type of course that lends itself to the spectacular side, where nerve racking gambles keep the gallery keyed up."[3]

The event was invitation only, and when the idea of hosting a tournament was mooted, Bobby Jones confessed, "The prospect of annually entertaining my old playmates and the later arrivals from the upper crust of competitive golf was quite attractive." As president of the club, Jones had the privilege "to invite a limited number of men whom I considered likely to grace the tournament because of their past accomplishments in the game, their present stature, their promise, or even my own feeling of friendship for them."[4] An example of this was Fred Haas, who would later become famous as the man who ended Byron Nelson's streak of 1945 when, as an amateur, he won the Memphis Open. He would go on to turn professional and made the Ryder Cup team in 1953. Haas recalled, "I was nineteen when I was first invited by Bobby Jones to play in the Masters. He had heard that I had won the Southern Amateur which was his favorite tournament."[5] Later, that casual approach was changed to a more regulatory basis for invitation. Unsurprisingly, at the start of the Masters' life, a great deal of the media and spectator interest focused on host Bobby Jones. Despite his official retirement after completing the Grand Slam in 1930, the American public remained in thrall to Jones and to whether or not he could repeat his deeds of 1930 and before. There was even an expectation that he might win his own tournament. Much of this was driven by the media, who had a longstanding love affair with Jones.

However, many inside the game were not so sure. Grantland Rice, for example, a close friend and admirer of Bobby's, said, "No one can say in advance how the nerve strain will affect him, what his mental attitude will be against the keen blades of so many stars, all after his scalp."[6] As it turned out, Bobby never seriously threatened in his appearances at the Masters, despite flashes of his own brilliance. His once wonderful putting was, by now, especially fallible. When reflecting on his first appearance he was honest enough to admit, "I simply had not the desire nor the willingness to take the punishment necessary to compete in that kind of company. I think I realized, too, that whatever part I might have in the Masters Tournament from then on would not be as a serious contender."[7]

The first Masters was won by Horton Smith. Smith was, perhaps, an underrated player, but from the time of his first tour victory in 1928, he compiled a very impressive record that saw him win 32 titles, including two Masters victories. He was also a five-time Ryder Cup player. For this inaugural event, all the top players were present apart from Gene Sarazen, who was abroad on an exhibition tour. Sarazen later explained his thinking in regard to 1934. "I remember," he said, "the return address on the invitation had Cliff Robert's name on the envelope. 'Aw the hell with this,' I said. 'I thought it was some kind of promotion to sell stocks or real estate. But the invitation the next year said Bobby Jones on it. Now *that* was something.'"[8] Sarazen certainly turned up in 1935 and it was, perhaps, his holed second shot for an albatross two at the 15th hole in the final round, and the ensuing publicity surrounding this shot, that really gave the tournament its Masters status. This single stroke helped Sarazen to a tie with Craig Wood with "The Squire" winning the 36-hole play-off. Horton Smith was a repeat winner in 1936 when his total of 285 beat Harry Cooper by one shot. This was just one of a number of near misses Harry had in the majors. Ralph Guldahl was not present at the first three Masters for the simple reason that he did not match the criteria set out by Jones. He was clearly not yet deemed to be among "the upper crust" of golf. Looking at the list of contestants for the first Masters, it is surprising that Guldahl did not gain an invitation in 1934, as there were many invitees whose achievements did not come close to his runner-up spot to Johnny Good-man in the National Open of 1933. However, in the time between June 1933 and April 1934, his stock had fallen so much that his performance at North Shore was a distant memory. In 1935, his form was so bad that there was no hope of an invitation, and while 1936 was his comeback year, the force of this resurgence was not seen before the invitations were dispatched. Still, the years from 1937 to 1939 would see Guldahl more than make his mark at Augusta.

Ralph Guldahl's successful 1936 ensured his appearance at the 1937 Masters. The Masters, in its early years, notably because of the invitation-only policy, was a relatively small event. Paul Runyan recalled, "Drinks were on the house for everyone at the first tournament, including the gallery."[9] And Byron Nelson later wrote of the tournament's intimacy and how "you would get to enjoy a lot of Southern hospitality. Every year, several members would host an early evening party with country ham and all the trimmings. Everyone felt free and easy and we all had a wonderful time."[10] Such luxury in the Depression era was a rare treat for professional golfers. It is not clear how much of this hospitality Ralph and Laverne Guldahl enjoyed, as according to one report, "While the other pros lived in luxury at the two swanky hotels, Ralph and his wife and baby held down expenses by residing at a cheaper hotel where no orchestras played."[11] It seems that despite the comeback in 1936, the Guldahls were still watching the pennies.

One of the features of the Masters was the pre-tournament "auction" or sweepstakes, where players could be bought for a certain price, and whoever picked the winner would receive 30 per cent of the total pool. For 1937, this stood at $14,357, the highest to date. Unsurprisingly, the top prices were fetched by holder Horton Smith and host professional Ed Dudley. Both were bought for $1,200. Guldahl fetched $1,050 along with Cooper and Picard. This figure suggests that Guldahl's recent form had not gone unnoticed by the members at Augusta. And in the betting, it was Harry Cooper at 9–1 with Dudley, and Smith at 10–1. Bobby Jones was at 14–1 along with Guldahl, Snead and Nelson.

The first round headlines were made by Nelson, who shot 66 on a warm and windy day. Jones, in contrast, shot a 79. Nelson later recalled this as being one of his greatest-ever rounds and the statistics back him up. He hit every par five in two, every par three in one, and every par four in two. He had 34 putts and 32 shots. It is hard to imagine any player in history (maybe Hogan) playing such precision golf in a major championship. Although he would go to become one of the game's greatest players,

Nelson did not arrive on tour in the same explosive way that Snead did. His progress was more gradual, with two second-place finishes in 1934; a single win and a number of high finishes in 1935; and a similar record in 1936. However, 1937 saw him establish himself with three titles, including his Augusta triumph, as well as a place on the victorious Ryder Cup team.

"There's No Doubt About Nelson's 'Moxie' Anymore," read one headline in the aftermath of Byron's inward 32 and a final total of 283. Before 1949 there were no green jackets presented to the winner at Augusta. Instead Nelson received a gold medal from Bobby Jones. Years later he admitted that this win "was the most important victory of my career. It was the turning point, the moment when I realized I could be a tough competitor. Whenever someone asks me which was the most important win of all for me, I never hesitate. It was the 1937 Masters, the one that really gave me confidence in myself."[12] And yet the day before there was no hint that Nelson would win. Back then, and unlike the U.S. Open, it was one round per day unless rain intervened. And on the penultimate day, Nelson seemed to have played himself out of contention with a 75 in the third round and a total of 213. In contrast, Guldahl birdied four of his last six holes for a 68 and 209. In describing Guldahl and his round, O.B. Keeler, writing in the local *Atlanta Journal*, wrote, "He is a hardy Norseman from Texas who looks like a screen actor from Hollywood. And the gentle Viking simply clicked off a card of 68 on Saturday to pick up seven strokes on Lord Byron and spill him out of the lead."[13] Going into the final round, it was Guldahl on 209, Dudley on 212, with Cooper and Nelson on 213. All of that would change on the final day.

In 1959, when reflecting on his creation, Bobby Jones wrote, "The finishes of the Masters have almost been dramatic and exciting. It is my conviction that this has been the case because of the make-or-break quality of the second nine. This nine, with its abundant water hazards, each creating a perilous situation, can provide excruciating torture for the front runner trying to hang on. Yet it can yield a very low score to the player making a closing rush."[14] Jones had any number of examples to call on to support his view, and 1937 would surely have been among this list.

History has recorded that the event was decided on the 12th and 13th holes, and even after a gap of almost eighty years, it is hard to disagree with this conclusion. Nelson, after an opening 38 for the final round, trailed Guldahl by three shots as he entered the back nine. As noted, the 12th and 13th are seen as having decided the tournament. However, what has not always been sufficiently documented, but was also important, was the fact that playing just ahead of Nelson, Guldahl birdied the very difficult

From their earliest days in Texas, the careers of Byron Nelson (above) and Ralph Guldahl were intertwined (courtesy Tufts Archives).

10th hole and so went four shots clear. Nelson, however, was up to the task and matched Guldahl's three. The importance of this putt was certainly recognized by Nelson's final round partner, Wiffy Cox. Although he was a nine-time winner on tour and a Ryder Cup player in 1931, Cox was known for being a difficult and at times volatile customer. However, on this occasion, he proved to be just the right partner for the young Nelson. As Byron later recalled, after the birdie on the tenth, Cox said to him, "Kid, I think that's the one we needed."[15] A 2–3 on numbers 12 and 13 saw him take a lead that he never relinquished. Nelson's back nine was 32 and his final total was 283. Guldahl, in contrast, went 5–6 on 12 and 13 by visiting Rae's Creek on each hole.

Since the inception of the Masters in 1934 up to the present day, the 12th hole at Augusta has seen triumph and disaster in equal measure. Although only requiring a short iron, Bobby Jones suggested caution, saying, "The inclination here is to be well up, or to favor the left side where the green is wider."[16] In 1937, Ralph Guldahl was one of the first cases of a contender falling foul of this hole. O.B. Keeler, who was one of the few who witnessed, at first hand, Sarazen's albatross in 1935, described how events unfolded. "The pin at the short twelfth," he wrote, "was in a narrow, dangerous part of a green, with a brook just in front and plenty of trouble behind. Guldahl, instead of playing cautiously for the more ample section of the green, had gone for the flag, and a combination of fade and wind had plumped him into the burn."[17] Guldahl was not the last player to misjudge the wind at this hole. Later, however, and in an early example of his strength of mind, he did not appear to have many regrets. Instead he put the mishap down to his overall approach to tournament golf. "Last winter in the Masters Tournament," he said later that year, "I took the ... gamble at the 12th hole of the last round and lost again.... I went for it, cut the shot too fine and plumped into the creek.... Everybody said I should have played safe, but that isn't my nature. Against fields as fast as these today, it's my hunch that boldness pays. Ten years ago you could ease into a title by the back door when the pacesetters cracked, but with so many top-notchers fighting for that prize today, somebody is sure to be hot on the last round."[18] His bold approach would be rewarded two years later.

The six at number 13 was one that Guldahl later claimed taught him a valuable lesson. He told Grantland Rice, "After a fine drive around the bend I saw I needed either a four wood or a two iron to get home.... I finally picked out a two iron. I was still thinking about the four wood when I started my backswing and caught the brook for a 6 in place of a 4."[19] Guldahl steadied himself after this, and after a birdie four at the 15th hole he had pars at each of the final three holes. However, his final round score of 76 (six more than Nelson) gave him a total of 285—two shots behind the winner. Ed Dudley was a further shot back on 286. Much has been made by golf historians regarding the rivalry between Byron Nelson and Ben Hogan, with the common denominator of the Fort Worth caddy-yard featuring prominently. However, before that wonderful rivalry got under-way in earnest, Augusta 1937 marked out another rivalry which had its roots in the tough school of junior golf in Texas. As Nelson recalled many years later, "After Ralph beat me so bad when we were both kids in Texas, it was nice to be able to top him at the Masters in '37."[20] The beating Nelson referred to was when both were in their teenage years. Nelson took up the story: "One year I was considered the Fort Worth amateur champion and Ralph was the Dallas amateur champion. A match was arranged with a round at Katy Lake, Fort Worth and at Bob O'Link in Dallas. We started out at Bob O'Link and we were supposed to play 36 holes but he gave me such a beating, I don't think we even played much of the final 18."

For a first Masters, finishing second could be seen either as a fine performance or, because of his weak finish, a major setback. If it was the latter, however, Guldahl's new-found confidence helped him overcome any lasting sense of disappointment, and he returned the following spring with high expectations. The "Masters" name was now being widely used, and the continued presence of Bobby Jones ensured large crowds and massive media attention. The invitation-only event saw all the top players take part, and there was one new invitee who would go on to contribute richly to Masters history: Ben Hogan.

At the start of the tournament, however, it was the weather that made the news. Grantland Rice suggested, "The caddie master should be Noah,"[21] and because of the downpours, the first day's play on Friday was washed out. This resulted in one round on Saturday, two on Sunday, and the 18-hole finale was played on Monday. The bad weather somewhat altered the betting, with the "pool" buyers opting for Snead and big Ed Dudley. Ed Dudley was an understandable choice, as he was Bobby Jones's pick as Augusta's first-ever professional and remained there until 1957. So his knowledge of the course was second to none. He was also a golfer of the highest quality with fifteen tour wins and four Ryder Cup appearances. And although he did not win a major title, he had twenty-four top ten finishes with ten of these coming at Augusta. So, with the weather conditions, this reasoning was sound, as it was reckoned that only the longest of hitters could reach the four par-fives in two. And Snead, especially with his capacity to hit a high draw, was certainly in this group.

In the end, however, it was not long hitting that was the determining factor, but putting. Certainly, as far as Ralph Guldahl was concerned, it was his trusty old putter (so important in his comeback) that went cold. After the third round, Picard led on 215, one shot ahead of an impressive quintet—Guldahl, Gene Sarazen, Ed Dudley, Harry Cooper and Craig Wood. Henry Picard was the tour's "nice guy," a man who was popular with the fans, the media, and his fellow golfers. He was also regarded as one of the great stylists of this era and as one of the finest long iron players in an era that included Nelson, Snead and Hogan. Picard would go on to win the following year's PGA title when he beat Byron Nelson in extra holes. In total he had twenty-six tour victories and he was also a two-time Ryder Cup team member. But coming into Augusta, he was having problems with a sore thumb. However, in the lead-up to the first round, he sought the advice of his mentor, the noted teacher Alex Morrison. Unlike today, when many top players use the interlocking grip (notably Tiger Woods and Rory McIlroy), back then, almost all golfers were wedded to the Vardon grip. Francis Ouimet and Gene Sarazen were notable exceptions. However, on the advice of Morrison, Picard changed from his conventional Vardon grip to the interlocking model and immediately found his game.[22]

In the end, the championship came down to a three-way fight between Guldahl, Picard, and Cooper. In those days, the leaders did not go out last, and Guldahl played with host Bobby Jones roughly an hour ahead of Picard. Guldahl got off to a fast start that included an eagle three at the second hole, but Picard went out in 32 and was firmly in command. In Grantland Rice's report, he recalled following the final round in the company of Tommy Armour. And the "Silver Scot" had some interesting observations on the proceedings. He commented, "When they hear of Picard's 32 out, it will have the same effect as a bomb exploding under your right or left ear. In place of playing golf, they'll try to play Picard. It can't be done but we all try it."[23] It appears, however, that Guldahl and Harry Cooper did not hear the bombs because, despite Picard's fast start, both drew close on the back nine. But a three-putt by Guldahl on both the 70th and 72nd holes saw him lose his chance. Three-putting two of the last three greens may have owed something to his belief that he needed to be aggressive and get at least one more birdie to win. However, this was one of the rare occasions when Guldahl's putter let him down during his great years. Picard parred both holes and won by two from the Dallasites with a total of 285. His last round was 70 with the joint runner-ups shooting 71 each. Second place for the second year running was an excellent performance, but Ralph Guldahl had bigger plans for 1939.

When Walter Hagen asked before a tournament, "Well boys, who's gonna be second?," it was seen a part of the "Haig's" charm and was lapped up by fans and media alike. The fact that it was part of Hagen's renowned gamesmanship was put to one side. Hagen was colorful and this confidence was part of his image. In terms of image, Ralph Guldahl was probably as far as he could get from Hagen and was seen as being introverted and lacking in personality. It was suggested that his personality was "so devoid of excitement and color that even natural promoters like Harlow and Corcoran were hard pressed to generate stories that made him seem interesting."[24] So when, just before the 1939 Masters, he announced that he intended to win, his words were seen as arrogant and cocky. In fact, his words could be deemed to be "super confident," as seen by an extract from an eve-of-tournament interview with Henry McLemore. "I've been runner-up here twice and I'm sick of getting nosed out," he told the writer. Guldahl continued, "I'm gonna get this one. You can write, right now, quoting me, that I'm going to win. There isn't a man in the field hitting the ball harder or squarer than I am. I'm ready to shoot a little golf."[25]

Perhaps Guldahl liked the fighter's talk he used at Cherry Hills when he referred to Gene Tunney and his strategic approach to boxing. In any event, Augusta 1939 was not the first instance of "fighting talk" ahead of a golf tournament. After his win at Cherry Hills in 1938, Guldahl returned to his then home club of Braidburn to play in the New Jersey State Open. He was so confident of winning that he promised to throw his clubs into the pond at the 18th hole if he failed. In the event, he finished in joint second place, three shots behind Pine Valley professional Ted Turner.[26] And later that year, before the PGA Championship at Shawnee, Guldahl irked his fellow professionals by saying that he did not need even one practice round at the venue, as he had played there four years ago and that taught him all he needed to know.[27] At Shawnee, Guldahl's words were proven to be hollow, as he did not feature in a championship won by Paul Runyan. However, at Augusta, he was as good as his word.

The buildup to the 1939 Masters was similar to the previous year with rain dominating proceedings. Instead of staring on Thursday, the first round was played on Friday with another on Saturday and 36 holes on Sunday. Admission prices were $2.20 per day or $5.50 for a season ticket. And in contrast to the National Open, where roughly 170 players contested the championship, Augusta hosted just forty-seven select invitees. In the pre-tournament betting, Guldahl was listed at 8–1 along with Snead and holder Henry Picard. The sentimental favorite, Bobby Jones, was at 40–1. Right from the start, Guldahl was in contention, and after two rounds, his score of 140 was tied second with Snead and just one behind Gene Sarazen. Gene's second round of 66 promised a second title to go with his "double eagle" win of 1935. Going into the last round on the final afternoon, it was Guldahl on 210—Sarazen on 211—and Snead, Billy Burke and Lawson Little on 212. There was plenty of class in the group pursuing Guldahl. Sarazen was a former winner, and at that time, he was the only player to complete the professional Grand Slam. And even though he was approaching the veteran stage in his career, he could still compete in the big ones, as evidenced by his tie with Lawson Little in the following year's U.S. Open. Burke won the National Open in 1931 in addition to twelve other titles on tour. He was also a Ryder Cup player. His performance at Augusta was seen as something of a comeback. And before he turned professional, Little had won back to back U.S. and British amateur titles in 1934 and 1935. Without doubt, he could claim to be "the greatest amateur since Jones." Furthermore, in his short professional career, he had already achieved three wins on tour, with the first of these coming at the prestigious Canadian Open. In truth, this trio performed well in the final round with Burke and Little shooting 70s for totals of 280 and Sarazen a 72 for 283. However, despite these fine efforts, the final drama mostly involved Guldahl and Snead—again.

After the Masters, W.D. Richardson, for many years the well-respected writer for the *New York Times*, reflected: "To the accompaniment of something new—a real hailstorm that spattered off players' domes like machine-gun bullets at a gangster's lawn party—another Masters tournament has passed into history, leaving behind another epochal performance, namely Ralph Guldahl's finish."[28] Using the word "epochal" to describe Guldahl's finish was not unwarranted, and in many ways the 1939 Masters had marked similarities to Nelson's win in 1937 and to Sam Snead's narrow loss in the U.S. Open of 1937. For example, with the leaders not necessarily going out last, Snead, playing ahead of Guldahl, shot 280, which was a new tournament record. Again, W.D. Richardson summed up the pressure Guldahl faced as he approached Augusta's treacherous back nine: "As the big, droop-shouldered Open champion came off the ninth green on that final swing, he heard the announcer on the 18th which is adjacent, call out: 'Sam Snead, 68, Total, 280.' That meant that he [Guldahl] had to finish in thirty-three strokes in order to win."[29] To add spice to the occasion, Guldahl was paired with Lawson Little, who was still in contention.

After the championship, Bobby Jones referred to the final round drama as "the greatest golf I ever saw,"[30] and while these comments may have understandably been laced with exaggeration from the host, the closing stretch ranks high on the list of great Masters finishes. Needing to play the back nine in 33, and in contrast to his final nine at Augusta in 1937, Guldahl did just that in a wonderful stretch of golf. He began with a birdie three at number 10, where he hit a four iron second to four feet. This was significant as Snead had earlier taken five here. And he followed this with a safe par at the treacherous 11th, and at the equally dangerous 12th, guarded by Rae's Creek, he had another comfortable par. In fact, his attacking policy from 1937 was still in evidence at this hole, as he took on the flag and left his iron shot six feet from the hole only to miss the birdie putt. Then came an eagle three at number 13, a par at the 14th, and a birdie four at the 15th. The eagle three at the 13th was not just important in terms of the title, it was also a form of redemption for Ralph Guldahl. Two years earlier when he lost to Nelson, after a perfect drive at number 13, he found Rae's Creek with a mis-hit two iron. This led to a bogey six. This year, what made his eagle so admirable was the length of his drive. It was recorded, "He had missed his drive at that par-5 hole. Others with better drives had elected to play short of the stroke-wrecking brook which has to be carried to reach the green."[31] W.D. Richardson again took up the story:

> Despite the distance to be carried in order to clear the creek—at least 230 yards—and a side-hill lie, big Ralph jerked out a No. 3 wood and tore into the ball, sending it on a low trajectory and in a dead line for the pin which was cut dangerously close to the right-hand edge—less than thirty feet from the creek. No sooner had the ball left the club-head than the crowd, greatest in Masters' history—more than 8,000 it was esti-mated—let up a roar, for it was plain to see that it would end up somewhere on the green which would have been an achievement in itself. But it did better than that. It ran almost up to the pin, stopping less than six feet away where he putted it in for an eagle 3![32]

This is where his courage, confidence, and his experience from 1937 kicked in as unlike that year, he was entirely committed to his club selection. Golf's "greatest finisher" was once again proving he was up to the task. In his 1937 final round, Guldahl played numbers 12 and 13 in a total of eleven strokes. In 1939, he took just six.

Despite this great burst of scoring, however, the job was not yet fin-ished. Ralph took a bogey five at the 17th when he was long with his second shot, and so as he approached the 18th tee, he knew he needed a four to win. History has shown that the final hole at Augusta, with its slight dogleg to the right, its uphill second shot, and its heavily bunkered green, can be treacherous, especially when the pressure is on. And unlike these days, when the final day pin position is towards the front left of the green, in 1937 it was much further back. In this regard, Guldahl initially opted for a four iron for his second shot, but then changed to a number three. It was the right call as his second found the back fringe, and two careful putts later, he was champion. He had won the Master with a record total of 279, which stood until Ben Hogan's victory in 1953. Again he had beaten Sam Snead at the death to win a major title, and as at Oakland Hills, he won knowing exactly what he needed to do on the back nine. In a reference to his superiority over Snead, he later admitted, "I don't know why but whenever Sam gets out in front of me, it inspires me to play my greatest golf."[33] In fact, there is evidence to suggest that Guldahl did know *why* he was able to get the better of Snead in the big tournaments: concentration. "That young man," Guldahl said, "is such a phenomenal golfer that if he could concentrate at the right time, he'd win most of the events. But I know that either from wearing his concentration powers down by such steady competition, or by not having the natural knack of concentration as Hagen and Jones did, he's usually good news for me when he starts ahead of me. I passed him in winning the National Open of 1937 and the Western Open of 1938 because I could mind my business more completely than he was able to do."[34]

By now Ralph Guldahl was seen as being the peer of Bobby Jones, and one scribe wrote of his Augusta victory, "After finishing second the two previous years ... the 279 he shot at the boys this time left them gasping like boated fish."[35] And an even greater compliment came from Associated Press golf writer Gayle Talbot, who wrote, "Every time he steps on the tee these days, Ralph Guldahl leaves a little less doubt that the is the super golfer of today and possibly the best there has ever been."[36] Another report concurred when asserting, "When Emperor Bobby Jones made his grand slam in 1930 ... they were certain they would never see the likes of him again, but there is a big shaggy-headed guy at large who threatens to top Jones and establish himself as the greatest player who ever lived."[37] History has shown that such claims were somewhat exaggerated, but at the time they were entirely understandable, as for a few short years, Guldahl was unstoppable.

And the tributes flowed not only from journalists but also from his peers. Grantland Rice interviewed Tommy Armour after the Masters and the "Silver Scot" had this to say when asked how Guldahl compared to Hagen and Jones: "I'll admit Guldahl hasn't their color—the crowd attraction Bob and Walter had. But he has all the golf shots—all the courage—all the determination—all the concentration needed to win championships." And, in regard to Guldahl's finish, Armour went on: "He wasted no time. None at all. He played the first four holes of that final nine, all hard pars, in three under par. He caught and passed Snead in four holes."[38] Until the era of Arnold Palmer, it is doubtful if anyone had the crowd appeal of Jones and Hagen, and so it was no criticism of Guldahl that he could not match this illustrious pair in that regard. However, the other comments from Armour are more telling, as these, in Armour's words, were what won championships.

And there was also praise from an unlikely source. It will be remembered that PGA President George Jacobus had some very harsh words for Guldahl and his behavior in the aftermath of the 1937 Ryder Cup. After the Masters, however, he was fulsome in his praise for the new champion. "He was marvellous winning that Masters," Jacobus said. And he continued, "What a fighter, he's great under pressure. It gets him fighting mad. That ability to get mad spells the difference between a great competitor and one who is only fair.... When some fellows hit a bad shot they say, 'aw well, what about it.' A player like Guldahl, though, gets burned up. His brilliant concentration is brought into play and he performs amazingly."[39] There was a certain irony here, as after Southport, 1937, the anger in Guldahl was roundly criticized by Jacobus, whereas now, it was seen as a quality which had the capacity to drive him on to great achievements. From within the game, and from the media, these were heady tributes, but 1939 was the apex of Guldahl's Masters career, as he never again featured prominently at Augusta.

After his National Open win of 1937, Guldahl again spoke of how he looked forward to the "gravy" that would come his way from off-course endorsements. One of these was from Camel cigarettes, which, in these pre-"smoking can damage your health" days, sponsored a number of athletes. "Camel's mild and rich tobaccos don't jangle your nerves,"[40] said Guldahl, with the unwritten message for golfers that a few Camels could help steady your putting stroke. And there were further endorsements. After his win at Augusta, Guldahl's photo adorned many newspapers as he took delivery of the 15,000th model of the aptly named Studebaker Champion, priced at $660. "I've long been sold on Studebaker quality and performance," said Guldahl. "In fact I already own a Studebaker Eight.... This new Studebaker Champion, it's got plenty of championship form and a perfect follow through."[41]

On the course, it was exhibitions that provided the extra cash, and in this regard, Guldahl took part in an exhibition four-ball at the Helfrich Field Club in Indiana on May 10. The game involved three other local pros, one of whom was Bob Hamilton, who would go to defeat Byron Nelson in the final of the 1944 PGA Championship. What was symptomatic of the Depression era was that Guldahl himself sent a telegram to the club shortly after his Masters win offering to play for $200 or the gate receipts minus expenses.[42] There were very few agents in those days (apart from

Fred Corcoran and Bob Harlow) and so players often had to market themselves. As it turned out, the club found a sponsor, and so Guldahl received his $200 and the 1,500 fans got in for free to see a match that Guldahl and his partner won. Guldahl shot a 69, which was the best score from the four players.

Ralph Guldahl was now reigning Masters and National Open Champion, and it was no surprise when he was installed as a 6–1 favorite for the U.S. Open. That year the nation's greatest major returned to Pennsylvania, but not to the famous Merion course. For 1939, it was played for the one and only time at the Philadelphia Country Club, otherwise known as Spring Mill. Spring Mill was one of America's earliest clubs and one of the first six members of the USGA. A nine-hole course was opened in 1892 and the club graduated to 18 holes in 1927. Just like at Augusta, Ralph Guldahl was not shy in displaying his confidence. As one journalist reported, "Name me another golfer who came up to the Open and flatly declared he felt sure of winning. Guldahl did that a few days ago."[43] His confidence seemed well placed. As part of his usual thorough preparation he visited the course in late May and shot an impressive 68.

In general, the media fancied Guldahl's chances, boldly claiming, "Regardless of what the bookmakers say, the player most likely to win the National Open Championship ... is Ralph Guldahl who won it in 1937 and 1938."[44] Guldahl also showed he was capable of attempting to gain an advantage by getting into the minds of his opponents. "They talk about the pressure of a big tournament," he said, "especially on the fellow who knows everyone expects him to do something. Well it's tough all right but it's nothing compared to the pressure on those who've tried and failed." He then turned his sights directly on some who might seriously contend at Spring Mill: "I know I can win an Open. I've done it twice. But Dick Metz, Henry Picard and Sam Snead and those other chaps, they don't know they can. They'll be out there thinking I lost last time. What's going to happen to me this time?"[45] It was clear that Guldahl was determined to remind "handsome" Dick Metz, "nice guy" Henry Picard, and his four-ball partner Sam Snead, who was best under the intense pressure of a U.S. Open.

In the lead-in to the championship, the newspapers reported how this rugged course would test the players, especially if the expected wind stayed for the three days. These conditions would certainly suit the defending champion. Just a few days before the start, however, Guldahl's belief was dented a little when he discovered that the rough at Spring Mill was cut by half. He complained bitterly about this but to no avail. It will be recalled that Guldahl's strategic planning at Cherry Hills the previous year was instrumental in his victory. There, because of the small greens and heavy rough, he left the driver in the bag for almost the whole tournament. He now his superior ability in this regard would be taken away from him. Furthermore, his excellent chipping from the "U.S. Open" greenside rough stood to him in his two successive victories, and now this advantage would also disappear. As it turned out, he played steadily and finished at 288, just four behind Nelson, Shute and Craig Wood, who tied first, with Byron winning the play-off. If anything, Guldahl struck the ball better at Spring Mill than he did in the previous two years, but it was his putting that failed him. It will be recalled, for example, that he had seven single putts in his final round at Cherry Hills, but here, he averaged just over thirty-four putts per round. It was a good defense of his title, but this Open, then and forevermore, would be remembered as the title that Sam Snead lost because of his triple bogey eight at the 72nd hole when a five would have won.

The PGA that year was held in July at the Pomonok Club in New York, but the championship was initially overshadowed by a row involving the PGA and two-time winner Denny Shute. This arose as Shute was two days late paying his annual PGA dues and the committee wanted to ban him from playing. Ralph Guldahl was in the vanguard of a group, including Sarazen and Picard, who vocally opposed the PGA and who threatened to go on strike if Shute was not allowed to play. In the end, common sense prevailed and the holder was allowed to defend his title. As for the championship itself, Guldahl continued his decidedly mixed record in match-play and went out in the second round to the relatively unknown Clarence Doser. Henry Picard won his second major in a thrilling final by defeating Nelson at the 37th hole.

Any lingering disappointment over Pomonok was quickly dispelled when Guldahl won the inaugural Dapper Dan at the Wildwood Club in Pennsylvania. This tournament was the brainchild of *Pittsburgh Post-Gazette* editor Al Abrams, who founded a sportsman's club (the Dapper Dan) to raise money for charities through dinners, boxing matches, and in this case a golf tournament. It was one of the forerunners of the many tournaments today, such as the Byron Nelson Classic, which raise millions of dollars for worthy causes. Here Guldahl missed a six-foot putt on the 72nd hole to win the tournament in regular time, but he beat fellow Wilson players Denny Shute and Gene Sarazen in an 18-hole play-off the following day. Key to his win was a holed bunker shot at the 291-yard eighth hole for an eagle two, which helped him to a 70 against Shute's 74 and Sarazen's

One of the endorsements that came Guldahl's way during his great years was for Studebaker cars (from the collection of Studebaker National Museum, South Bend, Indiana).

75. The victory saw him net a first prize of $2,500 plus an extra $1,000 as his share of the play-off gate receipts. It was estimated that the crowd for the play-off was in excess of 5,000, which is remarkable considering the country was still officially experiencing the Great Depression. When we remember that the first prizes for the Masters and U.S. Open were $1,500 and $1,000 respectively, the Dapper Dan victory was very significant in material terms.

The following week, Guldahl traveled north to Canada, where he had many high finishes without coming away with a victory. The Canadian

Open that year was played at the Donald Ross–designed Lakemore Country Club in Brunswick. Again, the story of near misses north of the border continued when he finished second to Jug McSpaden. His prize was $400. And at the end of August that year, Guldahl teamed with Jug McSpaden in a better-ball tournament held at the Midlothian Club, Chicago. The event was special as it was held to commemorate Hagen's victory in his first National Open at the club twenty-five years earlier. All the big names competed, with the "Haig" fittingly partnering his friend and rival, Gene Sarazen. Ed Dudley and Billy Burke came out on top with Guldahl and McSpaden finishing a creditable second. Guldahl also had a chance to win the Hershey, but a final round of 76 saw him finish in joint fifth place, four shots behind surprise winner Felix Serafin. Serafin was a native of Pennsylvania and spent much of his time as professional at the Scranton Club in America's coal district. He did, however, play a number of times on tour and recorded four wins in total.

After this, and coming towards the end of what had been a stellar year, it was time for Guldahl to once again cash in on his fame and his 1939 performances. This involved a demanding fifty-day tour, starting in Ohio and ending, fittingly, in San Antonio, Texas. In total, he played forty-five matches while on the road. This was once again proof that while there was money to be made from Camel, Studebaker and especially Wilson, even the best of professional golfers during the Depression era had to leave home and go and chase the "gravy." For the series of matches it was estimated that Guldahl would make an average of $150 per appearance. This may seem like "small beer" for the Masters champion and a double National Open winner, but it was guaranteed cash, and in the 1930s, even for the best of players, this was an important detail. The tour also featured a question-and-answer session before each round, and the findings from these would feature prominently in an instructional book Guldahl was about to write. In time, this book would be seen as assuming great significance in his career.

Ralph Guldahl was now arguably at the peak of his powers, and the fact that he did not complete the hat-trick of U.S. Open wins in 1939 was offset by his victory at Augusta and by his other successes. He was the best player on tour and he was in demand from tournament sponsors and exhibition organizers alike. He was also the top name in the Wilson pecking order, as well as being sought after by the makers of non-golfing products. All told, 1940 promised to be another stellar year for the Guldahls.

6

The Decline

Close friendships on tour in the Depression era were not greatly in evidence, with Nelson and Jug McSpaden being a notable exception. In addition, based on a friendship that went back to the caddy yard at Glen Garden, Nelson and Hogan were close for a time. As Hogan biographer Gene Gregston recounted, "Byron and his wife, Louise, who had also met in Sunday school, and Valerie and Ben were usually a foursome at functions during a tournament. Valerie and Louise, both popular among the tour pros and their wives, became close friends." The Hogan-Nelson friendship cooled off during the 1940s, when both men vied for the top spot, but their wives continued to enjoy a healthy friendship.

As for Ralph Guldahl, there is little to suggest that he had many close friendships on tour. Indeed, Byron Nelson who knew him from their teenage days back in Texas said of Guldahl, "He was pretty much a loner."[1] Another report claimed, "He is single—a guy who doesn't mix with his fellows. He doesn't play bridge. He doesn't drink. He doesn't sing in the locker room quartets."[2] Being "single" (from age 19 he was married to Laverne) was not unusual in the highly competitive world of professional golf, although sharing travel costs and expenses, as was the case with Sam Snead and Johnny Bulla, does suggest a certain amount of camaraderie on tour. And we also saw how Snead recalled traveling with Guldahl on occasion, and there were the many exhibition tours featuring the pair. Indeed, Herbert Warren Wind claimed that Snead was "as close to Guldahl as anyone."[3] At this juncture, therefore, it is perhaps worth looking at the relationship between the pair in some detail.

It will be recalled that golf historian Robert Sommers suggested that in the late 1930s while Nelson and Snead were receiving all the praise, it was Guldahl who was the better player. However, in reference to Guldahl, Sommers suggested:

> When he and Snead won the Miami Four-Ball in 1939 and the Inverness Four-Ball in 1940, he played the better golf of the two, but Sam drew the crowds. Snead had that flowing, rhythmic swing.... Guldahl, on the other hand, squirmed himself into position, took a full shoulder turn, keeping his feet firmly anchored and moving his lower body very little, drew the club back with explosive speed, and struck the ball with what looked like an uppercut delivered with the force of a sledgehammer. It looked awkward but it worked. With a more athletic build, Snead's clothes fit as if they were tailored specifically for him; Guldahl's hung like wash on a clothesline.... Snead had the personal magnetism Guldahl lacked.[4]

There are a number of points here. First, the matter of Guldahl's swing, which will be looked at in some detail further on. Second is the question of personal appearance, and based on the evidence presented in photos here (and elsewhere), the criticism of Guldahl seems a little harsh. Guldahl was a big man, but a number of newspaper reporters, notably O.B. Keeler, referred to his "film star" looks, and his taste in clothes was always smart. On the question of personal magnetism, it would be hard to argue with Sommers's assessment, as Snead's athleticism combined with his quick one-liners gave him an appeal with the fans and the media that Guldahl could never match. Overall, what is apparent is that the two men were very different, and yet they seemed to get along very well. Certainly, it would appear that at one stage, anyway, Snead had a very healthy respect for Ralph Guldahl, as evidenced by some recollections in the mid–1980s.

"Ralph Guldahl and I used to play a lot of exhibitions together," Snead recalled.

> There was a time when he was the best player in golf. He won the U.S. Open two years running. He beat me out in the Open, beat me out in the Masters and beat me out in the Western—I mean, just by the skin of his teeth, naturally. But anyway, after these matches I'd have people coming up to me and saying, "That Guldahl is a son of a bitch." I'd say, "You never met him, how can you say that?" "That's what I heard." So I'd say, "Do you go by everything you year? That Guldahl is one of the most gentle people in the world. Wouldn't say 'boo' to anybody. Tends to his own business, which is more than I can say for some."[5]

Snead also took time to show the level of respect he had for Guldahl. "In my first run at the U.S. Open in 1937," Snead said, "I faced Guldahl, who deserves to be remembered as a hero. Nobody, it seemed, could beat him—including me, as it turned out. Hardly anybody remembers Ralph now, mostly because his game left him in the '40s, and that was it. He was never able to make a comeback. It's a shame, but there you are."[6] As we know, Snead never handed out compliments too freely, and so using the word "hero" about Guldahl represents a rare compliment. Overall, his words suggest there was both respect and a friendship between the two men.

On the other hand, Guldahl's friendship with Snead can be tempered by a story that Doug Ford recounted about an experience in Augusta in 1968.[7] Ford was another in the long line of Italian-American professionals, his original name was Fortunato. He was a widely respected player who won nineteen times on tour including victories in the 1955 PGA Championship and the 1957 Masters. He was a good friend of Snead's and the story in question came at a time when Sam was still competitive but Guldahl was definitely at Augusta to see old friends. According to Ford, he played a practice round with Snead in advance of that year's Masters and up ahead was Ralph Guldahl. Ford noticed that Sam was not being particularly friendly to his former four-ball partner, and when he remarked on this, Snead pulled an IOU from his wallet for $1,600. According to Sam, when the pair won the Miami-Biltmore four-ball in 1939, Guldahl took the first prize money and handed Sam an IOU.

Bob Goalby, the 1968 Masters champion, had the same experience on a fishing trip with Snead a few years later. The fact that Snead kept the IOU for roughly thirty years adds to the lore about his fondness for money. However, the story needs to be qualified on two counts. First, there is no record of a Guldahl version of events, and second, as the total first prize was $1,600, surely the IOU would have been for $800, as this sum would have been Snead's share. However, the story suggests that Snead never saw his portion of the first prize, and it should be recalled that by 1939, times were a lot better for Ralph Guldahl. One of Snead's biographers, Al Barkow, suggested that what made Snead particularly angry was that Guldahl never mentioned the debt, and that if he had, Sam would have been sympathetic. Barkow, who knew Snead well, recounted how Bob Goalby claimed that if Guldahl had just said, "I'm a little short but I'll get it to you when I can.... Sam would have told him not to worry about it, that he could pay it back when he had it. He might even tell him to forget about it. But when he didn't say a word, ever, that got to Sam."[8] This version of events is worth noting as Al Barkow, and others, have testified to the fact that, despite his reputation for tightness, there were many occasions when Snead helped out fellow pros or others who were in need.

In contrast to Snead, however, Guldahl's friend from his Dallas days, Harry Cooper, had different memories regarding the question of money. In 1990, Cooper, recalling Guldahl on tour, said, "His wife used to travel with a couple of dogs and the family and it apparently cost him quite a bit, and every once in a while he'd run a little short, and, and, uh, I loaned him money at times and he always paid it back. I'll say that. He never missed paying it back, and he was an unusual character." And Cooper added, "I got a very nice letter from him recently, but just before he passed away. I liked Ralph. But, boy, he was sure a slow player."[9]

Overall, on tour, it seems that Ralph and Laverne kept to themselves, but there is no evidence that they were anything but well thought of by the other pros and their wives. Indeed, not long after Guldahl's first U.S. Open win in 1937, Laverne recalled, "They were nice, those wives of the other pros. Some were rooting for Sam Snead but most of them were rooting for Ralph. Most of them root for the one who needs the money most."[10] It is interesting, therefore, to look at how Ben Hogan's official biographer, James Dodson (who had access to the family papers), sheds some light both on Ralph and Ben's relationship as well as on Guldahl's decline.

It will be recalled that Guldahl and Hogan, along with Ted Longworth, traveled together to one of their first tournaments, the 1930 St. Louis Open. Not long after, unsurprisingly, their lives diverged as a result of marriage, club jobs, and the different up and down paths their tour careers took. As we know, the word "friend" was not a word which many people associated with Hogan, and yet James Dodson used the word in regard to Ben and Ralph's relationship.[11] Perhaps this was because of the early days of competition in and around Dallas and Fort Worth, or perhaps it was borne out of a mutual respect. Whatever the reason, Dodson was in no doubt that Guldahl's success and decline were a salutary lesson for Ben Hogan. In his biography of Hogan, Dodson suggested that at the peak of his fame, "A river of commercial opportunities flooded Guldahl's way, all of which proved mentally distracting to the naturally shy and amiable Texan." And he went on to succinctly describe Ralph Guldahl's golfing demise. "After capturing his lone Masters title in 1939," Dodson wrote, "never complaining but struggling poignantly to rediscover his winning form and losing his competitive fire with each passing year, brilliant Ralph Guldahl became a casualty of his own big success and soon abandoned the professional game entirely."[12]

It was this experience, the author believed, that taught Hogan an important lesson. "Ben Hogan watched his friend's meteoric rise and fall very carefully," Dodson wrote. One can surmise from comments he made later on that he eventually took from Ralph's cautionary tale the wisdom of remaining focused and perhaps even working harder to protect whatever got you to the trophy ceremony. "The minute you believe whatever they write about you and let that change things," he remarked a decade later, more or less at the center of the same kind of media storm that had enveloped and ultimately undone likeable Ralph Guldahl, "is the minute you go no further."[13]

Whether Ralph Guldahl ever believed "whatever they wrote about him" is open to question, as all the evidence suggests he was a very grounded individual. But many would agree with the idea that he lost his "competitive fire," and perhaps the "river of commercial opportunities" had something to do with this. In the lean Depression years, and especially when considering his experiences in 1934–1935, it was hard to turn down opportunities to gain financial security either from contracts or from exhibition tours. However, as is often the case, the reality of his decline was more complex, and when the reigning Masters champion embarked on his quest for more glory in 1940, there were no indications of what lay ahead.

In March of 1940, at a snow-delayed Greensboro Open, a number of pros were chatting in the locker room when the question was raised as to who was best when "the chips were down." "Ralph Guldahl," said Henry Picard, "nerve control, that's what he has better than anybody." A number of other players nodded in agreement, a group that included Ben Hogan, Ky Laffoon, and Leonard Dodson.[14] It was hard to disagree with this assessment, especially the reference to "nerve control," as Guldahl's ability in this regard, plus his unmatched levels of concentration, were backed up by the facts. Between 1936 and 1939 he had won the Masters, the National Open twice, and the prestigious Western Open on three successive occasions. He had also won a number of other tour events. So it was not surprising that he was favorite for just about every tournament he started in 1940.

In the early part of the year, Guldahl's form could be described as reasonable. He and Sam Snead failed to defend their Miami International Four-ball title. On the other hand, however, the pair tied with Jug McSpaden for second place at the New Orleans Open, just one behind Jimmy Demaret. And it was a good payday, with the trio splitting $3,200 for the second-place tie. Jimmy was the "fourth" Texan after Guldahl, Nelson and Hogan. He came from Houston and his game was honed when he was assistant to Jack Burke, Sr., at the River Oaks Club. Like Nelson, he made gradual progress on tour in the mid to late 1930s. For example, he had a single victory in both 1938 and 1939. However, for the first half of 1940, Jimmy was just about unbeatable and the success at New Orleans was his third victory in a season that saw him win six times. Apart from Demaret's continuing hot streak, the New Orleans stop was also notable for the size of the crowds. The sponsors introduced a "free in" policy, and Fred Corcoran claimed that the 38,000 strong galleries constituted a record for a tour event.

It was when the tour came to the Carolinas, and with Augusta in sight, however, that Guldahl's game really came back to life. He missed out on the North and South at Pinehurst because Laverne was ill, but at Greensboro, as defending champion, he finished tied third. And then, in the week before the Masters, he placed second at the Land of the Sky Open in Asheville to Ben Hogan with a score of 276. Hogan shot 273 for his third victory in the space of two weeks, as he also won the North and South and the Greensboro. Ben's win at Pinehurst would be his first individual victory on tour. Greensboro and the Land of the Sky Open were back to back tournaments, and journalist Laurence Leonard from the *Greensboro Daily News* received a close-up insight into Guldahl's thinking about the U.S. Open, which was almost three months away.

Right after Greensboro and before he and Laverne headed to Asheville, Guldahl and Leonard had a meal. The weather was cold and windy and Leonard was struck by how the two-time winner was already thinking ahead to the National Open. Guldahl noted, "It's going to be like this at Canterbury. Perhaps not this cold, but windy. Quite windy. That is a windy course, a tough one with relatively narrow fairways and a definite premium on accuracy."[15] Despite finishing third at Greensboro and before he would finish second at Asheville, Guldahl already had his eyes on the biggest prize of all.

Based on their recent form, it was not a surprise when Hogan and Guldahl were installed as co-favorites at Augusta at a price of 6–1. However, there was a third co-favorite, the form player Jimmy Demaret, and it was Guldahl's fellow Texan who would win the first of his three Masters titles. In fact, it was a Texas one, two, three, but neither Guldahl or Ben finished in one of these places. Instead it was Lloyd Mangrum (brother of Ray) who was second and Byron Nelson who was third. Guldahl started his defense with a 74 and was never a factor after that. He eventually finished in 14th place, 12 shots behind Jimmy Demaret's score of 280. His response to this disappointment was to go straight to Canterbury to practice for the U.S. Open, which would be held there in early June.

Before Canterbury, however, Guldahl and Snead were booked to appear in another exhibition swing in May. This was another Wilson-inspired tour intended to spread the golfing gospel (and Wilson sales) to British Columbia and then down the West Coast with stops in the Spokane region. Sadly, Snead's mother died suddenly and there were doubts about some of the exhibition matches. However, 1935 PGA champion Johnny Revolta stepped in. Revolta was another staff member of the Wilson team and he was also a colleague of Guldahl's on the victorious Ryder Cup team.

He would be a comfortable substitute for Snead. In one memorable match at the Manito Club, Revolta and Guldahl came up against Spokane champion Ken Storey and Marvin "Bud" Ward. Local man Ward was one of America's finest-ever amateurs who was twice National Amateur champion, but what enhanced his career even further was his performance at the U.S. Open of 1939 at Spring Mill. Here he finished just one shot out of the play-off, which saw Byron Nelson beat Craig Wood and Denny Shute. Against such opposition the professionals needed to show some form, and Guldahl did not disappoint, carding a 66 that contributed to a 3–2 victory for himself and Revolta. A dance to honor the visiting professionals and their wives was held that night.

A few weeks later, and in the lead-up to Canterbury, Guldahl went on another exhibition tour with Snead. This was another Wilson project and added to the "gravy" Guldahl spoke of after his first National Open victory. However, in a mirror image of the recent tour of Spokane, a family bereavement interrupted the matches for a while. This time it was a loss to Ralph and his family as his father, Olaf, died from a heart condition, aged 63. He had been suffering from poor health for the past year, and it had forced him to retire from the Continental Gin Company. The Norwegian-born Olaf had become increasingly concerned about the well-being of his relatives "at home" regarding how they were being affected by the war in Europe and was listening for news on the radio when he passed away.[16]

After his tour with Snead, Guldahl, as usual before the National Open, got to the Canterbury course over a week early. Despite his modest showing in the Masters, he went into the U.S. Open at Canterbury, Ohio, as one of the favorites. This was not surprising, given that he won the Western Open at the same venue in 1937 and because of his recent U.S. Open form. Early on in his preparations, Guldahl was in a confident mood and when asked whom he thought would win answered, "Ralph Guldahl." He was, however, in for a surprise. The wind he had forecast back in March was there, and on the eve of the championship, Gayle Talbot described the conditions. "A strong west wind blew in off Lake Erie," Talbot wrote, "flapping the refreshment tents at Canterbury golf club and foretelling grief for the big field that tees off tomorrow in the opening 18-hole round of the National Open Golf Championship."[17] However, the narrow fairways with a premium on accuracy that Guldahl had anticipated, were not present. When he saw the width of the fairways that would feature in the championship proper, Guldahl's confidence dissipated somewhat and he immediately took Sam Snead to be the winner. "Canterbury is a slugger's paradise," he said. "The fairways are the widest I can remember playing on in a National Open. They are at least 15 yards wider than when I played over them in the Western Open of 1937."[18] And he went on to say, "Snead outdrives me from 15 to 20 yards consistently…. I just finished a three-week exhibition tour with Sam during which he played top-notch golf."[19]

In addition to the wind, there was also heavy rain. This made the course play especially long and would have an important effect on the final outcome. Despite the wider fairways, Guldahl predicted that nobody would beat 290, and even wagered Vic Ghezzi $25 to back this up. As the tournament unfolded, however, neither Guldahl's vote of confidence nor the wide fairways helped Snead, who started with a blistering 67 but finished with an 81 for 295. In contrast, Guldahl had a solid championship, starting with rounds of 73 and 71, and despite a 76 on the Saturday morning, he finished with a 70 for a joint fourth place, only three shots back of Gene Sarazen and Lawson Little. Their final scores were 287, and so Guldahl lost his bet with Vic Ghezzi. A third player also came in with 287: Ed "Porky" Oliver. However, because of a weather warning, Oliver teed off thirty minutes before his official time and was disqualified. Many felt the ruling was grossly unfair but it was there in black and white for all to see: "Competitors shall start at the time arranged by the committee. Penalty disqualification." Despite some tears, to Oliver's credit, he accepted the ruling with dignity. Little fulfilled his immense potential by winning the play-off by virtue (according to Sarazen) of his power hitting on the soft fairways. Guldahl's assessment of the course as a "sluggers paradise" may have had some truth in it.

In the aftermath of Canterbury, Guldahl had some blunt but somewhat prophetic words for Snead and his failure to feature at the U.S. Open. "Snead?" he said. "I don't know what's the matter with the fellow. He's got the best swing in the business. He's almost 40 yards ahead of most of us and straight down the middle. Canterbury was a pitch and putt course for him. If he couldn't win there, I don't know where he'll win the Open."[20] Perhaps this was a reaction to Sam's failure to deliver on Guldahl's prediction that Snead would win. And there were some complimentary words, notably in regard to Snead's swing and his driving prowess. But these were also the comments of a professional golfer who knew what it took to win the U.S. Open, and sadly, history proved Guldahl to be correct in expressing his doubts about Snead.

Despite these words, business was business and Guldahl would soon team up with Snead for the Inverness Invitational Four-ball played at the Inverness Club in Toledo, Ohio. Inverness was right up there with Oakmont,

Oakland Hills, and others, when it came to golfing royalty in America. The original course, which opened in 1903, was designed by Donald Ross, and it hosted the National Open in 1920. This championship was famous for a number of reasons, but two stand out. First, it was won by the Jersey-born Ted Ray, who would remain the "last British man" to win the title until Tony Jacklin's success at Hazeltine in 1970. Second, and of great importance, the club offered full use of all its facilities to all professionals competing. S.P. Jermain, the first president of the club, was on record as saying, "We want to make sure Inverness becomes the perfect host."[21] Whereas before, professionals might have to change in their hotel or in a particular area of the clubhouse, now all facilities, such as the locker room, were open to them. These facilities also included the dining room, and a section in the official USGA program read, "The golfer's dining room in the Clubhouse will be reserved exclusively for all contestants."[22] These were such groundbreaking gestures that they prompted the professionals, led by Walter Hagen, to present a cathedral clock to the Inverness members. The clock, which stands today in the clubhouse, was inscribed as follows:

> God measures men by what they are
> Not what they in wealth possess
> This vibrant message chimes afar
> The voice of Inverness.

This liberal and hospitable approach was also in evidence during the Inverness Four-ball. As we know, players' wives could not always afford to travel with their husbands, but if they did, there were certain stops which were more attractive than others. As we saw earlier, the early Masters championships fell into this category, and another was the Pinehurst resort, which had hosted the North and South Open since 1902. The founders and owners of Pinehurst, the Tufts family, were not always convinced as to the social standing of the professional golfers. However, to make sure that Pinehurst remained America's foremost golf resort, it was important that the leading players came to Pinehurst, at least once a year. Indeed, to ensure that the 1936 PGA championship was held at the venue, the family paid the PGA $12,000. Denny Shute was the winner. And so the pros, and especially their wives, had access to the wonderful facilities on offer, such as the spas, beauty parlors, and lavish dining rooms. All of this was set in the beautiful surroundings of the North Carolina Sandhills.

At Inverness, the hospitality for wives came in the form of bridge rooms where the women could play while the men were at work, and the beautiful lunches served in between rounds. In addition, the players' wives were part of one of the elite weeks on the Toledo social calendar. "The current weekend promises to be unusually gay," read one report, "with the many visitors and parties in their honor all centered about the Invitational Golf Tournament."[23] The report was accompanied by photographs and descriptions of the social elites and their tastes in fashion, and in this regard, the wives of the golfing stars were not neglected. For example, "Mrs. Jimmy Thomson wore a light blue and Dubonnet two piece dress and ... Mrs. Billy Burke was in yellow crepe,"[24] were just two instances of the attention lavished on the golfing wives. Compare this to Sam Parks, National Open champion of 1935, recalling a drive "from one tournament site to the next one through dead-flat west Texas at night and turning off his headlights for a moment or two to look into the distance for the glare of a town where he might get a cup of joe and a sandwich, gas up, rest his eyes."[25] And as early in Ben's career as 1939, his wife Valerie was talking of "the long days in a four-door sedan, drafty hotels, lumpy beds and unpredictable diner food."[26] The Inverness setting was certainly far removed from some of the less glamorous stops on tour.

The tournament itself also had the feeling of luxury, with only sixteen invitees displaying the best of American golf. Among the eight pairs, for example, were the holders, four-ball specialists Henry Picard and Johnny Revolta. Another star pairing was "Lord Byron" teaming up with "Sir Walter." Nelson had recently become professional at Inverness, and as host, he recalled, "They asked me to play with Hagen because it would have been unfair for the other players to be paired with him as his game wasn't very sharp." As the course was long, Nelson also recalled Hagen saying to him on the ninth green, "Play hard, Byron, and I'll see you on the 14th tee."[27] (The 14th was beside the clubhouse.) Only Hagen, who was approaching fifty, could get away with this, but in truth, he was there to boost the crowd and media interest and he delivered on both counts. This was the only tournament in which Byron finished last. However, there was no doubting that the star attraction was the team of Ralph Guldahl and Sam Snead, who duly delivered in this complicated seven rounds of medal/match-play event and took away the $1,500 first prize. Jimmy Demaret and Dick Metz placed second. This was another good week for L.B. Icely and Wilson.

The final major of the year, the PGA, was held at the Hershey club in Pennsylvania. The club was the brainchild of philanthropist and chocolate magnate Milton Hershey. As well as building modern factories and a model town for his staff and their families, Hershey also built some golf

The biggest attractions at the 1940 Inverness Four-ball. Back then, smart neckties were an important part of the golfer's wardrobe. Snead and Guldahl won the tournament (courtesy Inverness Club).

A group photograph at the 1937 Inverness Invitational with Guldahl at the extreme right on the back row. Between them and throughout their careers, this group won 33 major championships (courtesy Inverness Club).

courses to encourage leisure activities. The club opened in 1930 and the PGA of 1940 was its first step into the "big time." It was the founder's largesse that funded the club, and the salary of host professional Henry Picard. Apart from his retainer, Picard received a like for like bonus from the owner each time he won a tournament. He was a strong favorite to retain the title on his home course.

Ralph Guldahl was also one of the favorites, although he freely admitted that he preferred medal play. Up to 1940, his form in his three previous appearances in this match-play championship was modest, as on each occasion he had only reached the final 32. Even in the early days in Dallas, he would invariably win the medal for best qualifier, but then sometimes lose to less fancied players in the knock-out stages of local tournaments. And when the PGA came around, he was rarely favorite, as he was in the National Open. However, the evidence suggested that there were no serious issues with match-play, as Guldahl had a 100 per cent record in the Ryder Cup and his first tour win at Riviera was in a knock-out tournament. And, as the championship unfolded, it seemed as if he might complete the third and final leg of the "American Slam." Apart from Picard and Guldahl, the other favorites at Hershey were Craig Wood, whose power would suit the long and heavy Hershey course, and Ben Hogan, who was having a wonderful year.

In the qualifying medal, Guldahl's form was modest, but he comfortably qualified with a score of 149, nine shots behind Dick Metz. After that, Guldahl displayed good form throughout the championship, as in when he came up against Ben Hogan in the quarter finals. Hogan was leading money winner at that stage of the season and was favorite to take his first major title. He and Guldahl were well acquainted from matches in Dallas and Fort Worth in the late 1920s. On those occasions, Guldahl usually had the upper hand, and it was the same story in Hershey, where he was approximately eight under par when the match ended on the 34th green. In the end, the title came down to four men: Snead, Nelson, Guldahl and Jug McSpaden. In one semifinal, Snead beat McSpaden comfortably, but in the other, Nelson had to work very hard to beat his fellow Texan on the final hole. The pair were level after 35 holes but a poor drive by Guldahl on the final hole saw Nelson win with a chip and putt par. The golf was good, with Nelson approximately 69–71 and Guldahl 70–71 for the 36 holes. Including the 1937 Masters, this was the second time that Glen Garden triumphed over Tenison in the latter stages of a major. Nelson went on to beat Snead one up in the final, and so made Sam wait for this first major.

Guldahl's second victory was in August 1940 and was the only hosting of the Milwaukee Open. However, instead of marking a strong end to what had been a decent season, this tournament can retrospectively be seen as the beginning of the end for Ralph Guldahl. Not only was this his final tour victory, it sowed the seeds of a lengthy dispute with Johnny Bulla that gained Ralph a great deal of adverse publicity.

In an era of colorful characters such as Ky Laffoon, "Wild Bill" Mehlhorn and Leonard Dodson, Johnny Bulla could match any of them. He was the North Carolina–born son of a Quaker preacher who frowned on golf. "He tried to keep me from it," Bulla recalled. "He wouldn't let me caddie on Sunday.... It was like musicians, or actors, or anything that wasn't manual labor was wrong. That's just the consciousness they grew up with."[28] But Bulla persevered, and like many others, he started golf by caddying. In Bulla's case, his golfing education came at the local Burlington Club, where he later became the professional. His golfing CV shows just one tour victory, the 1941 Los Angeles Open, and he also won a number of regional tournaments. In addition, he had several top-ten finishes in the majors, including two second places in the British Open, both of which came at St. Andrews. In 1939, he finished two shots behind Dick Burton and in 1946 he tied runner-up with Bobby Locke when his friend, Sam Snead, claimed his only win in golf's oldest championship. Bulla and Snead were good friends who, in their early days on tour, traveled together. Both were raw and unmarried and with very little money and so it made sense to split their expenses and their winnings. And when Snead struck gold at the Oakland Open in 1937, he recalled Bulla "buying drinks for the crowd like he owned a saloon." Snead then added, "We had a cool $1,200."[29] Later, however, Snead told of how, in fact, Bulla had drawn back from splitting their winnings because Snead was playing poorly. This cost him $600 but it did not affect the friendship between the pair.

Bulla was also the first pro to travel to tournaments piloting a plane. This was loaned to him by the drugstore chain Walgreens, with whom he had a contract. This was in the form of endorsing Walgreens golf balls, and it led to Bulla's being banned from the PGA Championship for a number of years for playing a "three for a dollar" drugstore ball not available from professional shops. The Walgreens connection almost damaged his friendship with Sam Snead. Bulla claimed, "L.B. Icely, who ran the Wilson company, he didn't want Sam to travel with me—Sam was on Wilson's advisory staff—but Sam told him, 'Look, you can tell me what to do on my golf, but don't tell me who my friends are.' Icely kept me out of the PGA, wouldn't let me join because I was selling in a retail outlet."[30] In many ways, Johnny Bulla was something of a maverick and enjoyed the tag of being seen as "the poor man's champion."[31]

The 1940 Milwaukee Open was played at the North Hills club in Menomonee Falls, Wisconsin. The tournament was sponsored by the local Chamber of Commerce and offered a purse of $5,000 with a first prize of $1,200. After three rounds, Bulla led Guldahl by three shots. However, playing together on the last day, Guldahl put in one of his famous finishes and a final round of 67 saw him win with a score of 268 as Bulla faded with a 75. That, however, was only part of the story, as this tournament marked the first of a number of instances when Bulla complained about Ralph Guldahl's slow play. Guldahl always believed that Bulla's grievance came from his passing him to win at Milwaukee. Journalist Billy Sixty who wrote for the *Milwaukee Journal* for sixty years, described the final day and how Guldahl "played golf with his heart and his head as well as his clubs." Sixty, says Guldahl, "wore Bulla down playing on John's jumpy nerves by deliberating over pitches and putts hole after hole, until Bulla just about hopped out of his spiked boots." Sixty went on to develop his theme by suggesting that Guldahl used the tactic of "putting out" to unnerve Bulla. For example, if an approach putt stopped a few feet away from the hole, rather than mark and step aside, Guldahl would putt out, but not before he had lined up his three-footer from every conceivable angle. This meant Bulla had to wait even longer.[32] There is more than a hint of a suggestion here that Guldahl's slow play was not purely accidental, and it was also noted that Bulla was "jumpy" and perhaps easily distracted. Regardless, it became golf's most bitter feud. Guldahl was always a deliberate player, but it would appear that as his career progressed, he became even slower. It can be argued that his tardiness coincided with a decline in his play or might even have been part of the cause of his much publicized regression.

In the years that followed, matters got worse between Guldahl and Bulla. For example, in 1941, Bulla walked in from the Asheville Land of Sky Open rather than finish a round with Ralph Guldahl. After that, according to Fred Corcoran, Bulla said, "I'll never play with him again as long as I live, even if I'm leading by nine strokes going into the last round."[33] Guldahl claimed that the feud was simply because Bulla was a bad sport, owing to Ralph's beating him in the Milwaukee Open and again at Asheville. A form of *rapprochement* was reached at the Inverness Four-ball of 1941 when Guldahl, partnered by Dutch Harrison, was drawn against Bulla and Sam Byrd. At the end of the match, which Guldahl and his partner lost, it was reported that Guldahl offered his hand to Bulla and the gesture was accepted. However, no words were exchanged.

Opinion was generally mixed on the issue. For example, Jack Grout, a friend from the early days in Dallas, concurred with the slow-play image of Guldahl when writing a letter to his sweetheart, Bonnie, before the Hurst Invitational tournament in 1941. "Darling Bonnie.... I play the 1st round with Ralph Guldahl at 1:50 o'clock Friday. When you're paired with him you're in for a long day because he plays too slow. There will be a large gallery out every day. I sure hope I can so some good."[34] Grout shot 74 and Guldahl 75. Byron Nelson, generally regarded as the most affable of professionals, admitted that he had to work at "staying calm and not becoming impatient" during his semifinal win over Guldahl in the 1940 PGA.[35] Henry McLemore, who had criticized Ralph's occasional tantrum in the past, offered the following commentary: "Guldahl is slow, there can be no doubt of that. He wiggles, he waggles, he squirms and he jiggles before he makes a shot off the tee.... Guldahl—and I am sure he does not do it with malice aforethought—is unfair to his fellow professionals."[36] McLemore took the time to also reprimand Bulla for his behavior. Johnny Bulla was no stranger to controversy: earlier that year at the U.S. Open, Bulla was in trouble with the USGA for being one of the threesome, along with Ed Oliver and "Dutch" Harrison, who teed off early in the last round of the National Open at Canterbury to avoid the predicted bad weather. This saw Oliver disqualified when his score equaled that of Little and Sarazen.

To be fair to Guldahl, he admitted to the charge of playing deliberately. In another collaboration with Art Krenz titled "Low Scoring Necessitates Playing Slowly," he argued that it was this deliberate approach that helped him hit his majestic three wood second to the 13th hole at Augusta *en route* to winning the 1939 Masters. It will be recalled that this single shot set up an eagle three for Ralph and significantly contributed to a one-shot victory. "Snap judgment on my part would have been disastrous,"[37] was his verdict. And, in regard to his Masters victory, his pace of play received some unexpected support from Bobby Jones. Jones, in his heyday, was known as a brisk player who just stepped up to the ball, had a single waggle of the club, and hit the ball. He was on record as saying, "Whenever I hesitated or took a second waggle, I could look for trouble."[38] However, when witnessing Guldahl's sensational finish at Augusta, which included his deliberating over a number of putts, Jones remarked, "If I could play like he does by playing slow, I'd be willing to finish in the dark every round."[39] It seemed that even for the greatest, it was the result that mattered and not how long it took the player to complete his round. Guldahl further justified his deliberate approach on the basis that scoring was getting lower and competition keener, and so every single shot must be thought out carefully. It was hard to argue about rising standards, but many players, such as Snead and Nelson, played at a much brisker pace.

The feud with Bulla got so bad that the PGA drew up a code of conduct to deal with any future instances, but there is little doubt that the affair did far more damage to Guldahl than it did to Johnny Bulla. The sight of perhaps the game's best player being dragged through the newspapers in this manner was not just unedifying, it also raised questions about his state of mind on the golf course. Indeed, one newspaper claimed Guldahl had said that "the Bulla incident and the wide publicity it was given had a tremendous effect on him and his game falling apart."[40] In the ruthless world of professional golf (especially in the tough late 1930s and early 1940s), a strong case can be made to the effect that a champion golfer should have been able to contend with Johnny Bulla's behavior. However, the evidence suggests that whether it should have been the case or not, Ralph Guldahl's game was adversely affected by this series of incidents with Johnny Bulla.

In early 1941, Guldahl's game was just reasonable, with a tied third at his favored Greensboro Open being one of the few bright spots, along with a runner-up spot in the Miami-Biltmore four-ball event. Here, he and Snead were beaten in the final by the partnership of Hogan and Sarazen. He also had a joint fourth-place finish in New Orleans behind winner Henry Picard. But his form was not seen as a real cause for concern as he could generally be relied on to find his game in the lead-up to the Masters and the National Open. However, the Masters was won by Craig Wood with a score of 280, with Guldahl finishing well back on 300. The "Blond Bomber's" victory was welcomed by many after his near misses in the majors. In the 1930s he had lost play-offs for the Open Championship, the National Open and the Masters. He also lost to Paul Runyan in the final of the 1934 PGA. The 1941 National Open at Colonial was the last held until after World War II, and since it was played at Colonial in his native state, Guldahl was confident of a strong performance. The newspapers and a number of his colleagues shared this view. This confidence was based on some good scores in practice that were largely the result of some good putting. However, Guldahl's game did not stand up to the Open examination and with 300, his score was well behind winner Craig Wood, who won his second major with a total of 284. For the rest of the year, Guldahl's form continued to be erratic, with a second place at St. Paul, one shot behind Horton Smith, being his best showing. The PGA Championship was played at Cherry Hills, and with such happy memories of the course from 1938 and his U.S. Open win, Guldahl was very confident and predicted he would rediscover his best form there. However, despite some fine golf in the early stages, he lost 4–3 to Byron Nelson in the third round. Just as Guldahl seemed to have the "sign" over Snead, it was the reverse with Nelson. Vic Ghezzi would be the surprise winner at Cherry Hills when he beat Nelson in the final at the 38th hole.

It was not until the second half of 1942 that the tournament schedule became noticeably reduced due to America's participation in the war. But in the opening months of the year, Guldahl's form was poor, and in the Masters, the last until 1946, he finished a full 20 shots behind Nelson and Hogan, who tied on 280. (Byron won the play-off.) This four-round total from a recent champion was indicative of the state of Ralph Guldahl's game. Guldahl shed some light on his problems in late 1942 when he said, "I'm using my old compact swing again. My whole game went to pieces when I opened my stance and tried to hit my drives as long as Snead, Hogan and Little."[41] It will be recalled that when coming out of his slump of 1934–35, Guldahl vowed never again to tamper with his natural swing, but clearly he was now becoming desperate to arrest his slide. This rarely quoted confession can be retrospectively seen as casting serious light on what went wrong with Ralph Guldahl.

Physically, he was taller and broader than Snead. "The big stoop-shouldered Norwegian" was among the phrases often used to describe him. And he was certainly bigger than "Bantam" Ben Hogan. But his game never contained the power of his fellow Texan. Consistency was his great strength, allied to an excellent short game. As Snead, his arch rival and exhibition partner, said, "When Ralph was at his peak, his clubhead came back on the line and went through on the line as near perfect as anyone I've ever seen." Sam then added rather poignantly, "I don't know what happened to Ralph."[42]

Mutterings about the state of Ralph Guldahl's game began to surface in 1940, but in retrospect, 1942 can be seen as the time when the newspapers first started to openly and regularly ask, "What's wrong with Guldahl?" For example, in the PGA that year, Guldahl failed to qualify for the match-play stages with scores of 77 and 73, and there is a photo of him watching his exhibition partner and rival, Sam Snead, playing in the final against Joe Turnesa. Sam won his first major title here. The caption, however, is instructive as it cruelly read, "Ex-Champ is a pathetic figure lost in the gallery."[43] And following on, the accompanying article claimed that fans were saying, "Here comes that Poky Guldahl."[44] Unlike today, it was not unusual in the 1930s and 1940s for players to go and watch rivals and friends, especially in the head-to-head PGA Championship. And so these quotes attributed to some fans may be cases of creative journalism. However, there is little doubt that there was almost a sense of embarrassment at the rapid decline of Ralph Guldahl.

If 1942 was the year that Guldahl's decline was first openly debated, then for many, 1939 was the year it began. In that year, he was at his peak with major title victories in three successive years. As we know, Guldahl talked of the "gravy" that came on the back of being a major winner and this came in the form of advertising and exhibition tours. As seen earlier, in the fall of 1939, Guldahl undertook an extensive tour of the mid-Southern states. Often the pros held clinics before or after the match itself, but this time there was a difference. When Guldahl held his clinic before each exhibition match, he spent forty-five minutes answering questions from the galleries. However, instead of just passing on to the next question, he meticulously jotted down each question and answer. These would be reference points for an instructional book that Ralph believed would add more "gravy" to the Guldahls' pot, but which many felt was the beginning of the end for Ralph Guldahl.

Back in 1937, after his first U.S. Open victory, Guldahl was involved in an instructional book called *From Tee to Cup by the Four Masters*. This was the brainchild of Wilson Sporting Goods, and the other "masters" were Gene Sarazen, Johnny Revolta and Denny Shute. All four players could easily lay claim to the title "master," as each was a major champion. All were contracted to Wilson, and the book's aim, apart from promoting the firm's goods, was to show how these four players played the game, with the help of a series of photos and basic tips. The book was divided into a series of sections with each of the "masters" dealing with a particular area of the game. For example:

    Woods—Gene Sarazen
    Long Irons—Denny Shute
    Short Irons—Ralph Guldahl—five through eight iron
    Scoring Zone—Johnny Revolta
    Puzzle Shots—woods from sidehill lies—Ralph Guldahl

The book was full of short, bland comments, such as for a five iron, "Ralph Guldahl is shown in his well-balanced stance, poised for a well-timed smooth swing."[45] But there was not much more than this.

The 1939 book, *Groove Your Golf*, was different. The idea sounded good, with Bobby Jones writing the foreword and the language being as non-technical as possible, and so ideal for the average golfer. The language was basic mainly because Guldahl wrote the book himself. "No ghost writers for me," he was quoted as saying.[46] This was certainly a novel approach, as for most instructional books, the golfer uses a ghost writer who simply transfers certain swing thoughts onto the pages, accompanied by some action photos or drawings. The finished product emerges and the player waits for the royalties. Even the man who gave more thought to golf technique than any other player in the game's history, Ben Hogan, availed of the immense talent of Herbert Warren Wind when writing his seminal *Five Lessons* book.

Sam Snead had a book out at the same time which was definitely ghostwritten called *The Quick Way to Better Golf*. In addition to not writing the book himself, Snead had a very different approach as to what path an instructional manual should follow. "I have come to the conclusion," Snead said, "that only a limited amount of good golf can be imparted to the pupil by words alone. Golf is a matter of feeling and touch. I'm not equal to the job of telling you exactly how you should feel when you make the motions required for a good shot. I doubt if there are words that could do that job."[47] Instead of words, Snead relied on a number of photos of his majestic swing with the idea, presumably, that these images would give the average golfer a sense of how to achieve the "feel" he spoke of. This was a very different approach from Guldahl's book, which certainly relied on photos, but which also contained blow-by-blow advice. And unlike *Groove Your Golf*, Snead's book was less than one hundred pages long.

Still, business was business, and the two men did joint book signing sessions in an effort to boost sales.

That Guldahl had strong views on golf technique was not in doubt. And, as was his custom, he was quite happy to share these opinions when the issue was raised. This was even the case when the man who wrote the foreword for *Groove Your Golf*, Bobby Jones, was in the firing line. For example, when asked about Jones's swing, he was quick to scotch the notion that the thirteen-time major winner, and America's all-time golfing hero, had somehow found perfection in his swing. "No," Guldahl said, "this crop of pros doesn't think so, despite the popular belief to this effect. We think Bobby was too loose, too free."[48] So, just as Guldahl promised, when he came to write his book, the language was certainly straightforward, as was his approach on how best to learn to play the game. For example, he suggested that the way caddies, like the young Guldahl, learned the game was best. That was by way of trial and error, where a caddie saw plenty of golf, both good and bad, and then experimented until he found which way was best. "Adherents to this method of learning slowly eliminate their faults after a long period of experiment until they have a perfectly grooved game. Most of the leading professionals in the world today, myself included, learned their game in this manner."[49] Overwhelmingly the facts backed him up, as many of the game's greats, such as Sarazen and Nelson, had learned in this manner.

Guldahl went on to admit that unfortunately this was not possible for the majority of players, and so in order to improve, a golfer needed to study by way of books or supervised coaching. And this is where *Groove Your Golf* came in—as Guldahl confirmed. "It is the purpose of this book," he wrote, "to fill the gap between the player and the professional to make clear certain fundamentals to the player so that he can get the most out of his professional's teachings."[50] This was a novel approach, as what was suggested was that the book was not *instead of* professional teaching but would act as a form of bridge between the player and the teacher. The book, which consisted of just over two hundred pages, dealt with the mechanics of the swing, and when "flicked" gave a moving picture illustration of each stroke.

It was also very comprehensive, with particular attention paid to the short game, and the book also included sections for the left-handed player and for women golfers. And to this untrained eye, the suggestions seem sound, with a great deal of emphasis being placed on the importance of a good grip. Unusually both for then and now, the grip was not dealt with in any detail until page 55. Guldahl preferred to start with the driver. But when he did discuss the grip, the Vardon model, with three knuckles show-ing on the left hand, was Guldahl's preferred choice. It will be recalled that Olin Dutra advised Guldahl to use a more "fingered grip," and his influence is very prominent in *Groove Your Golf*. "The gripping," Guldahl wrote, "is done almost entirely with the fingers thereby creating a 'feel' that is usually lacking when one grips the club in the palms of the hand." And he went on to stress the importance of the left hand in this regard. "Too much emphasis," Guldahl wrote, "cannot be placed on the part the gripping of the left hand plays in the golf swing.... This is the first funda-mental in 'grooving your swing.'" These were basic yet vital principles and were very much in keeping with Guldahl's aim of dispensing advice in a way that was easy for the average golfer to digest.

During his great years, Guldahl was seen as one of the great pressure putters, and in *Groove Your Golf* he is seen as one of the early advocates of a shorter backstroke. In this regard he reasoned that first, "the club is under better control and is not apt to get out of its proper groove." And second, "the shorter backstroke encourages a firmer, more decisive and more complete follow through." Some years later, another double National Open champion and fellow Dallasite, Lee Trevino, was advocating a sim-ilar approach.

There were also some compelling words on Guldahl's strongest suit: concentration. Long before these days of "mind coaches," golfers had to figure it out for themselves, and Ralph's words on this subject make inter-esting reading: "Intense concentration, I believe comes from thinking about the proper execution of the shot at hand rather than the results.... No matter how good a player you are, you must always take your stance with a definite picture of how you are going to swing. No one swings from memory.... My point is that no one ever gets to the point in golf where he is so good he never has to consciously be aware of a number of things to keep his swing in the groove."[51] Even at a distance of roughly seventy-five years, these words have stood the test of time in terms of wisdom and clarity.

The book's authenticity is not in doubt, but the argument goes that by writing it himself, Ralph Guldahl was forced to think too much about *how* he swung the club, and so his natural, "self-taught" game suffered as a result. New York Yankees baseball legend Yogi Berra claimed that you can't hit and think at the same time, and perhaps Ralph was an early exam-ple of the "paralysis by analysis" theory in the game of golf. The eminent golf historian Al Barkow believed that Ralph, in search of truthfulness, was too honest, and he quoted Lloyd Mangrum, who believed that most pros would hire "an eighty-dollar-a-week liar who works for a newspaper and who shanks his words."[52] Certainly Barkow was in no doubt as to the damage writing *Groove Your Golf* did to Ralph's game. "Guldahl was honest," he wrote. "He holed himself up in a room with paper, pencil, and a mirror, and wrote his own book. For the first time in his life he had to figure out what he was doing. He agonized, he introspected, he watched himself in the mirror, and after he completed the book he couldn't break glass."[53] Noted player and teacher George Fazio put it concisely: "He didn't know enough about the swing to come back."[54]

If Guldahl's game suffered from writing *Groove Your Golf*, the evidence indicates that it did not happen immediately. As seen above, 1940 was a good year, despite the feud with Johnny Bulla. Two tour wins, plus a joint fourth in the National Open and a semifinal spot in the PGA, represented a decent year. The newspapers, however, certainly made the connection between his form and the release of his book. The controversial and always quotable Henry McLemore called it the author's jinx and referred to many other sports personalities whose form had suffered after their thoughts had gone into print. For example, famous track coach Lawson Robertson, McLemore argued, had not produced a single champion since writing his last book ten years previously.[55]

However, perhaps the most telling observations came much later from his own family. Laverne suggested the book was a mistake, and after his death, his son, Ralph Jr., had his say: "My Dad had never really noticed how he swung a club. The camera angle on the photos was slightly wrong. It looked like he was playing the ball too much off his right foot. So he adjusted his swing and got all out of kilter."[56] On viewing the book, it appears that "Buddy" may have had a point, as many photos of the address position for iron shots appear to show the ball being played from a position which is almost opposite the right heel. The comments of Laverne and "Buddy" are persuasive, and the facts back them up, as 1940, the year after the book's publication, was the last time Ralph Guldahl won a tournament.

Predictably, Gene Sarazen had his opinion, and claimed that Guldahl's troubles were due to "a tendency to close the face at contact, which his timing took care of for a number of years and then could take care of no longer."[57] This view would appear to rhyme with that of George Fazio when he claimed that Guldahl did not understand his own mechanics well enough: that when what he learned by trial and error was not enough, then there was no "fall back" position. And Fred Corcoran, who was always close to the action, remembered how he "made a Pathé sports film with

Some claimed that Guldahl's "homemade" swing saw him finish with the weight still on his right foot. This photograph seems to dispel the notion (courtesy Tufts Archives).

Joe Walsh and his camera crew at the Forest Hill course in Augusta about this time. Later, hoping to find his lost game, Ralph took Joe and his crew back to Augusta and replayed the film, shot for shot, trying to discover what had happened to his swing. He never found out."[58]

Perhaps the most insightful comments came from the man who

probably played more golf with Guldahl than anyone else: Sam Snead. Snead was not known for trying to help his fellow professionals. A top professional struggling with his game meant one less to worry about on Saturday or Sunday afternoon. Snead was well aware of the beauty of his own swing and how it compared to the less aesthetic technique of Ralph Guldahl. Recalling Oakland Hills and 1937, he said, "With all respect to Ralph, who was after all the winner, his way of shooting was old-fashioned and kind of stodgy. The sportswriters were saying I had the most perfect, most natural swing. And soon newcomers were studying my style."[59] However, given their shared history on the exhibition circuit, he made an exception in the case of Guldahl and offered him the benefit of his wisdom:

> I played a lot of exhibitions with Ralph during my first years on tour so I knew his swing. He didn't go into the service during World War II, but staying a civilian didn't help his hitting much. When I came back he couldn't hit his hat. We were playing together in Portland, Oregon, where I had a chance to see his problem first hand.... I said, "I'll bet you've played more golf with me than anybody you ever played with. I know your swing pretty well. Now if you want me to help you sometime...." He waved me away. "Aw, I'll get it," he said. He tried studying photos and movies of his swing and did a lot of practicing, but nothing much helped. Finally his wife told him, "Give Sam a try." So I took him and fixed his hands around the club. Goldie tried my new grip a few times and said, "It doesn't feel right." I said, "Well I wouldn't think it would. That grip is the one you used, when you were winning everything in sight. Now you've gotten away from it and you're doing something new—and that something new is wrong."

Sam believed that Guldahl had unknowingly fallen into bad habits and found it hard to revert to his old way, especially in regard to his grip. He said, "His grip was the bugaboo that was wrecking his whole game."[60]

It was understandable that Guldahl had too much pride to allow him accept help from Snead. Even Laverne, to whom he was devoted, couldn't persuade him to change his mind. After all, just a few years earlier, Guldahl had beaten Snead almost every time it mattered, and he would have seen taking advice from his adversary as a sign of weakness on his part. Maybe he should have listened to Laverne.

In the summer of 1941, Guldahl himself gave a very frank interview and opened up about what had gone wrong. "I just don't feel right standing up to the ball," he said. "That's the whole thing, I can't seem to get comfortable." He went on, "I can't line the hole up as I used to. I really should take a month off and do nothing but practice." And he concluded, "I've noticed a tendency to play too much to the left.... I know that swinging too fast has caused me to slice. It's jerky. Other players have told me about it."[61] To say there were a number of mixed messages here would be an understatement. His address position; lining up to the hole; the need to practice and not play; his alignment; and swinging too fast: If these comments reflect anything, it is a man who was totally confused about how to address his loss of form. Perhaps here we are back to George Fazio's view that in order to find the solution you need to understand your swing in the first place. And Guldahl's comments, for example, that he did not feel comfortable standing to the ball suggest that in his formative years, and in his great days, the stance and address were instinctive. As his son suggested, he never really thought about his swing, he just "did it."

Guldahl's comments about other players telling him his swing was too quick are also pertinent regarding what went wrong. In those pre-guru days, golfers tended to share ideas or ask each other for opinions or offer their views to the scribes. Some pros even sat down and watched "then and now" movies of his swing. One report claimed, "Fellow pros aren't agreed on what is wrong with Ralph's game. Many of them though think he has worried so about his failure to start clicking that he has lost the ability to concentrate."[62] As the power of concentration may have been Ralph's greatest strength, then it would appear that his dramatic decline after *Groove Your Golf* was due not just to a deterioration in the technical aspects of his game, but also to a loss of mental focus. Perhaps this was the most serious blow of all.

When America entered the war in December 1941, the tour, like every other aspect of American life, was affected. Some questioned if professional golf had any place in this new world, but President Roosevelt believed maintaining morale was a vital weapon of war. And in a letter to the media and the American Golf Associations, John B. Kelly, assistant U.S. director of Civilian Defense in charge of physical fitness, spelt this policy out more succinctly. "Dear Sir," he wrote, "This is a time when golf really must score for the physical and mental conditioning of American citizens under wartime pressure." As John Strege suggested, it was "a direct order to play on."[63] For tournament director Fred Corcoran, it was a question of how many of his star names would be drafted and how this would impact on the quality of the fields. Or with a rubber shortage, would there be enough golf balls, and with oil at a premium, would golfers be able to travel from tournament to tournament? Unlike stars like Snead and Demaret, who enlisted in the Navy, or Hogan, who joined the Army Air Force, Guldahl was 4-F and was not drafted. In this regard he was like Byron Nelson, who, with Jug McSpaden, won thousands of tournament dollars in war bonds, as well as raising thousands more for the war effort through a series of exhibition matches. Hollywood was also to the fore in fundraising, with golfing enthusiasts Bing Crosby and Bob Hope predictably leading the way.

Perhaps by comparison, Ralph Guldahl was a less conspicuous figure during these years, but like many of his profession, he did make a contribution to some American Red Cross "Ryder Cup" matches at Oakland Hills. For example, with the 1939 match canceled due to war in Europe, those selected to represent America were challenged in 1940 to a match by a team picked by Gene Sarazen. "The Squire" was apparently still angry at his non-selection in 1939 and challenged captain Walter Hagen to a contest which would see all proceeds donated to the Red Cross war effort. Hagen's team included luminaries such as Nelson, Picard and Snead, while those Sarazen called on included Hogan, Cooper and Armour. The matches were played at Oakland Hills, and it was very much a happy return for Guldahl to the scene of his first National Open win. He beat Craig Wood 2–1 and helped Hagen's team to a 7–5 victory. And in 1942, there was a similar fundraiser when Craig Wood was captain of an official Ryder Cup team that included Snead, Hogan, Nelson and Demaret. Guldahl's form did not merit his selection. However, captain of the opposition was "Sir Walter," who rated Guldahl very highly throughout his career. And Hagen did not forget Ralph and selected him for his team, but Guldahl lost his singles match to Vic Ghezzi 3–2. Overall, the official U.S. team won the matches by 10–5 and the considerable sum of $25,000 was raised for the Red Cross.

In between these matches, in 1941, there was another "Ryder Cup" match: this time at the Donald Ross–designed Detroit Club. This was to raise funds for the United Services Organizations (USO), a nonprofit body designed to provide entertainment for American troops. If FDR believed that the pursuit of leisure activities was good for citizens' morale, then he also believed that entertainment was similarly important for the military. In this regard he called on Hollywood, and among those to answer the presidential request were stars such as Bogart, Bacall, Sinatra and Cagney. Unsurprisingly, Hope and Crosby were also prominent. Where golf could help was by raising money for the cause, and the match in Detroit featured a "Ryder Cup" team led by Hagen versus a squad led by Bobby Jones. Jones played and his presence swelled the crowd to a reported 12,000. He also beat Henry Picard and led his team to victory. Ralph Guldahl was on Hagen's team and enjoyed mixed fortunes. In the foursomes, he and his old partner, Sam Snead, were trounced 7–6 by the powerful duo of Craig Wood and Lawson Little, but in the singles, he beat Sarazen 2–1. It total, a sum of $25,000 was raised for the USO.

And Guldahl also got close to the war effort when, in the years 1943–44, he became professional at the San Diego Country Club, which had been leased by the giant Rohr Aviation Company. His main task there was to give lessons to the staff and so help boost morale during the war years. The company was a massive supplier of aircraft for the war effort and saw golf as an ideal leisure activity for its thousands of employees, who would pay $4 per year for playing privileges. In this way and with the spending power of the new Rohr recruits, the move also benefited the San Diego Club, which had struggled to recover from the Depression years.

The tour was most affected by the war in 1943, with only a handful of events taking place. Most notable of these was George May's All-American extravaganza at the Tam O'Shanter club in his home state of Illinois. May was one of golf's great showmen, and in 1953, he became the first person to show live televised tour golf. His plan in 1943 was to boost morale and to raise money by selling war bonds to the large galleries estimated to be close to 100,000 for the week-long event. In this regard, he put up a total purse of $11,900, with $2,500 for the winner. As well as the professional event, there were also sections for women players such as Patty Berg, and for the amateurs. May's tournament was also the first to openly welcome African American golfers. Jug McSpaden won, but Ralph Guldahl missed the cut. The slump continued.

A sense of normalcy came to the tour in 1944 with 24 tournaments being played. Byron Nelson enjoyed nine victories while the other half of "The Gold Dust Twins," Jug McSpaden, won five times in addition to a four-ball win with Nelson. But for Guldahl the same story continued, and for three stops on the West Coast at Oaklands, San Francisco and Portland, it was reported that his winnings were "not a nickel." Even the Texas Victory Open, played in his home city of Dallas, did not inspire him and bring a change of fortune. Here Nelson won by ten and the Victory Open eventually became the Byron Nelson Classic, which exists to this day. In an attempt to arrest his slide, Guldahl announced in late 1944 that he would leave his job with Rohr and devote himself to the tour as of January 1, 1945. Around this time, however, it was clear that even if Ralph said he wanted to play the tour full time, then Laverne and Buddy did not. Laverne later recalled, "Our son, Ralph Jr., was getting to be a teenager, and I had been away off and on since he was two and a half.... And then one year—1945 or '46—we almost got it. Our trailer skidded off a snowy road in New Mexico."[64] Throughout his career, Guldahl had traveled almost all the time with Laverne, and when his wife had had enough, that was more or less it. He did try traveling alone for a while but he never enjoyed it.

In 1945, the tour was even more restored to its prewar status with over thirty tournaments taking place. For Guldahl, it was the same as the previous year, but in truth, nobody noticed: 1945 was the year of Byron Nelson's streak of eleven straight victories and eighteen in total. Snead and Hogan won most of what was left. However, it was the quality of Guldahl's golf that continued to be a worry, with a score of 311 at his favored stop in Greensboro being one of many low spots during the year. And his thinking in regard to leaving Rohr and focus more on tournaments seems to have backfired, as in February 1945, he was appointed head professional at the famed Medinah Club in Chicago, where he assumed teaching and shop duties as well as looking after the caddies. In theory, with Guldahl's record and reputation, this move should have been ideal for a famous golfer who was playing less tournament golf and who was looking to put down roots. The reality, however, was different.

One of the perks of being a triple major championship winner was the chance of the comfort and security of a job at a prominent club with a large and relatively affluent membership. Medinah was certainly this. In the Chicago district, which was home to some of the nation's most prestigious clubs such as Olympia Fields and Flossmoor, Medinah was one of the jewels. Both Tom Bendelow and A.W. Tillinghast were involved in the design of the course, and the club held a number of tour events in the 1930s. For example, the Medinah Open, won by Harry Cooper, was held there in 1930, as was the Chicago Open of 1937, won by Gene Sarazen. The club also hosted the Western Open of 1939 and would go on to hold the National Open, the PGA Championship and the Ryder Cup. When assuming his duties in Chicago, Guldahl followed in the footsteps of Tommy Armour, who, as well as being a multiple major winner, was one of the highest ranked teachers in the game. Up to that point, Guldahl, while teaching at a number of clubs, was primarily known as a tournament player. The respective personalities of the two men were very different, with the teetotal Guldahl on the one hand, and on the other, Armour holding court in the locker room, usually with an iced glass in his hand. As Tim Cronin recounted, "They were opposites as personalities. Where Tommy was loud, Ralph was quiet. But both could play, and Medinah still wanted a player as its head pro. Guldahl was adept on the course and with the membership as well."[65] Cronin further explained, "Guldahl's playing record and his personality combined to win him the job after Armour was let go. He might have stayed forever, but for one thing. His wife Laverne couldn't handle the hay fever season.... That's the only reason he left."[66]

"Buddy" Guldahl later expressed his views, and according to Tim

Cronin, he said, "That was a horrible mistake, leaving after '48. First of all, he would have made a killing in the shop selling to the gallery. Second he would have had a darn good chance of winning. What did Cary Middlecoff shoot, 286. My dad would have done that any day, because No. 3 is where he played the majority of his golf. He knew the course." The U.S. Open "Buddy" referred to was that of 1949, and certainly whoever was head professional at an Open venue could count on an exceptionally good week in the shop. The championship was won by Cary Middlecoff with a score of 286. Ralph Guldahl finished ten shots back and he won $100. It was his last U.S. Open. Buddy's views were that if Guldahl, Sr., had stayed, playing almost daily at Medinah would have given the two-time National Open winner an advantage over the other pros. Tim Cronin reminds us, "In 1948, Claude Harmon, the head pro at Winged Foot, and someone who only occasionally ventured out on the tour, won the Masters. Guldahl winning at Medinah is conceivable in the era just before golf pro and pro golfer irrevocably widened."[67]

It is understandable that Ralph, Jr., might hold this view, as the Guldahls were a closely knit and loyal family unit. However, his thoughts do not take into account his father's form around this time, and whether the desire, so apparent in the 1930s, was still there. Still, finishing ten shots behind the winner was a decent total and entitled "Buddy" to think of what might have been. In regard to the comparison with Claude Harmon, it should be noted that as well as winning the Masters in 1948, Harmon reached the semifinals of the PGA Championship that year, and was clearly a man in form. Retrospectively, Tim Cronin's words that "he might have stayed forever," are the most apposite as well as being the most poignant. A double National Open winner and a Masters champion being host professional at one the nation's most prestigious clubs might have seen Ralph Guldahl enter his later years in a setting worthy of his place in golf's history. But it was not to be.

While he was in Chicago, Guldahl was involved in a serious car crash in which George Payton, a very promising young professional, was killed. Along with the two other passengers, Guldahl was shaken but only sustained cuts and bruises, and by the end of the year, there was talk of a comeback. "Ramblin' Ralph Plans Comeback" read one headline, while the same newspaper reminded readers of certain aspects of his past: "They will remember him as just about the slowest, most fidgety, goat getting golfer they ever saw."[68] Like the missed putt at North Shore in 1933, it seemed that slow play and the rows with Johnny Bulla would always follow Ralph Guldahl.

As it turned out, the revival did not materialize, and contrary to the "comeback" story above, it is debatable just how seriously Guldahl considered this option. In 1946, it was more of the same. The Masters was held for the first time in four years and generated great excitement. Byron Nelson was the defending champion and was installed as 3–1 joint favorite with Ben Hogan. In the end, Hogan shot 283 but lost by one shot to surprise winner Herman Keiser. At the other end of the scoreboard, with a score of 27 over par, Guldahl had a particularly bad week. This total included a first round of 85. To place this performance into context, his showing in 1946 was 36 shots worse than when he won in 1939.

The National Open that year was played at Canterbury, where Guldahl had won the Western Open in his great years. However, this time he failed to make the cut in a tournament won by his fellow Dallasite, Lloyd Mangrum. He did not appear at the 1947 Masters, but he did play in the National Open at St. Louis and shot 304–22 shots behind Lew Worsham and Sam Snead. Lew won the play-off. In 1947 also came the resumption of the Ryder Cup matches, which had been canceled due to the Second World War. The matches were played at Portland, Oregon, and the American recorded an 11–1 victory. Snead was on the team, as were fellow Texans Nelson, Hogan, Demaret and Lloyd Mangrum, but unsurprisingly, Guldahl's name was never mentioned. And to cap off his year, Guldahl's contract with Wilson ended. He had been with the company since he first came to prominence, and we saw the faith shown to him by L.B. Icely and his team during his slump. This faith was rewarded spectacularly, and despite signature names like Snead and Sarazen being contract players, for a time, Ralph Guldahl topped the bill in company advertisements. Yet, unlike Guldahl, Snead and Sarazen enjoyed "lifetime" contracts with Wilson. The separation was yet another mark of how far he had fallen. The blow was softened somewhat as Ralph joined the Golfcraft Company and his name appeared on the firm's products for a number of years. Unlike Wilson, however, it was not part of golf's elite equipment group. Golfcraft's marketing strategy was aimed at department stores such as Gimbels and not at the PGA-approved professional shops, a situation similar to that of Johnny Bulla and his Walgreens golf balls.

In 1948, Ralph Guldahl gave an interview during which he attempted to explain his difficulties in recent years and why there was little hope of a return to the old days: "Well, in 1940 I had trouble with my back…. Then came the War and I didn't play any tournament golf at all…. I'm tied up at the Medinah Country Club in Chicago for seven months and don't get time for practice and competition…. But I'm not kidding myself. The new crop of golfers is young and big and strong and eager. I never was a long driver and against some of these fellows I'd be outdriven by 25 yards."[69] There were a number of messages here. His back problem could without doubt have affected his play. These comments about the war and the absence of golf suggest that there was very little competition and therefore few financial opportunities. However, with the exception of 1943, there was a comparatively healthy number of tournaments. Nelson, for example, played in fourteen tournaments in 1942 and twenty in 1944. And when they could get leave of absence, Snead and Hogan competed and won tournaments. And these years of 1942–1944 were before he took up his post at Medinah. We have already seen that Medinah wanted a top professional and so it is hard to imagine too many objections to his playing tournaments. And the comments about the new crop of players and their length advantage seem a little strange since, during his best days, he was never the longest hitter but still found a way to beat Snead, Little, Thomson and all the power players. Overall, what does come across are the thoughts of a man who had lost the willingness to take what Bobby Jones referred to as the "punishment" of competition at the highest level.

As Ralph Guldahl entered the twilight days of his tournament career, his name still featured in the sports pages. Invariably, however, these bulletins had more to do with his demise or his glory days, such as—would his National Open record stand? There were occasional flashes of brilliance like the 1948 Tam O'Shanter, when he led after two rounds of 64–73 before fading. However, in the Masters of that year, Guldahl shot 303, a full 24 shots behind winner Claude Harmon, who tied Ralph's Augusta record of 279.

His mother Anna died in November 1950, and it was around about this time that Ralph Guldahl more or less retired from competitive golf at the relatively young age of 39. His name would feature in the occasional exhibition match and he did play in the Western Open in 1950, where he finished a respectable 13th and won $322. There were also random appearances in local West Coast events, and in one of these, a pro-am at Agua Caliente, he was in the company of future women's "great," Mickey Wright. But in general he just drifted away from headline golf. There might be an occasional note in the newspapers to say he would *not* be playing in the U.S. Open, but not much more than that. Typically there was no fanfare, nor were there press conferences, just a quiet move into the insurance business in San Diego. Had he wished, as a past winner, he could have continued playing in the Masters and meet up with some old colleagues, but he chose not to.

It would be unfair to say that his break with golf was absolute, for as we have seen, he did make the occasional appearance in the early 1950s. But if tournament golf as a livelihood was no longer a realistic option, why not use his name to continue to make some money from exhibitions? As a relatively recent three-time major winner, he surely would have some credit left in this regard. This, however, would have meant traveling and the more you read of his interviews from the 1940s, the clearer it becomes that Guldahl, Laverne and Buddy wanted to put down roots and live the life of a "normal family."

There would also have been the option of a prestigious club job— even after his experience at Medinah. He had a number of club posts during his career. Indeed, one of the features of his life was the number of times he moved club. Perhaps there is a clue here, as the itinerant pattern of his life as a club pro could indicate he was not always suited to this particular calling. However, he did return to club life in what was to be a happy and peaceful final chapter in the life of Ralph Guldahl. And this phase of his life also saw him return to Augusta and take his rightful place with the other former champions.

Epilogue

Ralph Guldahl's time selling insurance lasted roughly twelve years. Along with Sam Snead, Jimmy Demaret and others, he did make an uncredited appearance in the 1951 movie bio of Ben Hogan—*Follow the Sun*—but apart from that, he became almost invisible as far as golf was concerned. Ralph's name still appeared on Golfcraft clubs and, because of his famous name, "Buddy" got a mention when he returned some good scores in junior competitions in the San Diego area. And, if it was near his home in San Diego, Guldahl would play an exhibition match. In this regard, he, Olin Dutra and Paul Runyan were present for the opening of the South Course at Torey Pines in 1957. The course would host the memorable U.S. Open of 2008, when Tiger Woods beat Rocco Mediate in a play-off. Similarly, if pre-qualifying for the U.S. Open was near his home, he would try to make it—but unsuccessfully. And invariably at U.S. Open time, his name would feature in the build-up with either references to the missed putt in 1933, or more probably his back-to-back wins in 1937 and 1938. His name also featured in 1954, when Fred Corcoran gave golf fans the benefit of his years of experience in the game when he outlined a "best of" list under a number of categories. Unsurprisingly, he nominated Snead as having the best swing; Nelson was deemed as having come the closest to mechanical perfection; best under pressure was Sarazen; Hagen was the most colorful; Craig Wood the handsomest; and Ralph Guldahl as being the most deliberate. The article was just a printed version of "shooting the breeze," but despite an outstanding record, it seemed that Guldahl was best remembered by one of golf's most influential figures as being slow![1]

However, in 1961, he experienced a form of redemption when he re-entered the world of golf. This was when he was appointed head professional and director of golf at a new club opening in Tarzana, California.

The club was located in the northwestern district of Los Angeles, not too far from Riviera, where Guldahl had his first success. His duties included teaching, playing with members, and running club competitions. Originally the country club was named Deauville, but it quickly became the Braemar club, and Guldahl remained there for the rest of his life. On many fronts the move back to golf benefited him, and it was as if the game had rediscovered Ralph Guldahl. Certainly this was the case in terms of recognition for what some might say were long overdue awards.

In fact, the awards began before he reached Deauville: in 1954, he was inducted into the Helms Foundation Golf Hall of Fame along with fellow Wilson player Patty Berg, and amateurs Willie Turnesa and Bud Ward. Here he was following in illustrious footsteps, as fellow Texans Babe Zaharias, Ben Hogan and Byron Nelson were early recipients of this honor. Then in 1963, he was inducted into the PGA Hall of Fame alongside his former rival and sometimes exhibition partner, Johnny Revolta. Since it was started in 1940 by Fred Corcoran and PGA president Tom Walsh, the Hall of Fame had inducted many of the game's greats, never more so than the first inductees of Jones, Hagen, Sarazen and Ouimet. And yet, while this was an honor Guldahl was proud to accept, not everyone was impressed with the tardiness of the award. One critic wrote, "They didn't put him in golf's Hall of Fame until they made room for such historic characters as Olin Dutra and Mike Brady. He made it ten years after Snead and Hogan."[2] These comments are somewhat unfair to double major winner Olin Dutra, who won the U.S. Open in 1934, three years before Guldahl. However, it did seem strange that Brady, who never won one of the game's "Big Four," was inducted before Ralph, although Mike twice lost play-offs for the U.S. Open. And while Guldahl won his majors before Snead and Hogan started, their combined total of 16 in the 1940s and '50s warranted their induction as early as possible.

In 1972, Guldahl was received into the American Golf Hall of Fame along with Patty Berg, Bobby Locke and Billy Casper. And a similar honor was bestowed on him in 1981 by the World Golf Hall of Fame. For this award, his co-inductee was another Dallasite and one more Tenison Park product, Lee Trevino. Again this could be seen as highlighting the "forgotten man" image of Ralph Guldahl. Trevino first won the U.S. Open at Oak Hill in 1968 and was inducted thirteen years later, while Guldahl entered forty-four years after his win at Oakland Hills. However, the World Golf Hall of Fame only started in 1974, and so Guldahl's induction was relatively quick. And as he said, "It's nice to be remembered."

More locally, he was inducted into the Texas Sports Hall of Fame in

1969. A fellow inductee was Betty Jameson, who was a three-time major and one of the founding members of the LPGA tour. In fact, Betty was born in Oklahoma, but having grown up in Dallas, she was very much seen as another member of the Texas production line. And there were certain parallels between her career and Guldahl's; before turning pro, Betty won a number of amateur titles in Dallas in her teenage years. Whether by coincidence or because he was back in golf, Guldahl's name began to appear on advertisements for Hill and Hill Kentucky bourbon— "For Men Who Know the Score." Ralph Guldahl was very much a teetotal man during his great years.

Guldahl also started to play some more golf and he quickly became a very popular figure with the members. The long-time receptionist at Braemar, Mary Renfrew, said, "I didn't know anyone who didn't like him. A real southern gentleman."[3] He also acquired a nickname at Braemar— Goldy[4]—which became such a part of his persona that it featured on his headstone. The members also encouraged him to take up his past-winners invitation to the Masters, and starting in 1964, he was happy to do this for a number of years. Apart from the club members, there was also some help from Clifford Roberts and from his former colleagues. When making the announcement of Guldahl's return to Augusta, Roberts told of how the club had written to him on several occasions and of how Ben Hogan had also tried to persuade him to return. But then, Roberts explained, "Claude Harmon went to the trouble to find him in California and told him about the sentimental angle of all former champions coming to the dinner and playing in the tournament."[5] In 1964, for the first time, all living champions attended the pre-tournament dinner. His appearance at Augusta was noted by the media, whom he told, "I just lost my zest for the game. When I tried I couldn't get it back. So I haven't tried. I'm just a weekend hacker now. I got a real thrill out of coming back."[6] Rounds of 79 and 80 were not those of a weekend hacker on the long and tough Augusta course. He also collected a few dollars from his trips, such as during Billy Casper's year of 1970, when he picked up $1,000, the same as all who did not make the cut. This group included former rivals Gene Sarazen and Henry Picard. And all the evidence suggests that Guldahl enjoyed his visits back to the scene of one of his greatest triumphs. He enjoyed catching up with his former rivals (maybe not Snead) and he was also in demand for interviews about the 1930s and how the stars of his era compared to Nicklaus and Palmer. In a way this was a chance to appeal to a whole new audience, whether these were younger journalists who interviewed him, or a new generation of readers to whom the name Ralph

Guldahl was unfamiliar. Even after Augusta decided to restrict participation in the Masters to those players who were deemed "active," Guldahl continued to play in the traditional pre-tournament, par-three event, and picked up a few Wedgwood plates for his play.

Ralph Guldahl was also present for what can be seen as a milestone in the history of "Seniors" golf in America. There had been a semblance of competitive "Seniors" golf in America since 1937, when Jock Hutchison won the inaugural Seniors PGA title at the Augusta National Club. Subsequent winners included Gene Sarazen in 1954. However, it was the Legends of Golf tournament in 1978 that gave birth to a "Seniors" professional circuit and is today the multi-million-dollar "Legends" tour. This first tournament was the brainchild of Fred Raphael, who was largely responsible for the award-winning television show, *Shell's Wonderful World of Golf*. The Shell show did a lot to popularize the game globally, and Raphael also showed foresight with the "Legends" idea. "I thought there was a whole generation of players," he said, "no one had really watched. I believed there was an interest in seeing some of the older players who did not have television exposure in their prime."[7]

The event was held in Ralph Guldahl's home state of Texas at the Onion Creek Club, which was founded and designed by Jimmy Demaret. It was recorded, "You could cut nostalgia with a knife in the thickly carpeted locker room of the Onion Creek Club where headline stars of three past generations assembled."[8] In addition to "nostalgia," however, there were three practical reasons why the event attracted enormous publicity and captured the public's attention. First, it was covered by NBC Television, with Arnold Palmer doing the commentary. Second, the quality of the field comprised true legends of the game such as Sam Snead, Julius Boros, Roberto de Vicenzo, Tommy Bolt *and* Ralph Guldahl. Gene Sarazen, at age 76, also took part. And third, the purse was enormous: first prize for this four-ball event was $100,000 per pair, and last place was $20,000. When you consider that Guldahl won $1,000 for each of his U.S. Open wins, this was serious money for him and for many of the other golfing legends. It was hoped that Ben Hogan would compete, and a place was kept for him to partner Jimmy Demaret up to the last possible moment. However, "the Hawk" did not come to Onion Creek, nor did he appear at any of the Legends tournaments. Not everyone was happy about this, and the following year, former PGA champion Walter Burkemo openly criticized him believing that Hogan should give a little back to the game. As was widely known, however, Hogan was never one for turning.

Just like old times, Guldahl got into training, and he prepared by losing thirty pounds. He admitted, "I'm not just excited.... I'm worried and I'm scared. I've lost 30 yards off the tee and it makes me mad. Old golfers don't fade away—they just lose distance."[9] As Fred Raphael alluded to, it was Ralph Guldahl's first time on television. In an exciting finale, Snead and Gardner Dickinson, with a better ball score of 193, beat Peter Thomson and Kel Nagle by one shot. This tournament is seen as giving birth to what is now the highly successful and lucrative Champions Tour. Guldahl partnered former Canada Cup winner (later the World Cup) Pete Nakamura, and the pair finished on 208, which featured a closing 65. He played in a few more Legends events, and while the prize money did not quite match the largesse of the first year, there was the guarantee of a decent check. For example, in 1979, Ralph teamed up with another former Canada Cup winner, Ireland's Christy O'Connor, and while the pair finished well down the field, they split $10,000 between them. And in one of his final appearances, Guldahl fittingly joined up with Harry Cooper in a Tenison Park reunion.

Ralph Guldahl died in his sleep on June 11, 1987, and he was survived by Laverne and "Buddy." Indeed, Laverne lived for another fourteen years. Ralph played golf right up to the time of his death. In 1978, he was replaced as head professional at Braemar by Tim Barry, but he would remain at the club as Professional Emeritus and acted in a consultative role. It seemed that the older he got, the more popular he became, and this was reflected in a bronze statue the Braemar members erected in his honor. It was a fitting tribute. Two years later, in 1989, Ralph Guldahl was posthumously inducted into the Hall Of Fame at his *alma mater*, the Woodrow Wilson High School in Dallas. This honor came sixty years after he led the school to victory in the state championship of 1929.

In early 1978, Tom Watson reflected on the year past when he assumed number-one status in the world of golf. His 1977 Masters and Open Championship victories over Jack Nicklaus confirmed this. But in an interview with *Golf* magazine, he was not taking anything for granted. "It might all end this year. It just might. I don't think it will but it has happened to others. Look at Ralph Guldahl who won everything in sight for two years and then virtually disappeared."[10] Thankfully, in the case of Tom Watson, it did not end, and despite some disappointments, he was still playing competitive golf up to and including his wonderful tilt at the Open Championship at Turnberry in 2009. However, his words back in 1978 tell us two things. First, Tom Watson was (and remains) a man with a fine understanding of the game's history. And second, roughly forty years after his first U.S. Open win, Ralph Guldahl was still a reference point for those golfers who burnt out very quickly. And it was this rapid rise and fall that probably precludes his name from being at the top table of golfers. Many of the possible reasons for this rapid "burnout" are offered in this book, and Byron Nelson, who knew Guldahl from his earliest golfing days, introduced a note of mystery to this question when he said, "I think I know what happened, but I don't want to say anything because of the people involved. He didn't lose it all at once, but it was pretty quick to be sure."[11] These comments suggest there *may* have been some personal issues involved, but without any further explanation from Byron Nelson, it is impossible to go any further down this particular path.

However, based on what we *do* know, if we look at the history of the game in the twentieth century, we can see that there are some golfers who, like Player and Nicklaus, can win majors in three different decades, and there are others, like Nelson, whose victories were largely condensed into a ten-year period between 1936 and 1946. Statistically, Nelson's achievements are far greater than those of Ralph Guldahl, but their respective careers show that how long a golfer can take the intense pressure of tournament golf can vary from player to player. A strong case can be made to the effect that a contributory factor in the decline of Ralph Guldahl was his unwillingness or inability to take the strain for more than ten years. And this is linked to his feud with Johnny Bulla, which Guldahl himself confirmed had affected him greatly.

In general, the game of golf has avoided confrontations of a serious nature. On one infamous occasion in 1947, Dick Metz put Fred Corcoran in the hospital with a single punch following a players versus PGA dispute. (The pair later made up.) But on the course, feuds or rivalries are not uncommon in golf any more than they are in other competitive sports. It is well known, for example, that there was no love lost between Bobby Jones and rivals George Von Elm and Chick Evans. Evans was the first amateur to win both the U.S. Open and Amateur titles in the same year, 1916. And Von Elm won the U.S. Amateur of 1926. Mark Frost recounted how Von Elm admitted that he "hated Bob's guts," and that as two people, Jones and Evans "simply repelled each other."[12] However, Jones's response was to let his clubs do the talking, and to do justice to both Evans and Von Elm, neither man allowed personal feelings to intervene when they met Jones in tournament golf. All parties publicly put on a show to honor the game of golf if nothing else. What marked out the Bulla-Guldahl episode was that it was more personal than many others, and more public, as evidenced by the many interviews with both men that appeared in the newspapers, and by the fact that Bulla walked in at Asheville, rather than play with Guldahl.

However, when taking all the relevant factors into account, a champion must learn to deal with such unpleasantness and not allow it to affect his performance. Reading about the accusations and counteraccusations is sad, more than anything else. Bulla was an eccentric maverick whose record did not come close to that of Ralph Guldahl, and so the onus was on the three-time major winner to deal with this distraction and get on with winning tournaments. Instead, it clearly bothered him, and it can be suggested that if a row and some bad publicity back in 1940 affected him that much, then perhaps his nerves were beginning to feel the strain already.

Just before the Bulla feud there was the release of *Groove Your Golf*, and the view from the media then and later on was that this damaged his game. And from the professional game, the authoritative voice of George Fazio was in no doubt as to the negative impact having to think about his swing had on his career. In addition, his wife Laverne and his son, Buddy, were of much the same opinion. These are compelling voices, but it can also be argued that the writing of *Groove Your Golf* just added to the troubles of a career that was already beginning to taper off. Guldahl himself did not use the book as an excuse, but rather referred to other factors such as injury and becoming tired of traveling. Most of all, what comes through, when taking into account all the aforementioned factors, was that Ralph Guldahl lost his *desire*. When Byron Nelson had won enough money to buy a cattle ranch, he more or less quit competitive golf. This was at the end of 1946, just one year after the streak of 1945. He recalled thinking, "What a relief to have it all over with. I packed up my clubs, sent them to MacGregor, and told them to keep them till I asked for them, which wasn't going to be for a long time."[13] Sam Snead, in contrast, won his favored Greater Greensboro Open in 1965, almost thirty years after his first win at Oakland in 1937. And he retained his desire until well into the 1970s. For example, in the 1974 PGA Championship, and at the age of 62, he finished third, only three shots behind winner Lee Trevino. And, as we saw, he won the first Legends of Golf event in 1978. And the third Texan, Ben Hogan, remained competitive into the early 1960s, thirty years after he first tried his luck on tour. Indeed, he almost won the U.S. Open of 1960 at Cherry Hills, the scene of Guldahl's second National title.

In the opening pages of this book, I suggested that I hoped to find out a little more about what happened to Ralph Guldahl. I could have added that I simply wished to find out more about Ralph Guldahl. His golfing record has been well discussed here, and it is clear from the evidence that his self-taught swing served him spectacularly well for a number of years. His swing was never a thing of beauty *à la* Snead, but its effectiveness was not in doubt. One writer described his swing as the "least aesthetic swing in golf but only because he had stripped it of every movement which did not contribute to the particular punch he wanted in every shot.... After taking his stance, Guldahl would squirm and wiggle like a man in a phone booth with a load of packages in his arms and then, finally satisfied with the way he had set himself, would draw back the club with explosive speed and hit the shot with a violent uppercut." Guldahl did not disagree too much with this view, commenting, "I sure didn't have a picture swing, but I felt it was smooth for a man of my height [6 feet 2 inches]. I did have a fast backswing."[14]

P.A. Vaile, a respected writer and analyst from that era, posed the question, "Is Guldahl the Last Word?" And Vaile went on, "The outstanding feature of Guldahl's stroke is the immobility of his legs and body. He takes the club away from the ball almost entirely by shoulder rotation and not as most good golfers do by leg movement and hip rotation.... This modern game of golf is getting to be played with as much economy of movement as possible. There is scarcely a superfluous motion in Guldahl's game."[15] In Vaile's description of Guldahl's swing, there are clear resonances with the swings of today—swings where there is much more emphasis on the movement of the upper body rather than the looser leg action of, for example, Bobby Jones. Perhaps Ralph Guldahl was ahead of his time in this regard.

Whatever the views on his action, all were agreed on the quality of his ball striking. Back in 1933, after watching him when he came so close to winning the National Open at North Shore, Bobby Jones commented, "He doesn't look like a golfer until he starts to swing a club, but he sure can hit that ball. When he hits one it stays hit."[16] And Henry Cotton, a keen student of the game as well as a triple Open champion, referred to Ralph as having a "very personal style." Henry was particularly interested in how Guldahl allowed "the club-shaft to slide" in his right hand. This idiosyncrasy, according to Cotton, did not allow the right wrist to "cock" in the accepted manner.[17] And if Guldahl's action could not match the grace of Snead's, similarly it was never spoken of in the same breath as Hogan's or Nelson's, both of whose swings (especially Ben's) are seen as templates for matchless efficiency that have stood the test of time. But Sam Snead was not known for handing out bouquets, and so his comments about Ralph having the most "grooved" swing of all are a fitting testimony to his abilities. The very stylish Horton Smith elaborated on this theme. "Uniformity is the most impressive thing about the mechanics of his game," Smith said. "He doesn't look too sound mechanically, but his left side is always out of the way so that he can swing past in a perfect follow through."[18]

In addition, Tommy Armour claimed that Ralph Guldahl had qualities which were essential for any champion—"First, magnificent skill in every type of shot—wood, iron or putter. Second, complete confidence is his swing. Third, the physical power needed to keep going and hit the stretch at speed."[19] Skill, confidence and an ability to finish strongly were certainly qualities which Guldahl displayed countless times during his career, especially when the stakes were at their highest. As he said, "I was always good in medal play and the big tournaments. I never had a real bad round like some, because I had good nerves and was able to concentrate. Hogan and I both got so engrossed on what we were doing we couldn't worry about what was happening on the golf course."[20] The reference to Hogan should not be seen in any way as an attempt at self-aggrandizement. The pair went back a long way, and Ralph Guldahl had earned the right to be mentioned in the same sentence as Ben Hogan.

It is also clear that Guldahl could, at times, be an outspoken and controversial figure, as evidenced during his trip to Britain in 1937 and in regard to the comments he directed at some of his colleagues after Sam Park's surprise U.S. Open win at Oakmont in 1935. And there was also his altercation with Dick Metz about stymies at the 1939 PGA Championship. No matter how much he tried to play this down, the incident did not look good. Then there were his occasional pre-tournament predictions that he would win, some of which he made good on, as in the Masters of 1939. However, it can also be argued that these qualities can often be a source of strength in the harsh world of professional golf, as they demonstrate a self-confidence and a mental toughness which are part of the champion's armory. His nemesis, George Jacobus, alluded to this after the 1939 Masters. Certainly Sarazen and Hagen were never shy about voicing their views, although in the case of "Sir Walter" the language may have been a little more diplomatic than that of his friend and rival.

In regard to "What happened to Ralph Guldahl?" I believe that a number of possible answers have been raised. However, the more I researched his story, the more I came to think of him as a man who had a wonderful career: a career which has not always been sufficiently recognized by the game and the wider public. Undoubtedly some of this lack of acknowledgment is due to his lack of color, when even at his peak he was seen as something of a sideshow to the "real" stars. For example, when writing her father Fred's biography, Judy Corcoran commented, "The late 1930s and the years leading up to the outbreak of World War II saw important changes in professional golf. As with any passage of time, and especially in sports, there was a changing of the guard. Taking center stage with Sam Snead were two young men from Texas, Ben Hogan and Byron Nelson, along with the colorful Jimmy Demaret right on their heels. These giants of the game became the new Big Four.... Ralph Guldahl was still playing and in fact had won two Open championships, but he lacked appeal."[21] I don't think for a moment that the "in fact" reference to Ralph Guldahl is in any way intended as a deliberate put-down, but the language is instructive. In the late 1930s, Guldahl was superior to the aforementioned "Big Four," and yet his two National Open victories are almost seen as an aside in terms of what was seen as the bigger picture of a PGA tour that needed new faces. The "lack of appeal" image dogged him throughout his career and, it appears, for long after.

Arguably, the lack of recognition owed more to the fact that he had such a dramatic decline. Notwithstanding this, in 1939, when writing a foreword for *Groove Your Golf*, Bobby Jones offered this opinion on Ralph Guldahl: "Ralph Guldahl's record to-date, even if he does nothing more in tournament golf, will entitle him for all time to rank among the great players of the game."[22] Jones's words "even if he does nothing more" are unintentionally prophetic, as after 1939, Guldahl won but two more tournaments. And some may argue with the assessment of Guldahl as "among the great players for all time." However, coming from the game's most authoritative voice at that time, the words of Jones are persuasive and the facts speak for themselves. Ralph Guldahl was an outstanding young player when he won numerous amateur tournaments in and around Dallas, and it also needs to be remembered that he won his first professional event at the age of 19. His second-place finish in the National Open in 1933 came when he was 22, and despite a slump for the next two years, he went on to achieve three major wins, two runner's-up spots at Augusta; three successive Western Opens; numerous other victories; a Ryder Cup place in 1937; and a place at the very top of golf's elite for a brief but glorious period, at a time when Sarazen was still competitive and Snead and Nelson had arrived on the scene. His was truly a career to be proud of.

Appendix

Ralph Guldahl Career Highlights

1928—Wins Dallas Junior Golf Championship
1929—Wins Texas High School Championship and Dallas City Championship
1930—Turned professional
1931—Motion Pictures Open—winner—beat Tony Manero 1 up in 36-hole final
1932—Phoenix Open—winner—Final Score—285
1933—U.S. Open—runner-up to Johnny Goodman—Final Score—288
      St. Louis Open—Winner—beat Orville White 8–6 in 36-hole final
1934—Westwood Golf Club Open—winner—Final Score—273
      Santa Monica Open—Tied Jimmy Thomson—Final Score—271
        Play-off, Thomson 70, Guldahl 74
1936—Western Open—winner—Final Score—274
      Augusta Open—winner—Final Score—283
      Miami Biltmore Open—winner—Final Score—283
      Shawnee Open—Joint Runner-up with Roland MacKenzie to Ed Dudley—
        Final Score—289
      Seattle Open—Tied MacDonald Smith—Final Score—285
        Play-off, Smith 65, Guldahl 71
      Centennial Open—Joint Runner-up with Phil Perkins to Billy Burke—
        Final Score—207
      Radix Trophy for best scoring average—Winner—71.63 per round
1937—Los Angeles Open—Joint Runner-up with Horton Smith to Harry
        Cooper—Final Score—279
      Oakland Open—Runner-up to Sam Snead—Final Score—272
      The Masters—Runner-up to Byron Nelson—285
      U.S. Open—Winner—Final Score—281
      Canadian Open—Runner-up to Harry Cooper—Final Score—287
      Western Open—Winner after play-off with Horton Smith—Final Score—
      288
        Play-off, Guldahl 72, Smith 78

Miami Open—Joint Runner-up with Horton Smith to Sam Snead—
Final Score—272

1938—The Masters—Joint runner-up with Harry Cooper to Henry Picard—
Final Score—287

U.S. Open—Winner—Final Score—284

Western Open—Winner—Final Score—279

Chicago Open—Runner-up to Sam Snead—Final Score—208

1939—Greensboro Open—Winner—Final Score—280

Miami Four-ball—Winner with Sam Snead

The Masters—Winner—Final Score—279

Dapper Dan—Winner after tie with Denny Shute and Gene Sarazen—
Final Score—287

Play-off, Guldahl 70, Shute 74, Sarazen 75

Canadian Open—Runner-up to Jug McSpaden—Final Score—287

Walter Hagen, Invitational Better Ball—Runner-up with Jug McSpaden

1940—Inverness Four-ball—Winner with Sam Snead

Milwaukee Open—Winner—Final Score—268

PGA Championship—Semifinalist

Land of the Sky Open—Runner-up to Ben Hogan—Final Score—276

New Orleans Open—Joint runner-up with Jug McSpaden and Sam Snead
to Jimmy Demaret—Final Score—287

1941—Miami Biltmore Four-ball—Runner-up with Sam Snead to Gene Sarazen
and Ben Hogan

*Major Championship Victories and Scores**

*Including the Western Open, which was considered a "major" in the 1930s

U.S. Open, Oakland Hills, June 1937

Ralph Guldahl	71–69–72–69—281	$1,000
Sam Snead	69–73–70–71—283	$800
Bobby Cruickshank	73–73–67–72—285	$700
"Lighthorse" Harry Cooper	72–70–73–71—286	$600
Ed Dudley	70–70–71–76—287	$450
Al Brosch	74–73–68–73—288	$375
Clarence Clark	72–75–73–69—289	$275
*Johnny Goodman	70–73–72–75—290	—
*Frank Strafaci	70–72–77–72—291	—
*Charles Kocsis	72–73–76–71—292	—
Henry Picard	71–75–72–74—292	$175
Gene Sarazen	78–69–71–74—292	$175
Denny Shute	69–76–75–72—292	$175
Ray Mangrum	75–75–71–72—293	$112

Paul Runyan	76–72–73–72—293	$112
Billy Burke	75–73–71–75—294	$87
Jimmy Demaret	72–74–76–72—294	$87
Sam Parks Jr.	74–74–72–74—294	$87
Pat Sawyer	72–70–75–77—294	$87
Vic Ghezzi	72–71–78–74—295	$50
Jimmy Hines	75–72–76–72—295	$50
Ky Laffoon	74–74–74–73—295	$50
Harold "Jug" McSpaden	74–75–73–73—295	$50
Fred Morrison	71–76–74–74—295	$50
Byron Nelson	73–78–71–73—295	$50
Bob Stupple	73–73–73–76—295	$50
Frank Walsh	70–70–78–77—295	$50
Leo Mallory	73–74–76–73—296	$50
Toney Penna	76–74–75–71—296	$50
Johnny Revolta	75–73–75–73—296	$50
Jimmy Thomson	74–66–78–78—296	$50
Dutch Harrison	74–71–74–78—297	$33
*Edwin Kingsley	72–76–75–74—297	—
Mike Turnesa	71–74–76–76—297	$33
Al Watrous	77–75–75–70—297	$33

*denotes amateur

U.S. Open, Cherry Hills, June 1938

Ralph Guldahl	74–70–71–69—284	$1,000
Dick Metz	73–68–70–79—290	$800
Harry Cooper	76–69–76–71—292	$650
Toney Penna	78–72–74–68—292	$650
Byron Nelson	77–71–74–72—294	$412
Emery Zimmerman	72–71–73–78—294	$412
Frank Moore	79–73–72–71—295	$216
Henry Picard	70–70–77–78—295	$216
Paul Runyan	78–71–72–74—295	$216
Gene Sarazen	74–74–75–73—296	$106
Vic Ghezzi	79–71–75–72—297	$106
Jimmy Hines	70–75–69–83—297	$106
Denny Shute	77–71–72–77—297	$106
George Von Elm	78–72–71–76—297	$106
Willie Hunter Jr.	73–72–78–75—298	$100
Olin Dutra	74–71–77–77—299	$50
Harold "Jug" McSpaden	76–67–74–82—299	$50
Johnny Revolta	74–72–77–76—299	$50

Jim Foulis	74–74–75–77—300	$50
Horton Smith	80–73–73–74—300	$50
Al Zimmerman	76–77–75–72—300	$50
Charles Lacey	77–75–75–75—302	$50
Tommy Armour	78–70–75–80—303	$50
Al Huske	76–79–76–73—304	$50
Johnny Rogers	71–76–73–84—304	$50
Charles Sheppard	79–73–74–79—305	$50
Joe Belfore	75–73–80–78—306	$50
Stanley Kertes	77–72–82–75—306	$50

U.S. Masters, Augusta, April 1939

Ralph Guldahl	72–68–70–69—279	$1,500
Sam Snead	70–70–72–68—280	$800
Billy Burke	69–72–71–70—282	$550
Lawson Little	72–72–68–70—282	$550
Gene Sarazen	73–66–72–72—283	$400
Craig Wood	72–73–71–68—284	$300
Byron Nelson	71–69–72–75—287	$250
Henry Picard	71–71–76–71—289	$175
Ben Hogan	75–71–72–72—290	$125
Ed Dudley	75–75–69–72—291	$100
Toney Penna	72–75–72–72—291	$100
Tommy Armour	71–74–76–72—293	$33
Vic Ghezzi	73–76–72–72—293	$33
Harold "Jug" McSpaden	75–72–74–72—293	$33
Denny Shute	78–71–73–72—294	—
Paul Runyan	73–71–75–76—295	—
Felix Serafin	74–76–73–72—295	—
*Chick Harbert	74–73–75–74—296	—
Jimmy Thomson	75–71–73–77—296	—
*Charles Yates	74–73–74–75—296	—
*Tommy Tailer	78–75–73–71—297	—
Jimmy Hines	76–73–74–75—298	—
Ky Laffoon	72–75–73–78—298	—
Frank Moore	75–74–75–74—298	—

*denotes amateur

36th Western Open, June 19–21, 1936, Davenport Country Club, Davenport, Iowa

Ralph Guldahl	68–67–75–64—274	$500.00
Ray Mangrum	66–67–74–70—277	$300.00

Byron Nelson	69–72–72–65—278	$200.00
Harry Cooper	70–69–70–70—279	$150.00
Zell Eaton	70–73–69–69—281	$95.00
Horton Smith	69–70–73–69—281	$95.00
Macdonald Smith	72–67–69–74—282	$80.00
Frank Walsh	72–69–70–73—284	$75.00
Johnny Revolta	73–69–72–71—285	$67.50
Toney Penna	70–70–73–72—285	$67.50
Ky Laffoon	70–73–74–70—287	$60.00
"Dutch" Harrison	74–71–73–70—288	$51.66
Jimmy Thomson	69–75–73–71—288	$51.66
Byron Harcke	74–69–73–72—288	$51.66
Lawson Little	67–73–76–73—289	$50.00
Abe Espinosa	76–75–68–71—290	$50.00
Albert O. Huske	71–72–77–72—292	$50.00
Pat Sawyer	74–73–74–72—293	$50.00
Terle Johnson	70–74–71–78—293	$50.00
Jack Grout	75–68–76–75—294	$50.00

37th Western Open, September 17–20, 1937, Canterbury Country Club, Beachwood, Ohio

Ralph Guldahl	72–73–69–74—288	$500.00
Horton Smith	72–71–72–73—288	$300.00
	Sept. 20 Play-off: Guldahl 72, Smith 76	
Paul Runyan	72–74–73–70—289	$175.00
Sam Snead	68–74–75–72—289	$175.00
Jimmy Thomson	70–77–72–73—292	$100.00
Dick Metz	70–76–76–71—293	$90.00
Harry Cooper	73–74–77–71—295	$80.00
James R. Foulis, Jr.	75–75–79–68—297	$75.00
Ray Mangrum	76–75–73–75—299	$70.00
Ky Laffoon	72–73–78–77—300	$65.00
Billy Burke	76–76–77–73—302	$60.00
*Maurice McCarthy	74–76–77–75—302	—
Jim Barfield	76–79–77–71—303	$51.66
R. Williamson	78–75–74–76—303	$51.66
Toney Penna	77–74–74–78—303	$51.66
Reggie Myles	76–75–79–74—304	$50.00
Ed Brook	76–79–73–76—304	$50.00
*"Chick" Harbert	74–80–79–72—305	—
Sam Parks, Jr.	76–74–78–77—305	$50.00
David Ogilvie, Jr., Cleveland	75–75–78–77—305	$50.00

*denotes amateur

38th Western Open, June 14–16, 1938, Westwood Country Club, St. Louis, Missouri

Ralph Guldahl	71–73–70–65—279	$750.00
Sam Snead	72–73–69–72—286	$450.00
Toney Penna	72–76–74–67—289	$300.00
Jimmy Thomson	76–76–71–69—292	$175.00
Leonard Dodson,	76–74–68–74—292	$175.00
Paul Runyan, N.Y.	72–73–74–74—293	$95.00
Bill Heinlein	78–75–70–71—294	$77.50
Jimmy Hines	73–73–76–72—294	$77.50
Frank Walsh	78–72–72–73—295	$70.00
Horton Smith	75–75–71–75—296	$60.00
Harry Cooper	75–75–70–76—296	$60.00
Ray Mangrum	72–72–76–76—296	$60.00
Abe Espinosa	74–78–77–68—297	$50.00
Tommy Armour	78–75–71–73—297	$50.00
Leland H. Gibson	73–75–76–73—297	$50.00
Floyd Farley	72–77–73–76—298	$50.00
Lawson Little	76–74–72–77—299	$50.00
Harry Bassler	77–77–74–72—300	$50.00
James R. Foulis, Jr.	78–76–73–73—300	$50.00
*Glenn Oatman	76–75–76–73—300	—
Ben Richter	79–72–74–75—300	$50.00
*Walter Blevins	79–74–71–76—300	—

*denotes amateur

Ryder Cup Matches, Southport, England, June 1937

FOURSOMES:

- Alf Padgham/Henry Cotton, GB, def. Ed Dudley/Byron Nelson, 4 and 2
- Ralph Guldahl/Tony Manero, U.S., def. Arthur Lacey/Bill Cox, GB, 2 and 1
- Charles Whitcombe/Dai Rees, GB, halved with Gene Sarazen/Denny Shute, U.S.
- Percy Alliss/Richard Burton, GB, def. Henry Picard/Johnny Revolta, U.S., 2 and 1

SINGLES:

- Ralph Guldahl, U.S., def. Alf Padgham, GB, 8 and 7
- Sam King, GB, halved with Denny Shute, U.S.
- Dai Rees, GB, def. Byron Nelson, U.S., 3 and 1
- Henry Cotton, GB, def. Tony Manero, U.S., 5 and 3
- Gene Sarazen, U.S., def. Percy Alliss, GB, 1-up

- Sam Snead, U.S., def. Richard Burton, GB, 5 and 4
- Ed Dudley, U.S., def. Alf Perry, GB, 2 and 1
- Henry Picard, U.S., def. Arthur Lacey, GB, 2 and 1

SCORE:
Great Britain 4—USA 8

Awards

1954—Inducted into Helms Foundation Golf Hall of Fame
1963—Inducted into PGA Hall of Fame
1969—Inducted into Texas Sports Hall of Fame
1981—Inducted into World Golf Hall of Fame
1989—Inducted into Woodrow Wilson High School Hall of Fame

Chapter Notes

Introduction

1. J. Dodson, *American Triumvirate* (New York: Alfred A. Knopf, 2012), p. 21.

2. A. Butt, *Taft and Roosevelt: The Intimate Letters of Archie Butt, Military Aide* (Doubleday, Doran, 1930), pp. 456–459.

3. *Milwaukee Sentinel*, January 31, 1914.

4. Dodson, p. 129.

5. *Springfield Republican*, April 6, 1939.

6. *Evening Star*, August 13, 1976.

7. *Pittsburgh Press*, June 14, 1942.

8. *Pittsburgh Press*, June 14, 1940.

9. *Spokesman Review*, April 28, 1964.

10. *Times-Picayune*, June 20, 1971.

Chapter 1

1. Historian Art Stricklin has suggested that Potter and Edwards were from Wales.

2. *Dallas Morning News*, October 1, 1935.

3. H. Jeblen Jr., "The Public Acceptance of Sports in Dallas 1880–1930," in *The Journal of Sport History* 6, no. 3 (Winter 1979): pp. 5–17.

4. *Ibid.*, p. 6.

5. *Dallas Morning News*, November 28, 1926.

6. A. Barkow, *The Golden Era of Golf* (New York: Thomas Dunne Press, 2000), p. 45. Art Stricklin suggested that the first prize was $1,666.

7. *Ibid.*

8. A. Stricklin, *Links Lore & Legends: The Story of Texas Golf* (Dallas: Taylor, 2002), p. 24.

9. *Oregonian*, February 22, 1922.

10. Lowe, p. 133.

11. *Prescott Evening Courier*, March 23, 1940.

12. Stricklin, pp. vii–viii.

13. *St. Petersburg Times*, August 3, 1939.

14. Nelson won eleven tournaments in a row.

15. G. Tindall and D. Shi, *America* (New York: W.W. Norton, 1993), p. 298.

16. *Pittsburgh Press*, June 28, 1937.

17. *Dallas Morning News*, March 4, 1923.

18. K. Cook, *Titanic Thompson* (New York: W.W. Norton, 2012), p. 197.

19. Cook, p. 197.

20. *Norwalk Hour*, August 8, 1931.

21. *Dallas Morning News*, January 1, 1969.

22. *Saturday Evening Post*, June 12, 1937.

23. *Pittsburgh Press*, June 28, 1937.

24. *Pittsburgh Press*, June 28, 1937.

25. C. Geer Dean, *Interlachen Country Club: A Century of Excellence 1909–2009* (Interlachen Country Club, Minnesota, 2009), p. 47.

26. *Pittsburgh Press*, June 28, 1937.

27. *The American Golfer*, April 1916.

28. *Tuscaloosa News*, March 23, 1930.

29. Harlow had worked alongside Gates since 1930.

30. J. Demaret, *My Partner Ben Hogan* (New York: McGraw-Hill, 1954), p. 53.

31. *Miami News*, February 1, 1946.

32. Dodson, p. 74. Jack Grout went on to become teacher and friend to Jack Nicklaus.

33. *Montreal Gazette*, October 25, 1938.

34. *Deseret News*, June 25, 1937.

35. *Pittsburgh Press*, June 30, 1937.

36. *San Jose Evening News*, January 26, 1931.

37. *Times Daily*, February 17, 1931.

38. *Dallas Morning News*, January 26, 1931.

39. *San Jose Evening News*, January 26, 1931.

40. *The Professional Golfer of America*, February 1933.

41. *Spokesman Review*, September 8, 1929.

42. *Norwalk Hour*, October 1930.

43. The Masters began in 1934.

44. T. Fitzgerald, "Ralph Guldahl: A Golfer's Golfer," in *Famous American Athletes of To-Day, Seventh Series* (Clinton, MA: L.C. Page), p. 242.

45. M. Blaine, *The King of Swings* (Boston: Houghton Mifflin, 2006), p. 256.

46. *Pittsburgh Post-Gazette*, June 7, 1933.

47. Blaine, p. 266.

48. Blaine, p. 269.

49. Blaine, p. 271.

50. *Golf Illustrated*, July 1933.

51. T. Flaherty, *the U.S. Open 1895–1965* (New York: E.P. Dutton, 1966), p. 86.

52. W.J. Curtis Sr., *Johnny Goodman* (Virginia: W.J. Curtis Sr., 1997), p. 73.

53. *Milwaukee Journal*, June 11, 1933.

54. Blaine, p. 283.

55. *Milwaukee Sentinel*, June 11, 1933.

56. *The American Golfer*, July 1933.

57. *Boston Herald*, December 9, 1936.

58. Fitzgerald, p. 246.

59. *Golfing*, March 1937.

60. *Golf Monthly*, July 1937.

61. *Golf Illustrated*, July 1933.

62. *USA TODAY*, April 13, 2015.

63. *St. Petersburg Times*, April 3, 1946.

Chapter 2

1. J.W. Finegan, *A Centennial Tribute to Golf in Philadelphia* (Golf Association of Philadelphia, 1996), p. 173.

2. *The Saturday Evening Post*, June 12, 1937.

3. *Dallas Morning News*, June 13, 1935.

4. *Herald Journal*, April 5, 1937.

5. *The Saturday Evening Post*, June 12, 1937.

6. *Evening Independent*, November 30, 1936.

7. *Evening Independent*, July 22, 1937.

8. *Evening Independent*, July 22, 1937.

9. *Pittsburgh Press*, July 1, 1937.

10. *Dallas Morning News*, June 14, 1937.

11. *Evening Star* (Washington D.C.) June 4, 1939.

12. *The Saturday Evening Post*, June 12, 1937.

13. *Pittsburgh Press*, July 2, 1937.

14. *Pittsburgh Press*, July 2, 1937.

15. *Pittsburgh Press*, July 2, 1937.

16. *Pittsburgh Press*, July 2, 1937.

17. G. Sarazen, and H.W. Wind, *Thirty Years of Championship Golf* (London: A&C Black Ltd., 1990), pp. 26–7.

18. *Richmond Times Dispatch*, May 19, 1939.

19. See p. 62.

20. *St. Petersburg Times*, December 7, 1936.

21. *Time Magazine*, June 27, 1938.

22. *Heraldo de Brownsville*, June 22, 1936.

Chapter 3

1. S. Snead, *The Education of a Golfer* (New York: Simon & Schuster, 1962), p. 37.

2. A. Barkow, *Sam* (Maryland: Taylor, 2010), p. 24.

3. *Pittsburgh Press*, July 2, 1937.

4. J. Steinbreder, *Golf Courses of the U.S. Open* (Dallas: Taylor, 1996), p. 101.

5. *Ibid.*, p. 102.

6. *Spokane Review*, June 7, 1924.

7. *Milwaukee Journal*, June 7, 1937.

8. F. Corcoran, *Unplayable Lies* (New York: Duell, Sloan and Pearce, 1965), p. 60.

9. Dodson, p. 119.

10. J. Corcoran, *Fred Corcoran: The Man Who Sold the World on Golf* (New York: Gray Productions, 2010), p. 35.

11. *Lawrence Journal-World*, June 4, 1937.

12. *The National Golf Review*, July 1937.

13. *Meriden Record*, June 10, 1937.

14. *Milwaukee Journal*, June 10, 1937.

15. Snead, p. 92.

16. *Deseret News*, June 25, 1937.

17. *Dallas Morning News*, June 14, 1937.

18. *Dallas Morning News*, June 14, 1937.

19. *Dallas Morning News*, May 12, 1940.

20. *Dallas Morning News*, June 14, 1937.

21. Corcoran, p. 206.

22. Flaherty, p. 97.

23. *Reading Eagle*, June 13, 1937.
24. *Sports Illustrated and the American Golfer*, August 1937.
25. *The National Golf Review*, July 1937.
26. *The National Golf Review*, July 1937.
27. USGA, July 1937.
28. *Harry Cooper Oral History* (USGA, 1990).
29. *Sports Illustrated and the American Golfer*, August 1937.
30. *Pittsburgh Press*, June 4, 1937.
31. Flaherty, p. 97.
32. H.W. Wind, *The Story of American Golf* (New York: A.P. Knopf, 1975), p. 275.
33. *Dallas Morning News*, June 13, 1937.
34. *Evening Star*, June 5, 1938.
35. *Reading Eagle*, June 14, 1937.
36. *San Francisco Chronicle*, June 13, 1937.
37. *The Professional Golfer of America*, July 1937.
38. *Reading Eagle*, June 14, 1937.
39. *Glasgow Herald*, June 29, 1937.
40. Nelson, p. 75.
41. *Times*, July 1, 1937.
42. *Times*, July 1, 1937.
43. *Times*, July 1, 1937.
44. Nelson always claimed the "Dip" was an optical illusion.
45. *Sarasota Herald-Tribune*, June 24, 1937.
46. *Dallas Morning News*, July 1, 1937.
47. *Dallas Morning News*, July 1, 1937.
48. *Evening Star*, July 1, 1937.
49. *Golf Monthly*, July 1937.
50. *Fairway and Hazard*, August 1937.
51. *Golfing*, September 1937.
52. *Golfing*, July 1937.
53. *Dallas Morning News*, July 21, 1937.
54. *Herald Journal*, July 23, 1937.
55. *Reading Eagle*, July 22, 1937.
56. *Reading Eagle*, July 22, 1937.
57. *The Professional Golfer of America*, July 1937.
58. *Ibid.*
59. *Ibid.*
60. *The Professional Golfer of America*, July 1937.
61. *Prescott Evening Courier*, July 26, 1937.
62. *Golf Monthly*, August 1937.
63. Nelson, p. 76.
64. Dodson, p. 135.
65. *Miami News*, August 2, 1937.
66. *Chicago Tribune*, July 5, 1937.
67. *Dallas Morning News*, July 4, 1937.
68. *Sydney Morning Herald*, July 12, 1937.
69. *Evening Star*, July 7, 1937.
70. *Evening Star*, July 7, 1937.
71. *Glasgow Herald*, July 9, 1937.
72. *Times*, July 8, 1937.
73. *Macon Telegraph*, July 21, 1937.
74. *The American Golfer*, September 1937.
75. *Herald Journal*, July 23, 1937.
76. *Prescott Evening Courier*, July 10, 1937.
77. *The American Golfer*, September 1937.
78. *Columbus Daily Enquirer*, July 10, 1937.
79. *Times*, July 10, 1937.
80. *Springfield Republican*, July 23, 1937.
81. *Daily Illinois State Journal*, June 21, 1937.
82. *Tuscaloosa News*, February 10, 1939.
83. Lowe, p. 130.
84. Sarazen and Wind, p. 192.
85. A. Barkow, *Gettin' to the Dance Floor* (New Jersey: Burford Books, 1986), p. 107.
86. Barkow, *Gettin',* p. 118.

Chapter 4

1. *Evening Independent*, January 3, 1938.
2. *Evening Independent*, January 3, 1938.
3. *Register-Republic*, December 10, 1937.
4. *Herald Journal*, January 3, 1938.
5. *Greensboro Record*, January 6, 1938.
6. *The USGA Official U.S. Open Program*, 1938, pp. 11, 25.
7. G.E. Brown III, *Cherry Hills Country Club 1922–1997* (Englewood, CO: Cherry Hills Country Club, 1998), p. 25.
8. J. Norland, *A History of Cherry Hills Country Club, 1922–1972* (Englewood, CO: Cherry Hills Country Club, 1972), p. 46.
9. *Milwaukee Journal*, June 7, 1938.
10. Norland, p. 40.
11. *Prescott Evening Courier*, June 13, 1938.
12. *Prescott Evening Courier*, June 8, 1938.
13. *Heraldo de Brownsville*, June 3, 1938.
14. *Milwaukee Journal*, June 9, 1938.
15. *Spokane Daily Chronicle*, September 9, 1938.

16. *Sunday Morning Star,* June 5, 1938.
17. *Pittsburgh Press,* June 13, 1938.
18. *Pittsburgh Press,* June 13, 1938.
19. *Pittsburgh Press,* June 13, 1938.
20. *Cleveland Plain Dealer,* June 13, 1938.
21. *Reading Eagle,* December 22, 1938.
22. *Cleveland Plain Dealer,* June 12, 1938.
23. *The Loop,* April 3, 2012.
24. *Miami News,* June 14, 1938.
25. *Miami News,* June 14, 1938.
26. R.T. Jones, *Golf Is My Game* (New York: Doubleday, 1960), p. 184.
27. *Montreal Gazette,* June 13, 1938.
28. *Spokesman Review,* June 17, 1938.
29. *Milwaukee Journal,* July 10, 1938.
30. *Esquire.*
31. Barkow, p. 105.
32. This is not to suggest that Grantland Rice, et al., were not also present.
33. *Berkley Daily Gazette,* July 9, 1938.
34. *Cleveland Plain Dealer,* July 19, 1939.
35. *The National Golf Review,* December 1938.
36. *Reading Eagle,* December 22, 1938.

Chapter 5

1. *Dallas Morning News,* January 2, 1939.
2. *Tuscaloosa News,* April 7, 1980.
3. G. Rice, "The Masters Fixture," in *The American Golfer* (New York: Random House, 1964), pp. 208–9.
4. Jones, p. 197.
5. C. Sampson, *The Masters* (New York: Villard, 1998), p. 39.
6. S.R. Lowe, *Sir Walter and Mr. Jones* (Chelsea: Sleeping Bear Press, 2000), p. 289.
7. Jones, p. 200.
8. Sampson, p. 33.
9. Sampson, p. 40.
10. B. Nelson, *How I Played the Game* (New York: Dell, 1993), p. 67.
11. *Herald Journal,* April 5, 1937.
12. Nelson, p. 67.
13. B. Nelson, *The Byron Nelson Story* (Ohio: The Old Golf Shop, 1989), p. 16.
14. Jones, p. 204.
15. Nelson, p. 66.
16. Jones, p. 228.
17. *The Saturday Evening Post,* June 12,

1937. The burn and the creek are better known as Rae's Creek.
18. *Sports Illustrated and the American Golfer,* August 1937.
19. *Pittsburgh Post-Gazette,* May 24, 1939.
20. Nelson, p. 226.
21. *Spokesman-Review,* April 2, 1938.
22. Many years later, Picard recalled that he hurt his thumb at the 1937 British Open and that it was a doctor who suggested the change. But Alex Morrison did teach the interlocking grip.
23. *Spokesman Review,* April 5, 1938.
24. Dodson, p. 128.
25. *Reading Eagle,* April 5, 1939.
26. Anecdote courtesy of Mike Moretti, New Jersey State Golf Association.
27. *Prescott Evening Courier,* July 10, 1938.
28. W.D. Richardson, in H.W. Wind, *The Complete Golfer* (London: W. Heinemann, 1954), p. 250.
29. Richardson, p. 251.
30. *Pittsburgh Press,* April 3, 1939.
31. *The Boston Herald,* April 4, 1939.
32. Richardson, p. 252.
33. *Evansville Courier and Press,* April 28, 1939.
34. *Esquire,* January 1939.
35. *Prescott Evening Courier,* April 3, 1939.
36. *Register Republic,* April 3, 1939.
37. *Register-Republic,* April 7, 1939.
38. *Dallas Morning News,* April 6, 1939.
39. *Omaha World Herald,* April 11, 1939.
40. *Pittsburgh Press,* October 4, 1937.
41. *San Jose Evening News,* May 2, 1939.
42. *Evansville Courier and Press,* April 19, 1937.
43. *Pittsburgh Press,* June 7, 1939.
44. *Idaho Statesman,* June 5, 1940.
45. *Dallas Morning News,* June 4, 1939.

Chapter 6

1. C. Sampson, *Texas Golf Legends* (Lubbock: Texas Tech University Press, 1993), p. 50.
2. *San Francisco Chronicle,* June 13, 1937.
3. Wind, p. 297.
4. R. Sommers, *The U.S. Open Golf's Ultimate Challenge* (New York: Atheneum, 1987), p. 117.

5. S. Snead and G. Mendoza, *Slammin' Sam—Sam Snead* (New York: Donald L. Fine, 1986), p. 87.

6. Snead, p. 97.

7. Barkow, p. 99.

8. Barkow, p. 99.

9. *USGA Oral History* (Far Hills, NJ: 1990), pp. 238–239.

10. *Deseret News*, June 25, 1937.

11. J. Dodson, *Ben Hogan: An American Life* (London: Aurum Press, 2004), p. 104.

12. Dodson, p. 103.

13. Dodson, p. 104.

14. *Dallas Morning News*, March 26, 1940.

15. *Greensboro Daily News*, June 6, 1940.

16. *Dallas Morning News*, May 12, 1940.

17. *San Francisco Chronicle*, June 6, 1940.

18. *Herald Journal*, June 2, 1940.

19. *Herald Journal*, June 2, 1940.

20. *Ohio Repository*, June 12, 1940.

21. *Toledo Blade*, June 10, 1973.

22. Inverness Club historian.

23. *Toledo Blade*, June 14, 1940.

24. *Ibid.*

25. A. Barkow, *The Golden Era of Golf* (New York: St. Martin's Press, 2000), p. 62.

26. J. Dodson, *American Triumvirate* (New York: Alfred A. Knopf, 2012), p. 153.

27. Nelson, p. 105.

28. A. Barkow, *Gettin' to the Dance Floor* (New Jersey: Burford Books), p. 87.

29. Snead, p. 40.

30. Barkow, p. 88.

31. *Gettysburg Times*, January 8, 1941.

32. *Milwaukee Journal*, August 6, 1940.

33. *Sarasota Herald-Tribune*, June 30, 1941.

34. R. Grout and W. Winter, *Jack Grout: A Legacy in Golf* (Indianapolis: Blue River Press, 2012), pp. 113–114.

35. Nelson, p. 106.

36. *Miami News*, March 30, 1941.

37. *Ottawa Citizen*, May 10, 1941.

38. Jones, p. 48.

39. *Daily Herald*, April 3, 1939.

40. *Pittsburgh Press*, June 14, 1942.

41. *Toledo Blade*, November 26, 1942.

42. *Richmond Times*, February 5, 1978.

43. *Times Daily*, June 3, 1942.

44. *Ibid.*

45. *From Tee to Cup to Green by the Four Masters* (USA: Wilson Sporting Goods, 1937).

46. *Prescott Evening Courier*, February 2, 1940.

47. S. Snead, *The Quick Way to Better Golf* (Sun Dial Press, 1938), p. 1.

48. *Pittsburgh Post-Gazette*, August 9, 1939.

49. R. Guldahl, *Groove Your Golf* (Indianapolis: Brookwalter-Ball-Greathouse, 1939), p. 9.

50. Guldahl, p. 10.

51. Guldahl, p. 207.

52. A. Barkow, *Golf's Golden Grind* (New York: Harcourt Brace Jovanovich, 1974), p. 135.

53. Barkow, p. 135.

54. Barkow, p. 135.

55. *Bulletin*, January 31, 1940.

56. *Chicago Tribune*, June 28, 1995.

57. Sarazen and Wind, p. 257.

58. F. Corcoran, *Unplayable Lies* (New York: Duell, Sloan and Pearce, 1965), p. 89.

59. Snead, p. 160.

60. Snead, pp. 214–5.

61. *Ohio Repository*, August 3, 1941.

62. *Ohio Repository*, August 3, 1941.

63. J. Strege, *When War Played Through* (New York: Gotham Books, 2005), p. 22.

64. Sampson, p. 52.

65. T. Cronin, *The Spirit of Medinah* (Chicago: Medinah, 2001), pp. 155–6.

66. Cronin, pp. 156–7.

67. Cronin, pp. 156–7.

68. *Milwaukee Journal*, December 16, 1947.

69. *Schenectady Gazette*, April 12, 1948.

Epilogue

1. *Lawrence World Journal*, December 21, 1954.

2. *Spokesman Review*, April 28, 1964.

3. Sampson, p. 52.

4. According to Sam Snead, he had the nickname of "Goldie" on tour.

5. *Augusta Chronicle*, April 2, 1964.

6. *Evening Independent*, April 9, 1964.

7. *Telegraph*, April 27, 1986.

8. *Mobile Register*, April 28, 1978.

9. *Daytona Beach Sunday News Journal*, April 28, 1978.

10. *Richmond Times*, February 5, 1978.

11. Stricklin, p. 50.

12. M. Frost, *The Grand Slam* (London: Time Warner, 2004), pp. 251–252.

13. Nelson, p. 165.

14. *Dallas Morning News*, December 22, 1968.

15. *Golfing*, June 1939.

16. *The Professional Golfer of America*, July 1933.

17. H. Cotton, *This Game of Golf* (London: Country Life Limited, 1948), pp. 230–1.

18. *Biloxi Daily Herald*, April 8, 1939.

19. *Dallas Morning News*, April 6, 1939.

20. *Dallas Morning News*, December 22, 1968.

21. Corcoran, p. 47.

22. Guldahl, Foreword.

Bibliography

Books

Barkow, A. *Gettin' to the Dance Floor*. New Jersey: Burford Books, 1986.
_____. *The Golden Era of Golf*. New York: St. Martin's Press, 2000.
_____. *Golf's Golden Grind*. New York: Harcourt Brace Jovanovich, 1974.
_____. *Sam*. Maryland: Taylor Trade Publishing, 2010.
Blaine, M. *The King of Swings*. Boston: Houghton Mifflin, 2006.
Brown, G.E., III. *Cherry Hills Country Club 1922–1997*. Colorado: Cherry Hills Country Club, 1998.
Butt, A. *Taft and Roosevelt: The Intimate Letters of Archie Butt, Military Aide*. New York: Doubleday, Doran, 1930.
Cook, K. *Titanic Thompson*. New York: W.W. Norton, 2012.
Corcoran, F. *Unplayable Lies*. New York: Duell, Sloan & Pearce, 1964.
Corcoran, J. *Fred Corcoran: The Man Who Sold the World on Golf*. New York: Gray, 2010.
Cotton, H. *This Game of Golf*. London: Country Life Limited, 1948.
Cronin, T.W. *The Spirit of Medinah*. Illinois: Medinah Country Club, 2001.
Curtis, W.J. *Johnny Goodman*. Virginia: W.J. Curtis, 1997.
Darwin, B. *Golf Between Two Wars*. London: Chatto & Windus, 1944.
Dean, C.G. *Interlachen Country Club: A Century of Excellence 1909–2009*. Minnesota: Interlachen Country Club, 2009.
Demaret, J. *My Partner Ben Hogan*. New York: McGraw-Hill, 1954.
Dodson, J. *American Triumvirate*. New York: Alfred A. Knopf, 2012.
_____. *Ben Hogan: The Authorised Biography*. London: Aurum, 2005.
Finegan, J. *A Centennial Tribute to Golf in Philadelphia*. Philadelphia: Golf Association of Philadelphia, 1996.
Flaherty, T. *The U.S. Open 1895–1965*. New York: E.P. Dutton, 1966.
The Four Masters. *From Tee to Cup to Green*. USA: Wilson Sporting Goods, 1937.
Frost, M. *The Grand Slam*. London: Time Warner, 2004.
Gregston, G. *Hogan—The Man Who Played for Glory*. California: The Booklegger, 1986.
Grout, R., and W. Winter. *Jack Grout: A Legacy in Golf*. Indianapolis: Blue Ridge Press, 2012.
Guldahl, R. *Groove Your Golf*. Indianapolis: Brook Walter Ball Greathouse, 1939.
Jones, R.T. *Golf Is My Game*. New York: Doubleday, 1960.
Lowe, S.R. *Sir Walter and Mr. Jones*. Chelsea, MI: Sleeping Bear Press, 2000.
Nason, J. *Famous American Athletes of To-Day Seventh Series*. Boston: L.C. Page, 1940.

Nelson, B. *How I Played the Game.* New York: Dell, 1993.
Norland, J. *Fifty Years of Mostly Fun—A History of Cherry Hills Country Club 1922–1972.* Colorado: Cherry Hills Country Club, 1972.
Sampson, C. *Texas Golf Legends.* Lubbock: Texas Tech University Press, 1993.
_____. *The Masters.* New York: Villard, 1998.
Sarazen, G., and H.W. Wind. *Thirty Years of Championship Golf.* London: A&C Black, 1990.
Snead, S. *The Education of a Golfer.* New York: Simon & Schuster, 1962.
_____. *The Quick Way to Better Golf.* Sun Dial Press, 1938.
Snead, S., and G. Mendoza. *Slammin' Sam.* New York: Donald L. Fine, 1986.
Sommers, R. *The U.S. Open Golf's Ultimate Challenge.* New York: Atheneum, 1987.
Steinbreder, J. *Golf Courses of the U.S. Open.* Dallas: Taylor, 1996.
Strege, J. *When War Played Through.* New York: Gotham Books, 2005.
Stricklin, A. *Links, Lore & Legends: The Story of Texas Golf.* Dallas: Taylor, 2002.
Tindall, G.B., and D. Shi. *America: A Narrative History.* New York: W.W. Norton, 1993.
Wind, H.W. *The Complete Golfer.* London: William Heinemann, 1954.
_____. *The Story of American Golf.* New York: Alfred A. Knopf, 1975.

Newspapers

Atlanta Constitution
Augusta Chronicle
Berkley Daily Gazette
Biloxi Daily Herald
Boston Herald
Bulletin
Chicago Tribune
Cleveland Plain Deale
Columbus Daily Enquirer
Courier
Daily Illinois State Journal
Dallas Morning News
Daytona Beach Sunday News Journal
Deseret News
Eugene Register Guard
Evansville Courier and Press
Evening Independent
Evening Star
Gettysburg Times
Glasgow Herald
Greensboro Daily News
Greensboro Record
Herald Journal
Heraldo De Brownsville
Idaho Statesman

Lawrence Journal World
Leader Post
Lewiston Daily Sun
Lodi Sentinel
The Loop
Los Angeles Times
Macon Telegraph
Miami News
Milwaukee Journal
Milwaukee Sentinel
Mobile Register
Montreal Gazette
New York Times
News & Courier
Norwalk Hour
Ohio Repository
Omaha World Herald
Oregonian
Ottawa Citizen
Pittsburgh Post Gazette
Pittsburgh Press
Prescott Evening Courier
Providence News
Reading Eagle
Register Republic
Richmond Times

Richmond Times Dispatch
St. Petersburg Times
San Francisco Chronicle
San Jose Evening News
Sarasota Herald Tribune
Schenectady Gazette
Spokane Chronicle
Spokesman Review
Springfield Republican
Sunday Morning Star
Sydney Morning Herald
Telegraph
Telegraph Herald
Times
Times Daily
Times-Picayune
Toledo Blade
Toledo News-Bee
Tuscaloosa News
USA TODAY
Washington Post
Washington Reporter
Vancouver Sun
Youngstown Vindicator

Journals and Magazines

The American Golfer
Esquire

North American Society for Sport History. Proceedings and Newsletter

Fairway and Hazard
Golf Digest
Golf Illustrated
Golfdom
Golfing
The National Golf Review

The PGA Magazine
The Saturday Evening Post
Sports Illustrated and the American Golfer
Time Magazine
The USGA Official Program, 1938

Miscellaneous

Club Historian, Inverness
Historian, Western Golf Association
USGA Oral History Collection

Index